Forced Migration

Forced Migration: Current Issues and Debates provides a critical engagement with and analysis of contemporary issues in the field using inter-disciplinary perspectives, through different geographical case studies and by employing varying methodologies. The combination of authors reviewing both the key research and scholarship and offering insights from their own research ensures a comprehensive and up-to-date analysis of the current issues in forced migration.

The book is structured around three main current themes: the reconfiguration of borders including virtual borders, the expansion of prolonged exile, and changes in protection and access to rights. The first chapters in the collection provide both context and a theoretical overview by situating current debates and issues in their historical context including the evolution of the field work and the impact of the colonial and post-colonial world order on forced migration and forced displacement. These are followed by chapters framed around substantive issues including: deportation and forced return; protracted displacements; securitising the Mediterranean and cross-border migration practices; refugees in global cities; forced migrants in the digital age; second-generation identity and transnational practices.

Forced Migration offers an original contribution to a growing field of study connecting theoretical ideas and empirical research with policy, practice and the lived experiences of forced migrants. The volume provides a solid foundation, for students, academics and policymakers, of the main questions being asked in contemporary debates in forced migration.

Alice Bloch is Professor of Sociology at the University of Manchester. She has researched and published extensively in the area of forced migration. Recent books include: *Living on the Margins: Undocumented Migrants in a Global City* (published by Policy Press and co-authored with Sonia McKay) and *Sans Papiers: The Social and Economic Lives of Young Undocumented Migrants in the UK* (published by Pluto Press and co-authored with Nando Sigona and Roger Zetter).

Giorgia Donà is Professor of Forced Migration at the University of East London co-director of the Centre for Migration, Refugees and Belonging and Fellow of the Higher Education Academy. She has researched and published extensively in the area of conflict and forced migration. Publications include *Child and Youth Migration: Mobility-in-Migration in an Era of Globalisation* (published by Palgrave Macmillan, co-edited with Angela Veale), *Research Methodologies in Forced Migration*, Special Issue for the *Journal of Refugee Studies* (with Eftihia Voutira), and *Child and Youth Migration*, Special Issue for the *International Journal of Migration, Health and Social Care*.

"This compelling anthology of case studies and critical reflections by an international group of scholars surveys the major issues around forced migration. Readers who want to understand the experiences of people pushed from their homes and government strategies of control will see farther and more clearly through the authors' lenses."

David Scott FitzGerald, *Co-Director, Center for Comparative Immigration Studies, University of California-San Diego*

"This collection of essays from leading figures in forced migration studies provides critical analysis that is as piercing and relevant as it is thoughtful. It encompasses some of the most intractable and contemporary problems of forced migration – urban displacement, protracted refugees, and forced return – with fresh insights. Uniting the various contributions is a deep concern for the clear emergence of expanded precarity and reduced rights, which appear as cause and effect of so much displacement in today's world. Indeed, these can be seen as unifying features in the experiences of most displaced people. This book shines a light on these experiences, and the processes which render those who are forced to move ever more vulnerable. This should be required reading for all migration studies students and scholars, as well as for policymakers and practitioners whose work involves any aspect of work on forced migration."

Laura Hammond, *Professor, Department of Development Studies, School of Oriental and African Studies (SOAS)*

"This volume is a welcome contribution to our understanding of the increasingly complex field of forced migration. Addressing the many challenges confronting forced migrants and those who support and live in communities alongside forced migrants, in a variety of contexts today, the volume points to the urgent need to re-conceptualise forced migration as well as the legal frameworks with which to respond. The collection will be of great value to academics, policy makers, and a broad range of professionals."

Marita Eastmond, *Senior Professor of Social Anthropology, School of Global Studies, University of Gothenburg*

Forced Migration

Current Issues and Debates

Edited by Alice Bloch and
Giorgia Donà

LONDON AND NEW YORK

First published 2019
by Routledge
2 Park Square, Milton Park, Abingdon, Oxon OX14 4RN
and by Routledge
711 Third Avenue, New York, NY 10017

Routledge is an imprint of the Taylor & Francis Group, an informa business

© 2019 selection and editorial matter, Alice Bloch and Giorgia Donà; individual chapters, the contributors

The right of Alice Bloch and Giorgia Donà to be identified as the authors of the editorial material, and of the authors for their individual chapters, has been asserted in accordance with sections 77 and 78 of the Copyright, Designs and Patents Act 1988.

All rights reserved. No part of this book may be reprinted or reproduced or utilised in any form or by any electronic, mechanical, or other means, now known or hereafter invented, including photocopying and recording, or in any information storage or retrieval system, without permission in writing from the publishers.

Trademark notice: Product or corporate names may be trademarks or registered trademarks, and are used only for identification and explanation without intent to infringe.

British Library Cataloguing-in-Publication Data
A catalogue record for this book is available from the British Library

Library of Congress Cataloging-in-Publication Data
Names: Bloch, Alice, 1964– editor. | Dona, Giorgia, editor.
Title: Forced migration : current issues and debates / edited by Alice Bloch and Giorgia Donáa.
Description: Abingdon, Oxon ; New York, NY : Routledge, 2018.
Identifiers: LCCN 2018025982 | ISBN 9781138653221 (hardback) | ISBN 9781138653238 (pbk.) | ISBN 9781315623757 (ebook)
Subjects: LCSH: Forced migration. | Refugees. | Emigration and immigration—Government policy.
Classification: LCC HV640 .F575 2018 | DDC 325—dc23
LC record available at https://lccn.loc.gov/2018025982

ISBN: 978-1-138-65322-1 (hbk)
ISBN: 978-1-138-65323-8 (pbk)
ISBN: 978-1-315-62375-7 (ebk)

Typeset in Goudy
by Apex CoVantage, LLC

Contents

List of illustrations and tables vii
Acknowledgements viii
List of contributors ix

1 **Forced migration: setting the scene** 1
   ALICE BLOCH AND GIORGIA DONÀ

2 **Conceptualising forced migration: praxis, scholarship and empirics** 19
   ROGER ZETTER

3 **Why critical forced migration studies has to be post-colonial by nature** 44
   PAULA BANERJEE AND RANABIR SAMADDAR

4 **Securitising the Mediterranean? cross-border migration practices in Greece** 60
   EFTIHIA VOUTIRA

5 **Protracted displacement: living on the edge** 74
   JENNIFER HYNDMAN AND WENONA GILES

6 **Deportation and forced return** 88
   NASSIM MAJIDI AND LIZA SCHUSTER

7 **Displacement and the pursuit of urban protection: forced migration, fluidity and global cities** 106
   LOREN B. LANDAU

8 Mobile technologies and forced migration 126
GIORGIA DONÀ AND MARIE GODIN

9 Second generation from refugee backgrounds: affects and
transnational ties and practices to the ancestral homeland 145
MILENA CHIMIENTI, ANNE-LAURE COUNILH AND LAURENCE OSSIPOW

10 Reflecting on the past, thinking about the future: forced
migration in the 21st century 163
GIORGIA DONÀ AND ALICE BLOCH

Index 174

Illustrations and Tables

Figure

4.1 The narrow strip of water that separates the Greek island of
Lesbos from Izmir, Turkey   61

Image

4.1 Local responses and the legacy of the past   64

Table

4.1 Arrivals and Fatalities in the Mediterranean Sea, 2014–2017   64

Acknowledgements

This book has evolved from years of conversations with each other and with colleagues working within the field of forced migration, often at the bi-annual International Association for the Study of Forced Migration conferences.

Thank you to Barbara Harrell-Bond who continues to inspire us both. We would like to thank the chapter authors for their contributions. We have very much enjoyed the opportunities that editing this book have provided to work with many of the leading scholars in the field. We would also like to thank Catherine Gray who first approached us during her time with Routledge and helped us shape the book and Gerhard Boomgaarden, Senior Publisher for Routledge, who has worked with us since and providing valuable input which has informed the book as published. Thanks also to colleagues from Routledge past and present Alyson Claffey and Diana Ciobotea, for keeping us informed and helping us through the process.

Alice would like to thank colleagues in the Department of Sociology at the University of Manchester, particularly Claire Alexander, Wendy Bottero, Bridget Byrne, Brian Heaphy, Sue Heath, Graeme Kirkpatrick, Vanessa May, James Rhodes and Penny Tinkler. Thanks also to the many colleagues who have provided support and advice over the years including: Suki Ali, Leah Bassel, Kirsten Campbell, Milena Chimienti, Allan Cochrane, Shirin Hirsch, Amal Treacher Kabesh, Sonia McKay, Kate Nash, Sarah Neal, Liza Schuster, John Solomos and Fran Tonkiss. Finally thank you to Rachel, my wonderful daughter.

Giorgia would like to thank colleagues who work and have worked in Refugee Studies at the University of East London, Paul Dudman, Anita Fábos, Patricia Ellis, Afaf Jabiri, Maja Korać, John Nassari, Phil Marfleet, Siraj Sait, Helen Taylor and Tahir Zaman. Thanks also to the many colleagues, friends and family who have provided support and friendship, including: Gargi Bhattacharyya, Michele Biancotto, Cristina Carli, Carlo Donà, Irene Donà, Matteo Donà, Meri Gava, Erika Cudworth, Liz Egan, Cigdem Esin, Anna Gobbo, Tim Hall, Laura Hammond, Diane Ball, Firew Kefyalew, Helen Kim, Aura Lounasmaa, Lorena Marcassa, Valerio Marcassa, Keith Piper, Natale Possamai, Branislav Radeljić, George Shire, Corinne Squire, Maria Tamboukou, Meera Tiwari, Rachel Tribe, Angie Voela, Georgie Wemyss, Eric Woods and Nira Yuval-Davis. A special thank you to all my undergraduate and postgraduate students at the University of East London for the most inspiring conversations and inspirational lives.

Contributors

Paula Banerjee is Professor and Vice Chancellor of Sanskrit College and University. She was the former President of International Association for Studies in Forced Migration and Dean of Arts of University of Calcutta. She is best known for her work on women in borderlands and women and forced migration and has published extensively in these areas including: *Statelessness in South Asia* (2016), *Unstable Populations, Anxious States* (edited 2013), *Women in Indian Borderlands* (edited, 2012) and *Borders, Histories, Existences: Gender and Beyond* (2010).

Alice Bloch is Professor of Sociology at the University of Manchester. She has researched, written and published extensively in the area of forced migration. Recent books include: *Living on the Margins: Undocumented Migrants in a Global City* (2016, with Sonia McKay) and *Sans Papiers: The Social and Economic Lives of Young Undocumented Migrants in the UK* (2014, with Nando Sigona and Roger Zetter).

Milena Chimienti is a sociologist and Professor at the University of Applied Sciences and Arts Western Switzerland – HES-SO Geneva, School of Social Work (HETS). She has researched and written mostly on the sociology of migration, sex work and processes of marginalisation and forms of agency, both individual and collective. Her publications include: A 'continuum of sexual economic exchanges' or 'weak agency'? Female migrant sex work in Switzerland. In: Skilbrei M-L, Spanger M (eds), *Understanding Sex for Sale: Meanings and Moralities of Sexual Commerce*, London: Routldege (2018, with Marylène Lieber); The failure of global migration, *Ethnic and Racial Studies*, 41(3); 424–430, 2017; *Undocumented Migrants: Policy, Politics, Motives and Everyday Lives*, Special Issue for *Ethnic and Racial Studies* (ed 2011, with Alice Bloch).

Anne-Laure Counilh is a social geographer, and researcher at the University of Applied Sciences and Arts Western Switzerland – HES-SO Geneva, School of Social Work (HETS). Her research interest lies in the area of migration, transnational mobilities and socio-spatial interactions. Her PhD focuses on migration of transnational migrants from West Africa in Mauritania in 2014.

Giorgia Donà is Professor of Forced Migration at the University of East London, co-director of the Centre for Migration, Refugees and Belonging and Fellow of the Higher Education Academy. She has researched and published extensively in the area of conflict and forced migration. Publications include *Child and Youth Migration: Mobility-in-Migration in an Era of Globalisation* (ed 2014, Palgrave Macmillan, with Angela Veale), *Research Methodologies in Forced Migration*, Special Issue for the *Journal of Refugee Studies* (ed 2007, with Eftihia Voutira) and *Child and Youth Migration*, Special Issue for the *International Journal of Migration, Health and Social Care* (ed 2006).

Wenona Giles is an Anthropology Professor and Research Associate at the Centre for Refugee Studies, York University, where she teaches and publishes in the areas of gender, forced migration, globalisation, migration, nationalism and war. She co-leads the Borderless Higher Education (BHER) project that brings degree programmes from Kenyan and Canadian universities to refugees in the Dadaab refugee camps, Kenya and recently co-authored (with Jennifer Hyndman) *Refugees in Extended Exile: Living on the Edge* (Routledge 2017).

Marie Godin, PhD, is currently a researcher at the Oxford Department of International Development (ODID) at the University of Oxford. Her research interests lie in the area of migration and development, with a focus on diaspora engagement and gender, mobile technologies and political activism. She recently published 'Breaking the silences, breaking the frames: a gendered diasporic analysis of sexual violence in the DRC' in the *Journal of Ethnic and Migration Studies* (2018). Marie is also one of the co-editors of the book entitled *Voices from the 'Jungle': Stories from the Calais Refugee Camp* (Pluto Press, 2017).

Jennifer Hyndman is a Professor in Social Science and Geography at York University in Toronto. Her most recent book (co-authored with Wenona Giles) is *Refugees in Extended Exile: Living on the Edge* (Routledge, 2017). Hyndman is author of *Dual Disasters: Humanitarian Aid after the 2004 Tsunami* (2011), *Managing Displacement: Refugees and the Politics of Humanitarianism* (University of Minnesota Press, 2000), and co-editor with Wenona Giles of *Sites of Violence: Gender and Conflict Zones* (University of California Press, 2004).

Loren B. Landau is the South African Research Chair on Mobility and the Politics of Difference at the University of the Witwatersrand in Johannesburg. His work explores mobility, governance and urbanisation across the global South. He is author of *The Humanitarian Hangover: Displacement, Aid and Transformation in Western Tanzania* and editor of *Exorcising the Demons Within: Xenophobia, Violence and Statecraft in Contemporary South Africa*. He has a PhD in Political Science from the University of California, Berkeley, and an MA in Development Studies from the London School of Economics.

Nassim Majidi, PhD, is an Affiliate Researcher at Sciences Po's Centre for International Studies (France) and Research Associate at the African Centre for

Migration and Society at Wits University (South Africa). As the co-founder of Samuel Hall, a think-tank of the Global South, she leads evidence-based research and policy development on migration and displacement.

Laurence Ossipow is an anthropologist and Professor at the University of Applied Sciences and Arts Western Switzerland – HES-SO Geneva, School of Social Work where she has been responsible for the research for the school for many years. She is a specialist of issues relating to migration, social inclusion and citizenship and has conducted a number of research projects in this field.

Ranabir Samaddar belongs to the critical school of thinking and is considered as one of the foremost theorists in the field of migration and forced migration studies. His writings on migration, labour, colonialism and the nation-state have signalled a new turn in critical post-colonial thinking. Some of his monographs include: *The Marginal Nation: Transborder Migration from Bangladesh and West Bengal* (1999) and the co-authored, Beyond Kolkata: Rajarhat and the Dystopia of Urban Imagination (2013). *Karl Marx and the Postcolonial Age* (2018) is his latest work. He is currently the Distinguished Chair in Migration and forced migration studies, Calcutta Research Group.

Liza Schuster is a sociologist at City University of London, working on forced migration, including forced return. She has published widely in the area of forced migration including comparative and multi-level analyses of Europe and European policy and on forced return where she has with area expertise in Afghanistan. She has led a number of funded projects on forced returns and has collaborated with colleagues at Kabul University.

Eftihia Voutira is Professor at the Department of Balkan, Slavic and Oriental Studies at the University of Macedonia. She taught at the University of Oxford in the Refugee Studies Programme and the Forced Migration and Refugees Studies Centre, American University, Cairo. She has done extensive fieldwork in the former Soviet Union, South and Central Africa, and the Middle East. She has published extensively on issues of refugee protection and humanitarian assistance including 'Cultures of Security and Refugee Insecurities' in *Policies of everyday life*, (2014) and 'Realising Fortress Europe. Managing Migrants and Refugees at the Borders of Greece', *The Greek Review of Social Research* (2013).

Roger Zetter is Emeritus Professor of Refugee Studies at the University of Oxford, retiring as Director of the Refugee Studies Centre in 2011. He was Founding Editor of the *Journal of Refugee Studies* from 1988 until 2001. He has regional expertise in sub-Saharan Africa, Europe and the Middle East. His teaching, research, publications and consultancy have included all stages of the 'refugee and displacement cycle'. He has been a consultant to many international and intergovernmental organisations and governments. Research funders include ESRC, Joseph Rowntree Foundation, Paul Hamlyn Foundation, MacArthur Foundation, MPI.

Chapter 1

Forced migration
Setting the scene

Alice Bloch and Giorgia Donà

Introduction

The last decade of the 20th century and the beginning of the 21st have been characterized by major geopolitical changes, which continue to shape patterns of migration, dynamics of human mobility and international responses to refugee crises and other forms of displacement. The collapse of the Soviet Union in 1989 corresponded with the ethnicization of political conflicts in Europe, Central Asia, South Asia and Africa. The 2001 attacks on the Twin Towers in New York marked the beginning of responses under the name of the War on Terror, creating further instability in the Middle East, increased Islamophobia, and more restrictionist measures in the securitization of migration (Geiger and Pécoud, 2017). Processes of globalization have changed the nature of conflicts and impacted on migration where on-going conflicts alongside new wars have led to persistent conflicts in which opposing sides are not interested in winning but in the enterprise of war itself (Kaldor, 2013). The intersection of the spread of new wars and increased securitization of migration have led to greater numbers fleeing persecution, generalized violence and human rights violations, and millions of displaced people who are unable to return to their countries of origin or to settle elsewhere.

While war, conflict, human rights abuses, individual and generalized persecution as well as environmental degradation and disasters are not in themselves new, the scale of global forced migration and displacement is unprecedented. In fact the numbers are higher than they have ever been. At the end of 2016 there were 65.6 million forcibly displaced people, of whom 22.5 million were refugees, 40.3 million were internally displaced and 2.8 million were asylum seekers. In 2016 alone 10.3 million people were newly displaced, 6.9 million internally and 3.4 million were refugees or asylum seekers (UNHCR, 2017). Added to this, UNHCR (2017) estimated that another 10 million persons were stateless. There is also an unknown and unquantifiable number of undocumented migrants of whom some will be clandestine entrants who may fear persecution but have not made an asylum claim and others will stay hidden for fear of deportation when their asylum claims are refused (Bloch, Sigona and Zetter, 2014).

Most countries in the world are affected by the past and current global crises as sending countries, as receiving countries and/or transit countries where the concern is not only the displaced generation but also future generations of children and families that may experience protracted insecurity, limited rights and poverty. The responsibility has historically and in contemporary times fallen on the nation-states that are close to the crisis which has disproportionately impacted on less developed countries of the global south and east. This is partially due to the geography of forced migration, the costs and risks of longer distance travel but also due to the maintenance of the post-colonial world order which has, as part of its agenda, the aim of keeping refugees out of the global north and west (Chimni, 2009). This means that developing regions, at the end of 2016, hosted 84% of the world's refugees (UNHCR, 2017). As more than half of the global refugee population is from Syria, Afghanistan and South Sudan, it is no surprise that Turkey, Pakistan, Lebanon, Iran, Uganda and Ethiopia host the largest numbers of refugees (UNHCR, 2017). The largest number of internally displaced people are in Colombia followed by Syria, Iraq, the Democratic Republic of Congo and Sudan, Nigeria and Yemen (UNHCR, 2017). The largest number of new internal displacements in 2016 occurred in the Democratic Republic of Congo (922,000), followed by Syria (824,000), Iraq (659,000), Afghanistan (653,000) and Nigeria (501,000) (IDMC, 2017). The data tells us that forced migration is uneven and that global responses and responsibilities are uneven.

Forced Migration: Current issues and debates focuses on contemporary key issues. The book traces continuities and discontinuities in histories and the experiences of forced migrants that unfold in the global and local landscapes. Overall, the book argues that forced migration movements are increasingly complex, leading to expanded precarity and reduced rights. These contemporary movements also challenge the language, legal frameworks and the strategies that continue to be adopted to understand and respond to involuntary movements. Not all the areas covered in the book are new, some are long-standing situations that remain current and central to on-going debates while others are more recent phenomena that demonstrate the shifting contours of the field or highlight areas that should be central to the field but remain marginalized, notably the experience of the second generation.

In conceiving and editing this book, our objective has been to showcase the changing debates and issues in order to produce a book that is contemporary and forward looking. We did not simply want to add to the existing literature or repeat much of what is already known. Instead we carefully considered present-day trends which the contributors to the book have addressed using interdisciplinary perspectives, through different geographical case studies and by employing varying methodologies. The combination of authors reviewing both the key research and scholarship and offering insights from their own research ensures a comprehensive and up-to-date analysis of the current issues in forced migration.

The book is structured around three main current themes: the reconfiguration of borders, the expansion of prolonged displacement, and changes in protection and rights and the impact of these on lived experiences. In response to increasingly restrictive state and international responses, the agency of migrants – from making the journey through to acts of resistance alongside new humanitarians – become visible as informal forms of hospitality and refugee-led initiatives emerge. These real-world changes call for rethinking concepts in the scholarly field of forced migration, and it is to these debates that we hope to contribute. However to understand the contemporary issues requires contextualization within historical trends, changing mobilities, communication technologies, labels and categories, language and rights and the lingering effects of the colonial and post-colonial world order. It also requires a generational perspective as displacement is not only significant for the generation that are displaced but for future generations too (Loizos, 2007).

The contemporary forced migration landscape

Forced migration is a general term that includes both refugees and asylum seekers and those who are internally displaced by conflicts, famine, development projects, chemical or nuclear wars or natural and environmental disasters. As an academic field forced migration studies grew out of refugee studies, a field that evolved in the 1980s with the changing profile of refugees, their movement from the south to the north, and the responses of these northern states that set out to contain refugees in the global south (Chimni, 1998). Scholars working in the field were concerned with rights and responsibilities at a time when these rights were being eroded. While forced migration is meant to be more inclusive as a field, Chimni (2009) argues that parameters of refugee studies and forced migration studies are both problematic because they contribute in exactly the same ways to the hegemony of the post-colonial world order. In this book, Zetter (Chapter 2) and Banerjee and Samaddar (Chapter 3) contribute to the debates about the field of study, the labels used and the post-colonial context.

Research and scholarship has a tendency to use the terms *refugee*, *forced migrant* and *forcibly displaced* inter-changeably and without critique or reflection. Throughout this introduction we use different terms, some specific – *refugee, asylum seeker* – and some general – *forced migrants, forcibly displaced* – to capture the field and to contexualize the chapters that follow. We hope that it is clear, at each point, why we have chosen the descriptors that we have and that we understand the politics of the labels and their significance in relation to lived experiences. One of the difficulties with categories and with understanding lived experiences is that individuals do not fit neatly into bureaucratic boxes. As Zetter notes in Chapter 2, categories are blurred. For example, conflicts and war can lead to human rights abuses, poor economies, weak states and therefore migration (Castles, 2003, 2013). Individuals often have mixed motives for their migration and can be part of mixed migration flows (Bloch, 2008; Crawley and Skleparis, 2018). However, these differences, as Crawley and Skleparis observe, are 'not merely an issue of semantics. Categories have consequences' (2018: 59). Therefore unpacking the different categories and the associated rights is an important foundation for understanding current issues; however limited they might be these issues are nevertheless central to global governance, regional and state policies and lived experiences.

The overarching framework for refugee protection is the 1951 Geneva Convention and the 1967 New York Protocol Relating to the Status of Refugees. To be granted refugee status requires the crossing of an international border and this is what makes refugees different from internally displaced people. The 1951 Geneva Convention defines a refugee as a person who,

> owing to a well-founded fear of being persecuted for reasons of race, religion, nationality, membership of a particular social group or political opinion, is outside the country of his nationality and is unable, or owing to such a fear is unwilling to avail himself of the protection of that country; or who, not having a nationality and being outside the country of his former habitual residence as a result of such events, is unable or, owing to such fear, is unwilling to return to it.

Only a relatively small minority of those considered at risk by UNHCR are in fact recognized as refugees and therefore afforded the protection of that status. This protection also includes the principle of non-refoulement, which advocates that no person should be returned to a country where they are at risk of persecution but as Majidi and Schuster show, in Chapter 6, the principle of non-refoulement is routinely breached through forced deportation. In addition to non-refoulement, refugees have other freedoms and rights that are closely linked to, but not as extensive, as those of citizens such as welfare rights and the right to work. These rights vary in different geographical contexts.

The numbers of refugees relative to internally displaced people has changed dramatically over the years. By the end of 2016 there were 40.3 million internally displaced persons, which was almost four times the number of refugees (UNHCR, 2017). This has led some to argue that the 1951 Geneva Convention and the 1967 New York Protocol Relating to the Status of Refugees are no longer fit for purpose or at the very least are limited in terms of the protection they offer forced migrants in the present-day context (see Cohen, 2007; de Wind, 2007). Moreover there are criticisms that they ignore the gendered aspects of forced migration, rooted in the dated perceptions of refugees as male, visible and public political activists and in so doing misses the private spheres where women can be subjected to persecution or the more hidden roles of women in conflict (Valhi, 2001). Women constitute 49% of the world's refugees and in many internally displaced contexts, they are the majority due, in part, to gender norms and the social discrimination that negatively impact on access to the opportunities and resources needed to make longer journeys (Nawyn, Reosti and Gjokaj, 2009; Ferrant and Tuccio, 2015). Others (see Hathaway, 2007) have made counter arguments about the need to keep the 1951 Geneva Convention due to the uniqueness of refugee's protection needs.

Regardless of the strengths and limitations of the current protection regime, which some of the chapters that follow interrogate, around three-quarters of the world's nation-states are signatories to the 1951 Geneva Convention and the 1967 Protocol. In short, it has a wide global coverage but not all signatory states adhere to the Convention and this is linked to state sovereignty over borders and the asylum system. The concept of asylum is not actually defined by any international legal instrument though 'the right to seek and enjoy in other countries asylum from persecution' is contained in the 1948 Declaration of Human Rights. However, it is up to nation-states to determine asylum cases (Goodwin-Gill, 2014).

Asylum seekers – those who are waiting for their case for refugee status to be determined – make up a small proportion of those in the forced migrant spectrum; at the end of 2016 there were 2.8 million asylum seekers (UNHCR, 2017). One consequence of this nation-state sovereignty has been variation and unevenness in recognition rates. For example, while 60% of asylum applicants from Iraq were granted refugee status in Germany; the proportion in Sweden was just 7% (Toshkov, 2014). There are numerous examples of such disparities in status determination across country contexts that partly reflect the arbitrary and subjective nature of the asylum determination process and partly the post-colonial frameworks within which decisions are made (Bloch, 2000; Nash, 2015).

Another consequence of state sovereignty in the context of the European Union and the Dublin Convention, which restricts asylum applications to the first safe country of asylum, is that many potential asylum seekers arriving in Europe enter via the southern member states (e.g., Italy and Greece) and try to go overland to countries further north. Many simply end up with little chance of making a claim or having it determined properly or end up as undocumented migrants or in transit where they try repeatedly to make a journey but their mobility is blocked or they are returned to the first safe country (Brekke and Brochmann, 2015; Schuster, 2011). As border regimes have become increasingly restrictive so too have the blurred boundaries between international refugee protection and the sovereignty of nation-states. The 1951 Geneva Convention requires states to recognise everyone who has crossed a border regardless of how the border was crossed and what, if any, documentation was used. This demonstrates an understanding of the need for some to use irregular routes to make a journey (UNHCR, 2010). However, states punish irregular or non-compliant migrants by detaining them and/or deporting them (see Majidi and Schuster, Chapter 6). While this section has set the contemporary forced migration landscape and highlighted on-going and emerging shifts, dynamics and responses, the next section examines a significant reconfiguration in this landscape that needs to be considered in order to really grapple with the contemporary issues addressed in the chapters of the book.

Borders, borderscapes and bordering practices

A key feature of the geopolitical changes that have occurred and continue to take place globally is represented by the reconfiguration of borders, and bordering practices which have created borderscapes which compromise mobility and influence the right to seek asylum. Borderscapes express the spatial and conceptual complexity of the border as a space that is fluid and shifting; a space transversed not only by bodies but also discourses and relationships that redefine inside and outside, citizen and non-citizen, host and guest across state, regional, racial and other symbolic boundaries (Perera, 2007).

Individuals fleeing conflicts that try and cross international borders encounter physical borders such as walls and barbed wired fences and natural borders such as rivers and oceans but also bureaucratic borders and security checks. At every stage of the process those fleeing persecution experience obstacles. Current migration management policies create borderscapes, those regimes of border controls that reconfigure and redefine national borders, monitor the governamentality of borderzones, and enact everyday bordering practices. Borders are no longer simply the domain of nation-states. Now other actors, such as supranational actors (the EU), private parties (e.g., airlines and transport companies), public institutions, vigilantes who patrol border areas, service providers and citizens have a role to play in the reconfiguration of borderscapes and migration management (Broeders and Engbersen, 2007; Yuval-Davis, Wemyss and Cassidy, 2018).

Since 9/11 there has been a rise in what Vaughan-Williams (2008) terms the 'citizen detective' who are the subjects of surveillance and at the same time carry out surveillance by identifying and reporting migrants who are suspected of being 'illegal'. Thus bordering practices have also been assigned to non-state actors – citizens, employers and service providers – as part of the immigration apparatus and threats of raids and fines for non-compliance has shifted the responsibility of identifying the irregular and non-compliant non-citizens, to citizens (Bloch and McKay, 2016; Yuval-Davis, Wemyss and Cassidy, 2018).

The contemporary borderscape architecture has one main objective: to stop people entering nation-states by patrolling and policing external borders. This doesn't stop irregular migration and so once in a nation-state, the aim of borderscapes is to make the lives of those who are irregular, undocumented or refused asylum seekers as untenable as possible through exclusions to welfare and from the regulated parts of the labour market and by carrying out immigration raids that can result in arrest and can end with forced return (Bloch and McKay, 2016).

The international regime manages forced migration through policies of containment, which sustains the borderscapes that keep people in regions of origin. Most recently, the 2016 bi-lateral agreement between the European Union and Turkey provides an example of how the European Union has tried to keep forced migrants away from its borders. The on-going crises in Syria and Afghanistan resulted in an increase in the numbers risking dangerous and fatal crossings between Turkey and Greece. Of the around 200,000 migrants arriving in Europe after crossing the Mediterranean in the first half of 2016, more than three-quarters had arrived in Greece. While this is not the only route across the Mediterranean – Libya to Italy being another major route with greater numbers of fatalities – it was the huge increase in numbers making the crossing between Turkey and Greece in

2015 and early 2016 that precipitated the deal. The terms of the deal were that those arriving in Greece (an EU member state) irregularly would be returned to Turkey, regardless of whether they were intending to seek asylum. In exchange for the returns, Turkey was to be paid 6 billion Euros, Turkish nationals would be allowed to travel in Europe without visas and a voluntary humanitarian scheme to resettle Syrians in Turkey to European Union member states would be developed. According to Amnesty International, one of the main problems with the deal was the erroneous assumption that Turkey offered protection and was a safe place for refugees. Moreover, as of February 2017 just 3,656 Syrians had been resettled in EU member states while there were 2.8 million Syrian people still in Turkey (Gogou, 2017).

In addition to containment, the externalization of borders and border controls has affected migration routes. Long-standing border measures include Carrier Sanctions which are the penalty fines imposed on carriers (airlines, shipping and trucking companies) found to be transporting people with incorrect or no documents, the strengthening of physical borders through fences and surveillance, documentation with biometric data, the use of airports as immigration offices abroad, the proposed creation of processing centres, called 'hotspots' in African countries, offshore processing of applications and sea patrols (see Voutira, Chapter 4, on policing the Mediterranean). Such re-bordering of spaces extends state control beyond national territories to new zones in other national territories, thus creating new borderscapes.

In the European borderzone of the Mediterranean, Frontex – the European Border and Coast Guard Agency – has established diverse surveillance mechanisms to monitor, intercept, apprehend and push back migrants or to block their passage (Topak, 2014). Of course they don't stop the flows of forced migrants arriving in Spain, Italy and Greece from North Africa from the western and central Mediterranean or via the Eastern Mediterranean route from Turkey to Greece. The countries on the southern and eastern peripheries of the European Union have become places of arrival, destination and transit. Those that want to move have their mobility blocked by new fences, by new patrols and/or by the lack of resources. Those who do manage to find their way out of the periphery can and do get caught up in the rules of the Dublin Convention if they have been fingerprinted and find themselves on the Eurodac database of fingerprints. Eurodac is used to regulate mobility and monitor asylum claims (Tsianos and Kuster, 2016), and it is a significant tool in the arsenal of weapons used as part of the Dublin Convention to identify people for deportation back to the first safe country for the purposes of claiming asylum (Broeders, 2009; Schuster, 2011 and see Schuster and Majidi, Chapter 6). However, as the policing of borders changes so too do the strategies of the smugglers and agents who migrants pay to make their journeys and of migrants themselves who make choices at every stage of the process (Mainwaring, 2016).

The reconfiguration of borders is also visible in the formation of borderscapes where the struggle over freedom of movement and its monitoring and obstruction are articulated. The increased duration of the journey across borders leads to the formation of spaces of transit at the borders of countries and across continents (Collyer, Düvell and de Haas, 2012) and these spaces are visible across the sub-Saharan desert (Collyer, 2007), at the eastern border of Europe and Asia (Biehl, 2015), and inside Europe (Schapendonk, 2017, see Voutira, Chapter 4). New informal transit spaces like Sangatte and Calais in France housed those waiting to try and find passage to the UK have been destroyed with the unwanted waiting in limbo and trying night after night to make the journey across the channel (Schuster, 2003; Ibrahim and Howarth, 2015; see Donà and Godin, Chapter 8). These 'new' informal settlements are a global phenomenon whose prototype can be found in refugee camps. In these transit spaces of exception, individuals are located inside the borders of nation-states but they do not belong to them, they are 'in' the national spaces but they not 'of' them (Bauman, 2002). The existence of these spaces, which are located outside conventional forms of protection and citizenship, challenges assumptions about belonging, and about who is entitled to belong and about who has rights and who does not.

Such states of exception are not unique to Europe. Australia operates the most extreme example through its off-shoring of asylum seekers, who arrive by boat, to islands in the Pacific. The Pacific Solution was supposed to deter those who arrive in irregular ways and who will never be allowed to settle in Australia. But in terms of the right to seek asylum it means that borders and physical spaces are more than sites of exclusion they are also spaces where the sovereign states can and do dismiss human rights obligations (McAdam, 2013). The islands in the Pacific and the Mediterranean, the sea frontiers of nation-states, have become borderscapes of containment with detention centres, reception centres but also places that have invoked displays of volunteering and charitable good will (Sandri, 2018; see Voutira Chapter 4).

For forced migrants, the shift to everyday bordering practices permeates every domain of their lives – mobility, work, housing, health, education – leaving them vulnerable to exploitation and unable to access rights. The reality is that bordering is not just about keeping people out or removing them, it also compromises human rights. Restrictive border practices redefine who belongs and whose rights can be applied. This is visible in the emerging, diversifying and spreading conditions of prolonged displacement.

Prolonged displacements and durable solutions

Another significant reconfiguration in the forced migration landscape that needs to be considered is the complex reality of individuals, families and children across generations who live in prolonged exile. The term 'protracted refugee situations' refers to the conditions of those who 'lived in exile for more than five years, and when they still have no immediate prospect of finding a durable solution to their plights by means of voluntary repatriation, local integration, or resettlement' (Crisp, 2003: 1). At the end of 2016, 11.6 million refugees were in protracted situations of which 4.1 million had been in this situation for at least 20 years. Afghan refugees in Pakistan and the Islamic Republic of Iran has involved more than 2 million and has been going on for more than 30 years. It is estimated that there are over 40 major sites of protracted refugee situations waiting to be unlocked (Zetter and Long, 2012). While in 1990 the average protracted exile lasted 9 years, now the average is approaching 20 years (Milner, 2014; Milner and Loescher, 2011). These are hardly exceptional situations in fact they are arguably the norm with few situations of displacement satisfactorily resolved. Protracted refugee situations are found in the peripheral border areas of asylum countries in the global south where refugees are provided with a 'conditional form of asylum' where they have the right to non-refoulement but at the cost of almost every other right (see Hyndman and Giles, Chapter 5). If situations of prolonged displacement are to be unlocked, the international community must circumvent the rigidity of existing solutions, including durable ones, and search for new and innovative strategies (Zetter and Long, 2012). Durable solutions have been central to UNHCR's approach to refugee protection. One of the problems faced by UNHCR in finding solutions to protracted situations is the resistance of countries to resettle refugees. In 2016 almost 200,000 refugees were resettled to a safe third country; resettlement is an important component of shared responsibility though of those resettled, 96,900 went to the USA, 46,700 to Canada and 27,600 to Australia. Resettlement is very uneven and few states take meaningful numbers of refugees and the numbers resettled constitutes a tiny proportion of refugees globally. The UK for example agreed to take a maximum of 20,000 Syrian refugees under a resettlement programme over a five-year period between 2015–2020 but are no where near meeting that target.

Local integration is another durable solution but when refugees are not permitted to leave camps or to seek employment opportunities outside the camps, integration is impossible and the consequence is protracted limbo where generations are born in camps and remain in camps. The final durable solution is voluntary repatriation and here the emphasis is on voluntary. In 2016 552,200 refugees were returned which is about 3% of the overall refugee population. Most returns were to Afghanistan, Somalia and Sudan. As this book is being completed, Bangladesh and Myanmar are negotiating the return of Rohingya refugees who fled across the border to Bangladesh after attacks in Rakhine state. The Rohingya are stateless in Myanmar and those that have fled to Bangladesh are being contained and blocked from any opportunities to integrate and do not want to be returned.

Durable solutions are not providing a workable solution to global displacement and there is a global imbalance when it comes to responsibility for those that need protection. Hyndman and Giles, in Chapter 5, argue for an approach where governments assist outside of camps, but they are also aware that without political will protracted refugee situations will continue to exist. The consolidation and normalization of prolonged exile is the result of on-going practices of confined protection in the global south, most notably the maintenance of refugee camps, and increasingly restrictive practices in the global north that limit permanent residency and protection.

Forced migration and human rights

The issue of rights is very relevant within forced migration for two reasons: first because there are numerous examples of where rights are disregarded such as the use of detention and of non-refoulement and second because human rights offer a complementary protection and have been very influential in developing refugee jurisprudence (McAdam, 2014; Bosworth and Vannier, 2016). While refugee rights are state centred, human rights are based on personhood, and so, in theory, everyone, regardless of their immigration status or lack of a formal status, should have access to human rights but the reality is very different. Non-discrimination, equality and fairness are the cornerstones of human rights. More specifically relevant to forced migrants are the rights that include: freedom from torture or cruel, inhuman or degrading treatment or punishment; freedom from slavery; freedom of thought, conscience and religion; freedom from arbitrary arrest or detention; the right to freedom of movement and residence within the borders of each State; and the right to liberty and security of person. Protracted lives in camps and restriction of movement outside of the camps in borderzones into the nation-states (e.g., Rohingya refugees in Bangladesh), detention without time limits is used in some countries (Bosworth and Vannier, 2016) or mandatory detention in the case of Australia (McAdam, 2013), compulsory dispersal within countries rather than freedom to choose where to live and not accessing the asylum system are examples of how states routinely fail to uphold the rights of forced migrants.

Children's rights are also routinely breached. At the end of 2016, 51% of the global refugee population were children and there are also children in armed conflict, unaccompanied minors seeking asylum and children deprived of the right to family life and the right to education (UNHRC, 2016). The Convention on the Rights of the Child details the specific rights of the child. Article 3(1) states:

> In all actions concerning children, whether undertaken by public or private social welfare institutions, courts of law, administrative authorities or legislative bodies, the best interests of the child shall be a primary consideration.

Placing children in detention centres, in camps for protracted periods of time, leaving them destitute or in make shift borderzones and places of transit without protection are just some of the ways in which the rights of the child are breached.

While human rights do exist and are used in asylum determination cases there are endless examples of how forced migrants cannot access rights (Lewis et al., 2014). Those who experience prolonged displacement, especially in camps which are supposed to be monitored and controlled can in fact experience a litany of different human rights abuses where mobility is restricted, employment is limited or undertaken without payment, where there is malnutrition, violence, rape, abduction and murder (Brun, Fàbos and El-Abed, 2017; Verdirame and Harrell-Bond, 2005, see Hyndman and Giles, Chapter 5).

Global context and individual agency

The global context in which contemporary forced movements occur represents a new world order in which there is confluence of similar patterns of movements, with longer and more perilous migration journeys and restricted forms of official protection. Individuals reaching Europe are likely to have endured a journey across other continents in the south and east. In the global north and west restricted access is justified on the grounds that current migrants (especially those from regions associated with Islamic fundamentalism) represent a threat to national security or that migration management takes precedence over refugee protection. Globally, there is also a tendency to move away from long-term welfare systems towards short-term emergency responses. This means the erosion of permanent solutions and an increase in precarity of life (Paret and Gleeson, 2016). Precarity can be physical, social, economic, political, legal and psychological, and forced migrants are likely to experience precarity in multifaceted and interconnected ways. In the asylum system in the UK, individuals are not allowed to work, receive welfare benefits which are below the poverty line, and are exposed to humiliation and discrimination. Exclusionary practices fuel precarity.

However, even within this current context we see that forced migrants use the agency they have, however limited, and are resilient and active in their decision-making (see Landau, Chapter 7). The tensions between structure and agency have long been evident in refugee and forced migration research (see for example Zolberg, 1989 and Richmond, 1993). Agency in particular has been having something of a renaissance though in forced migration the reality is more a limited agency where constraints are analysed and decisions made within the context of structures such as border controls. The intersections of the micro and macro are central to understanding agency.

Mainwaring identifies two sites of migrant agency: resistance-based agency and what she terms as 'everyday forms of agency' (2016: 292). There are acts of agency at every step of the process, from the initial decision to migrate, to making the journey, what happens in transit and in destination countries and how people resist the state to for example, block attempts to forcibly deport. The most basic form of agency is autonomous action where individuals are able to 'reflect on their position, devise strategies and take action to achieve their desires' (Bakewell, 2010: 1694). The agency that any individual social actor will have intersects with gender, age, class and norms. Mainwaring highlights the role of power and in so doing contests the notion of agency as being equated with choice as being too simplistic.

Agentic actors and their actions are relational and fluid and can only be understood within the framework of structure. Within forced migration research the interplay between structure in the form of sovereign state power and agency are often visible but the meso level facilitators form a crucial element of the interactions. Forced migrants make decisions at different times, and their approach is dynamic and changes according to new information and opportunities that help resist and subvert state immigration controls and borderzones (Schuster, 2011; Mainwaring, 2016). The battle between agency and structure is on-going, and the chapters in this book show how forced migrants can and do lose that battle through reliance on sometimes unscrupulous agents and smugglers, by deaths at sea and other borderzones, by their lack of access to asylum systems and violations of human rights, through off-shoring and through the practice of forced returns.

Outline of the book

The chapters in the book address forced migration as an increasingly pressing social and political issue and encourage the reader to rethink contemporary issues in the field of forced migration from multiple perspectives: theoretical, historical, regional and empirical. The first part of the book, Chapters 2 to 4, provide an historical context and offer the reader an understanding of the main theoretical frameworks that have evolved within refugee studies and forced migration studies and both Zetter (Chapter 2) and Banerjee and Samaddar (Chapter 3) make the case for moving the focus to displacement. These chapters introduce the multiple overlapping categories of those with protection needs and add to Chimni's (2009) analysis and critique of how our understandings of the complex experiences, needs and rights of multiple categories of forced migrants that have been developed in the global north must be brought into dialogues with post-colonial perspectives developed in the global south. After all, the majority of the world's forced migrants are in the global south but the funding, production of knowledge and the attention of policy makers are almost exclusively in the global north (Chimni, 2009, see Landau, Chapter 7).

The theoretical chapters set the context by situating current debates and issues in their historical context. The authors draw upon the histories of the field of forced migration, the development of theoretical approaches to studying and understanding forced migration and social transformations more generally, as well as from the histories of migration in the regions in which the authors work. The chapter by Zetter builds on his earlier work on labels (1991, 2007) by suggesting that we need to move beyond the constraints of the label refugee to think about the 'turn' from refugee to forced migration and to consider forced displacement as a more suitable terminology. Zetter develops and elaborates an empirically based conceptualization framed around the drivers, patterns and processes of forced migration and does this by taking the reader through the shifting and developing theoretical perspectives that have, increasingly recognised the complexity of forced displacement from the last quarter of the 20th century through to the current time. Forced migration paradoxically incorporates compulsion and choice as well as agency and constraints and the chapter also provides an important entry point into distinguishing the diversity of protection needs and rights that transcend a 'status-based' criterion of eligibility.

Banerjee and Samaddar offer a post-colonial critique of an academic field which has been shaped by the restrictive framework of refugee studies since World War II. The authors draw from the experience of South Asia in order to highlight the colonial approach to race and racialization where difference, conflict and borders – both real and imagined – are created. They draw on the examples of the northeastern states and of the partition of India. The processes include and exclude and label some as inside and others as outside the nation-state as it is configured and reconfigured at different times and with different objectives. They argue that contemporary displacement cannot be understood without knowledge of the past and of the role of colonial administration and in so doing the chapter offers a post-colonial critique of the field of refugee studies. It is through post-colonial interventions that forced migration studies has come out of the restrictive (legal) framework of refugee studies and has evolved to embrace many other aspects of migration – notably displacement – and has now entered a critical post-colonial phase.

The chapter by Voutira draws on the work of French historian Fernand Braudel's analysis of the Mediterranean, which considers the sea to be a multitude of interconnected land masses and bodies of water without borders and a point of interconnections between ancient worlds. Voutira notes the irony of contemporary public discourse that almost exclusively identifies the Mediterranean space as a territorial border. As a result the main policy response at the European Union level has been the introduction of policing migration with the objective of securing the European Union's external, maritime borders rather than seeing it as a landlocked basin framed in political terms in Roman times, labelled 'mare nostrum'. Using Greece as a case study – and more specifically the 10 kilometre strip of water between the island of Lesbos in Greece from the shores of Izmir in Turkey – the chapter offers an overview of the current crisis and sets this overview within an historical context of asylum at sea and of the trauma and memory of three generations of Greek Asia Minor refugees which has affected responses to the arrival of refugees on the island. The chapter highlights the connections between the present and the past emphasizing how these impact on current forms of informal hospitality.

The remaining chapters of the book bring interdisciplinary approaches to understanding complex experiences, needs and rights of multiple categories of forced migrants in the global north and south. The chapters cover a range of countries and regions and place specific current issues within the context of refugee policies and state practices but also through the lens of everyday lives and lived experiences.

The chapters use different methodological approaches including interviews, surveys, ethnography, netnography and secondary sources. Some of the chapters bring together multi-sited research conducted over time while others present in detail a case study. All the chapters offer insights into the realities of forced migration.

Hyndman and Giles focus on protracted refugees situations. The majority of world's refugees are living in protracted exile, without permanent legal status, or a place to call home. The chapter traces the origins and evolution of the concept protracted refugee situations back to the case of Sudanese refugees in Kakuma, Kenya, in 2000. The challenge, they argue, is the long-term situation of the millions living in camps year after year and for some, decade after decade and generation after generation, without any possibility of ending the precarious situations that define their lives. Similar to Voutira, they note that the immediate humanitarian emergency captures a global audience but once that emergency is over and the subjects are no longer at risk of dying the attention goes and they cease to be of interest. Hyndman and Giles explore the realities of protracted refugee situations through the case of Somalian refugees in Dadaab, showing how camps become a site of existence, of palliative care, and little more. A new paradigm where governments have to be prepared to assist outside of camps rather than assisting in the form of food rations is needed. However this would challenge the current political consensus that refugees should be protected in the region of origin and not travel to the global north where they are seen as unwanted and undeserving and objects to be pushed back and securitized.

Majidi and Schuster focus on forced return, which is a form of deportation and the physical expulsion of those non-citizens who do not or who no longer fulfil the conditions for entry, stay or residence in a country. The chapter traces forced return from what was once an exceptional strategy to one that is now a normalized or central part of the border policy of nation-states. The chapter outlines the developments in deportation policy both theoretically and empirically. Deportation is a relatively recent area of research and scholarship with contentions in the literature about why it exists as a policy. While research initially focused on the country of deportation, there has been a recent turn that explores deportation as a business, as a form of control and most recently the experiences of those who have been forcibly returned. Majidi and Schuster draw on their research with Afghans who are facing and have experienced deportation from Australia, Europe, Iran and Pakistan to illustrate the lived experiences of those subjected to this practice. They argue that forced deportation cannot be seen as a durable solution (return) because re-integration is rarely the outcome and instead re-migration routinely takes place.

The focus of Landau's chapter is on urban refugees living in South Africa in a turn that sees research and scholarship moving away from the global cities of the old imperial metropolises and turning their gaze to the urban centres where displaced people both internally and across borders are becoming an increasingly significant part of the urban population but also a population that is more of interest to humanitarian organizations including UNHCR. More and more refugees live outside of camps and within urban areas where opportunities for work and physical freedom exist, in contrast to camp settings. Urban areas can be sites for settlement but also transit. Drawing on two projects and spanning five cities – Johannesburg, Maputo, Nairobi, Lubumbashi and Kampala – Landau explores experiences and compares refugees with 'economic' migrants noting agency, precarity and solidarity. He argues that it is necessary to rethink and reframe the meaning of durable solutions and humanitarian interventions within local contexts which vary in their institutional responses, or non-responses, to refugees and other displaced people. To do this policy makers need to properly engage in the global south and uproot themselves from their northern perspectives and literally 'shift frames'.

Donà and Godin's chapter adopts a comprehensive approach to examine the role of mobile technologies for belonging and survival in forced migrants' journeys, which are embedded in 'techno-borderscapes'. Transit migrants negotiate their movements in increasingly securitized spaces, in interactions with activists and spontaneous humanitarians, all of whom use smartphones and online platforms to communicate, organize and assist. The chapter examines the role of mobile phones among forced migrants in transit through a case study of Calais, where forced migrants lived outside conventional forms of protection and assistance while waiting to cross at the border between France and the United Kingdom. In this space, mobile technologies become multi-functional devices that intersect with all dimensions – practical, affective, economic, social and political – of forced migrants' lives.

Finally, the chapter by Chimienti, Counilh and Ossipow focuses on the second generation, that is the Swiss-born children of refugees. This is a group that is increasing in size and will continue to grow but to date little is known about their experiences as they are generally submerged within the literature on ethnic minority people. The focus of the chapter is on transnational links and activities with the ancestral home of their parents. It shows the connections and ruptures that can exist for the second generation and these will have longer-term impacts on their sense of belonging but also in relation to remittances, development and possible return. The chapter argues that experiences of second generation from refugee backgrounds should be more central to understandings experiences of forced migration and that the diversity of experiences and actions enables an understanding not only of transnationalism but also identity and belonging.

The chapters in their totality bring to the fore the tension that exists between exclusion and inclusion which limits paths to asylum, confines populations to live their lives in protracted refugee displacements and expels them through deportation, forcing the disappearance of forced migrants as political subjects. However, they demonstrate that marginalization and belonging can co-exist in global cities, which are both sites of precarity, inequity, exclusion and insecurity and yet in their very fluidity and connections to regional and global networks of trade and information exchange, can also be places of protection and belonging. A redefinition of inclusion and exclusion in changing geopolitical and social contexts is presented by the analysis of the increasing role of new social media in the lives of forced migrants, which open new spaces of belonging and create flexible connections and 'virtual integration' that re-defines identity, belonging and integration both for the refugee generation and their children.

Bibliography

Bakewell O (2010) Some reflections on structure and agency in migration theory. *Journal of Ethnic and Migration Studies* 36(10): 1689–1708.

Bauman Z (2002) Up the lowly nowherevilles of liquid modernity: Comments in and around Agier. *Ethnography* 3(3): 343–349.

Biehl KS (2015) Governing through uncertainty: Experiences of being a refugee in Turkey as a country for temporary asylum. *Social Analysis* 59(1): 57–75.

Bloch A (2000) A new era or more of the same? Asylum policy in the UK. *Journal of Refugee Studies* 13(1): 29–41.

Bloch A (2008) Zimbabweans in Britain: Transnational activities and capabilities. *Journal of Ethnic and Migration Studies* 34(2): 287–305.

Bloch A, McKay S (2016) *Living on the Margins: Undocumented Migrants in a Global City*. Bristol: Policy Press.

Bloch A, Sigona N, and Zetter R (2014) *Sans Papiers: The Social and Economic Lives of Young Undocumented Migrants*. London: Pluto Press.

Bosworth M, Vannier M (2016) Human rights and immigration detention in France and the UK. *European Journal of Migration and Law* 18(2): 157–176.

Brekke J-P, Brochmann G (2015) Stuck in transit: Secondary migration of asylum seekers in Europe, national differences, and the Dublin regulation. *Journal of Refugee Studies* 28(2): 145–162.

Broeders, D (2009) *Breaking Down Anonymity: Digital Surveillance Of Irregular Migrants in Germany and the Netherlands*. Amsterdam: Amsterdam University Press.

Broeders D, Engbersen G (2007) The fight against illegal migration: Identification policies and immigrants' counterstrategies. *American Behavioral Scientist* 50(21): 1592–1609.

Brun C, Fàbos AH, and El-Abed O (2017) Displaced citizens and abject living: The categorical discomfort with subjects out of place. *Norsk Geografisk Tidsskrift-Norwegian Journal of Geography* 71(4): 220–232.

Castles S (2003) Towards a sociology of forced migration and social transformation. *Sociology* 37(1): 13–34.

Castles S (2013) The forces driving global migration. *Journal of Intercultural Studies* 34(2): 122–140.

Chimni BS (1998) The geopolitics of refugee studies: A view from the south. *Journal of Refugee Studies* 11(4): 350–374.

Chimni BS (2009) The birth of a 'discipline': From refugee to forced migration studies. *Journal of Refugee Studies* 22(1): 11–29.

Cohen R (2007) Response to Hathaway. *Journal of Refugee Studies* 20(3): 370–376.

Collyer M (2007) In-between places: Trans-Saharan transit migrants in Morocco and the fragmented journey to Europe. *Antipode* 39(4): 668–690.

Collyer M, Düvell F, and de Haas H (2012) Critical approaches to transit migration. *Population, Space and Place* 18(4): 407–414.

Crawley H, Skleparis D (2018) Refugees, migrants, neither, both: Categorical fetishism and the politics of bounding in Europe's 'migration crisis'. *Journal of Ethnic and Migration Studies* 44(1): 48–64.

Crisp J (2003) *No Solution in Sight: The Problem of Protracted Refugee Situations in Africa*. Geneva: UNHCR.

de Wind J (2007) Response to Hathaway. *Journal of Refugee Studies* 20(3): 381–385.

Ferrant G, Tuccio M (2015) *How Do Female Migrant and Gender Discrimination in Social Institutions Mutually Influence Each Other?* Working Paper No. 326, Paris: OECD Development Centre.

Geiger M, Pécoud A (2017) International organisations and the securitisation of migration. In: Bourbeau P (ed) *Handbook on Migration and Security*. Cheltenham: Edward Elgard Publishing, 339–362.

Gogou K (2017) *The EU-Turkey Deal: Europe's Year of Shame*. Amnesty International. Available at: www.amnesty.org/en/latest/news/36-47.2017/03/the-eu-turkey-deal-europes-year-of-shame/.

Goodwin-Gill GS (2014) The international law of refugee protection. In: Fiddian-Qasmiyeh E, Loescher G, Long K, and Sigona N (eds) *The Oxford Handbook of Refugee Studies*. Oxford: University of Oxford Press, 36–47.

Hathaway J (2007) Forced migration studies: Could we agree just to 'date'? *Journal of Refugee Studies* 20(3): 349–369.

Ibrahim Y, Howarth A (2015) Space construction in media reporting: A study of the migrant space in the 'Jungles' of Calais. *Fast Capitalism* 12. Available at: www.uta.edu/huma/agger/fastcapitalism/12_1/Ibrahim-Howarth-Space- Construction.htm.

IDMC (2017) *IDMC Global Figures 2016*. Geneva: IDMC. Available at: www.internal-displacement.org/database/.

Kaldor M (2013) *New and Old Wars: Organized Violence in a Global Area*. Hoboken, NJ: John Wiley & Sons.

Lewis H, Dwyer P, Hodkinson S, and Waite L (2014) *Precarious Lives: Forced Labour Exploitation and Asylum*. Bristol: Policy Press.

Loizos P (2007) Generations in forced migration. *Journal of Refugee Studies* 20(2): 193–210.

Mainwaring C (2016) Migrant agency: Negotiating borders and migration controls. *Migration Studies* 4(3): 289–308.

McAdam J (2013) Australia and asylum seekers. *International Journal of Refugee Law* 25(3): 435–448.

McAdam J (2014) Human rights and forced migration. In: Fiddian-Qasmiyeh E, Loescher G, Long K, and Sigona N (eds) *The Oxford Handbook of Refugee Studies*. Oxford: University of Oxford Press, 203–214.

Milner J (2014) Protracted refugee situations. In: Fiddian-Qasmiyeh E, Loescher G, Long K, and Sigona N (eds) *The Oxford Handbook of Refugee Studies*. Oxford: University of Oxford Press, 151–162.

Milner J, Loescher G (2011) *Responding to Protracted Refugee Situations: Lessons from a Decade of Discussion*. Forced Migration Policy Briefing 6. Oxford: Refugee Studies Centre Policy Briefings.

Nash K (2015) *The Political Sociology of Human Rights*. Cambridge: Cambridge University Press.

Nawyn SJ, Reosti A, and Gjokaj L (2009) Gender in motion: How gender precipitates international migration. *Advances in Gender Research* 13: 175–202.

Paret M, Gleeson S (2016) Precarity and agency through a migration lens. *Citizenship Studies* 20(3–4): 277–294.

Perera S (2007) A Pacific zone? (In) security, sovereignty, and stories of the Pacific borderscape. In: Kumar Rajaram P, Grundy-Warr C (eds) *Borderscapes: Hidden Geographies and Politics and Territory's Edge*. Minneapolis, MN: University of Minnesota Press, 201–227.

Richmond A (1993) Reactive migration: Sociological perspectives on refugee movements. *Journal of Refugee Studies* 6(1): 7–24.

Sandri E (2018) 'Volunteer humanitarianism': Volunteers and humanitarian aid in the Jungle refugee camp of Calais. *Journal of Ethnic and Migration Studies* 44(1): 65–80.

Schapendonk J (2017) The multiplicity of transit: The waiting and onward mobility of African migrants in the European Union. *International Journal of Migration and Border Studies* 3(2–3): 208–227.

Schuster L (2003) Asylum seekers: Sangatte and the tunnel. *Parliamentary Affairs* 56(3): 506–522.

Schuster L (2011) Dublin II and Eurodac: Examining the (un)intended(?) consequences. *Gender, Place & Culture: A Journal of Feminist Geography* 18(3): 401–416.

Tsianos VS, Kuster, B (2016) Eurodac in the times of big business: The power of big data within the emerging European IT agency. *Journal of Borderlands Studies* 31(2): 235–249.

Topak ÖE (2014) The biopolitical border in practice: Surveillance and death at the Greece-Turkey borderzones. *Environment and Planning D: Society and Space* 32(5): 815–833.

Toshkov DD (2014) The dynamic relationship between asylum applications and recognition rates in Europe (1987–2010). *European Union Politics* 15(2): 192–214.

UNHCR (2010) *Convention and Protocol Relating to the Status of Refugees*. Geneva: UNHCR.

UNHCR (2017) *Global Trends: Forced Displacement in 2016*. Geneva: UNHCR.

Valhi N (2001) Women and the 1951 convention: 50 years of seeking visibility. *Refuge* 19(5): 25–35.

Vaughan-Williams N (2008) Borderwork beyond inside/outside? Frontex, the citizen – detective and the war on terror. *Space and Polity* 12(1): 63–79.

Verdirame G, Harrell-Bond B (2005) *Rights in Exile: Janus-Faced Humanitarianism*. New York: Berghahn Books.

Yuval-Davis N, Wemyss G, and Cassidy K (2018) Everyday bordering, belonging and the reorientation of British immigration legislation. *Sociology* 52(2): 228–244.

Zetter R (1991) Labelling refugees: Forming and transforming a bureaucratic identity. *Journal of Refugee Studies* 4(1): 39–62.

Zetter R (2007) More labels, fewer refugees: Remaking the refugee label in an era of globalisation. *Journal of Refugee Studies* 20(2): 72–192.

Zetter R, Long K (2012) Unlocking protracted displacement. *Forced Migration Review* 40: 34–37.

Zolberg A (1989) The next waves: Migration theory for a changing world. *International Migration Review* 23(3): 403–430.

Chapter 2

Conceptualising forced migration

Praxis, scholarship and empirics

Roger Zetter

Introduction

The number of internal migrants exceeded 244 million people in 2016 (UNSDGs, 2016). Although international migration is usually perceived to be a voluntary and a managed process, today's reality reveals a different picture (UN General Assembly, 2017), not least because in contrast to voluntary migration, a very significant migratory movement comprises people who leave their homes involuntarily, often spontaneously rather than as a premeditated decision. Millions of people migrate because of violence, armed conflict, human rights violations and repression, as well as because of natural disasters including the effects of climate change and environmental degradation. Often termed 'forced migrants' or 'forcibly displaced' people, many millions remain in their own countries, but many millions also cross international borders: in both cases the numbers have been rapidly increasing in recent years.

What do we mean by the terms forced displacement and forced migrant? To what extent have these labels gained traction in praxis and academic discourse and above all how might they be conceptualised? These are the questions this chapter seeks to address. Although neither 'forced migrant' nor 'forced displacement' is a 'term of art' in the same way as 'refugee', this more familiar label decreasingly fits the substantially growing numbers of people needing some form of protection and other forms of assistance, but are not subject to persecution – the determining criterion of refugee status and protection under the terms of the 1951 Geneva Convention on the Status of Refugees and 1967 Protocol (hereafter the 1951 Refugee Convention). Despite the lack of global consensus, the widespread use of labels such as 'forced migrant', 'forced displacement' and 'forcibly displaced persons', and their increasing institutionalisation, counter the more prescriptive and circumscribed international legal and normative meaning of the label 'refugee'. In the search for more all-encompassing definitions, these newer labels seek to capture the complex drivers, processes, impacts and consequences, and the multiplicity of categories – outlined above and discussed in more detail below – which characterise contemporary and emerging forced displacement dynamics.

However, like any new label, the emergence of forced migrant and terms such as forced displacement has been uncertain, problematic and contentious.

Ideally, a workable concept of forced migrant would enjoy consensus among scholars and practitioners. This is far from the case and I explore why this is so in the first two parts of this chapter. First I briefly examine praxis to illustrate how the increasing traction of the terms amongst international humanitarian and development stakeholders has yet to yield a coherent conceptualisation. The chapter then shifts its focus to the academic literature to trace the emergence and conceptualisation of the term 'forced migration' (and associated terms such as forced displacement) as a descriptive tool and its saliency to the contemporary dynamics of population mobility. This assessment finds an ambiguous and limited discourse on conceptualising the term, and an uneasy relationship to the more familiar but increasingly problematic label 'refugee'. Against this context, the third part of the chapter then seeks to develop and elaborate an empirically based conceptualisation of forced migration which is framed around two parameters – the drivers of forced migration, and the patterns and processes of this forced migration.

The chapter draws on, develops and refines two earlier explorations of the concept of forced displacement: a monograph for the Swiss Federal Commission on Migration (Zetter, 2014) and a Policy Paper for the Migration Policy Institute (Zetter, 2015). More generally it is set against the backcloth of my longstanding research engagement with the theory and practice of labelling in the context of humanitarian practices (Zetter, 1991, 2007).

Evidence from praxis

Evidence from praxis offers a preliminary entry point to this review. It reveals both the accelerating pace of the search for appropriate labels to capture the phenomenon of involuntary migration and also the diversity of such labels. At the same time, it also reveals how praxis has not yielded a coherent conceptualisation.

Perhaps the earliest example can be found in two significant regional refugee instruments – 1969 OAU (now AU) Convention Governing the Specific Aspects of Refugee Problems in Africa and the non-binding 1984 Cartagena Declaration on Refugees.[1] Whilst both instruments still use the label 'refugee' and include the determining criterion of persecution, their raison d'être was the perceived limitation of this term to capture other relevant drivers of forced migration such as 'external aggression, occupation, foreign domination' in the case of the OAU Convention or, in the case of the Cartagena Declaration 'because . . . safety or freedom have been threatened by generalised violence, foreign aggression, internal conflicts, massive violation of human rights'.

Like these earlier regional instruments, the more recent so-called 2009 Kampala Convention[2] has also come about because of the definitional limitations of refugee. By redressing the failure to give legal recognition to the far larger number of forced migrants who are displaced within their own countries – internal displaced persons (IDPs) – the Kampala Convention resonates with the need to widen the scope of the terminology.

By including these wider drivers of forced migration these three instruments offer a broader and more inclusive definition and one that resonates more closely with contemporary conditions and labels such as forced migrant or forced displacement. However, despite their relevance to contemporary circumstances, their application remains limited both to their regions of origin and as the basis for a firmer conceptualisation of the phenomenon.

Other recent international initiatives have similarly sought to identify and respond to the needs of different groups of forcibly displaced people. Significantly this praxis breaks away from the constraints of specific legal and normative categories and labels designated in international conventions. Yet it stills falls short of providing a coherent conceptualisation. For example, in 2012 the IOM adopted its Migration Crisis Operational Framework (MCOF), an operational tool for the IOM, its Member States and partners to better prepare for and address the needs of populations, regardless of their legal and normative status, affected by increasingly complex, large-scale migration flows and mobility patterns (IOM, 2013). More recently, the Migrants in Countries in Crisis Initiative (MICIC, 2016) constituted a multi-stakeholder initiative of states, civil society and international organisations, and private sector actors, which has produced voluntary and non-binding Guidelines to Protect Migrants in Countries Experiencing Conflict or Natural Disaster.

Significant in these initiatives is the use of the word crisis in conjunction with migration. This is an increasing trend in the way international actors are seeking to broaden the scope of their involvement with forcibly displaced people. It is echoed more recently in a report by the UN Special Representative on Migration overviewing trends on forced migration (UN General Assembly, 2017). Yet, again, whilst the descriptive category of affected people is expanded by these initiatives, the conceptualisation remains limited.

Displacement by natural disasters is further highlighted by another example of the search for a more all-embracing label for those affected. The 2012 Nansen Initiative, now superseded by the Platform on Disaster Displacement, is a state-led process to develop a consensus about how affected states can respond to the challenge of cross-border displacement by those who cannot claim refugee status in the context of disasters and the adverse impacts of climate change (Nansen Initiative, 2015).

The significance of disasters as a driver of forced migration was also recognised by the Hyogo Framework 2005–2015 (UNISDR, 2005), reinforced by the Sendai Framework 2015–2030 (UNISDR, 2015). These instruments offer some, albeit still weak recognition of vulnerable socio-economic groups who are not refugees and the scope for interventions such as disaster risk reduction (DRR), mitigation, resettlement and rights protection that might assist recovery. Adding to the descriptive categories, these initiatives have not, however, produced a firmer conceptualisation of the phenomenon of forced migration.

The impetus behind both the World Humanitarian Summit (WHS) (United Nations, 2016) and the United Nations High-level Meeting on Addressing Large Movements of Refugees and Migrants (United Nations, 2016a, 2016b) in 2016 was to seek new ways of addressing the global challenges presented by increasingly complex patterns and processes of international migration and population displacement including forced migration. On the one hand it could be argued that these summits acknowledged the declining ability of the international regime and international actors such as UNHCR to comprehend and respond to the changing dynamics of international migration, especially refugee flows (see Hammerstad, 2014). On the other hand, they offered significant global opportunities for elaborating the concept of forced migration and enhancing the way that this understanding could foster new approaches to addressing this major contemporary global phenomenon. And indeed both summits make frequent use of the term forced displacement.

Thus, the WHS specifically records the aim of 'reducing forced displacement' in its core pledge to 'leave no-one behind', noting that 'forced displacement is not only a humanitarian challenge, but also a political, development and human rights one'(UN, 2016: 7). However, having opened up the scope for elaborating the concept of forced displacement and its potential application, the WHS Outcome Report immediately follows this by narrowing down the definition in advocating 'a new comprehensive approach to addressing forced displacement based on meeting the immediate humanitarian needs of *refugees and internally displaced persons*' (emphasis added) (UN, 2016: 7).

Similarly, both the UN Secretary General's draft report (United Nations, 2016a) and the draft outcome report (UN, 2016b) of the United Nations High-level Meeting on Addressing Large Movements of Refugees and Migrants, as well as the more recent report of the UN Special Representative on Migration (UN General Assembly, 2017), discuss the complex drivers, patterns and processes of migration and displacement. Yet, as in the case of the WHS these reports carefully eschew extensive use of the label forced displacement or forced migrant. For the most part they stick to the politically acceptable formulation of refugees and migrants (including IDPs) highlighted in the title of the High-level Meeting. None of these reports offer a conceptualisation of the terms forced displacement or forced migrant.

The potential for the two forthcoming Global Compacts on refugees and migrants – the intended reconfiguration of the international response to large-scale population movements proposed at the 2016 High-level meeting – to offer a coherent definition and elaboration of the concept and label of forced migration seems limited. In summary, reflecting the complex dynamics of forced displacement, acknowledging the limitations of the label refugee, and recognising how significant the innovative international initiatives are in specific circumstances, they provide neither a coherent definition of forced migration nor a comprehensive response to the diverse needs of forced migrants. This is because what is missing is a robust conceptualisation of the terms. This is the analytical challenge.

Conceptualising forced displacement – the research literature

The interplay between the label refugee and the term forced migration dominates the research literature; but we are left with a term which is conceptually problematic and of uncertain methodological validity. Some researchers demarcate a sharp analytical distinction between the terms refugee on the one hand and forced migration and forced displacement on the other, stressing a dichotomy between them: others elide the two sets of terms or use them interchangeably. Whilst for some academics the starting point is the differentiation offered by the international legal and normative status of refugee, others question this exceptionality and advocate the more inclusive terminology such as forced migrant or forced displacement.

Although by no means agreed, legal and normative definitions of a refugee dominate the conceptual discourse and so this constitutes an important entry point for any analysis of the concept of forced migration and its relationship to the concept of the refugee. Legal scholars such as Hathaway, Goodwin-Gill and McAdam, and Chimni advance several claims for the distinctiveness of the term refugee and the singularity of this legally defined category separate from other categories of forced migrants. While scholars such as Goodwin-Gill and McAdam acknowledge the politically and legally contested nature of the concept of a refugee (McAdam, 2006; Goodwin-Gill and McAdam, 2007), Hathaway offers a legally positivist and purist's reading of the international legal and normative basis for the concept. Concerned at the 'scholarly shift away from "refugee studies" in favour of "forced migration studies"' (Hathaway, 2007: 349), Hathaway's counterargument is premised on an orthodox reading of the 1951 Refugee Convention and its unique protective strength. He argues that the specificity of the refugee's personal circumstances and her needs and rights are not defined by a particular phenomenon of movement, i.e., forced displacement or forced migration, but by their 'underlying social disfranchisement . . . [and] the unqualified ability of the international community to respond to their needs'. In other words, it is impossible to protect refugees without protecting and maintaining the legal regime that applies to them.

Echoing Shacknove's 'Arendtian' designation of the alienage of a refugee without rights (Shacknove, 1985), Hathaway argues that subordinating the singularity of the label refugee to what he terms wider 'systemic concerns' risks undermining the normative claims and entitlements of the refugee. In his reasoning, effective protection is contingent on clear-cut categorisation and on maintaining a legal regime applicable only to refugees so defined by the 1951 Refugee Convention as the 'most deserving' of migrants. Such a justification does indeed deny the wider 'systemic concerns' on which the concept of forced displacement or a forced migrant is predicated.

Other legal scholars such as McAdam accept that the legal and normative limitations to the concept arise, in part, because of this narrowly prescriptive interpretation. Her suggestion is to widen the legal compass of the concept to overcome the 'reluctance of States, academics and institutions to view human rights law, refugee law and humanitarian law as branches of an interconnected, holistic regime' (McAdam, 2006: 1). And yet, as I will argue below, contra Hathaway and McAdam, it is precisely the subjective and restrictive legal character of the Convention (even with a 'holistic regime' which extends to other international legal instruments) privileging political and social rights, that renders it no longer an indisputable instrument for those who should qualify for some forms international protection and assistance – forced migrants.

In reflecting on the 'turn' from refugee to forced migration studies, Chimni's starting point is also the distinctiveness of the concept of the refugee contingent on its grounding in international legal and normative standards (Chimni, 1998, 2009). But this is decidedly not because of the need to safeguard the protective strengths of the 1951 Refugee Convention as Hathaway argues. Rather, for Chimni the refugee label, as a legal and normative entity, is invoked by post-industrial countries as an instrument to reinforce their hegemonic interest in legitimising the containment of refugees in the global south by non-entreé regimes and by perpetuating what he terms 'the myth of difference' (Chimni, 1998). As he pointedly notes, 'legal categories are not merely devices for inclusion but also of exclusion' (Chimni, 2009: 11). In other words, Chimni's challenge concerns the conceptual subordination of the label refugee to the locus of political interest and power in the global north, but not the wider relevance of the concept as a whole to contemporary drivers, patterns and processes of forced migration. Yet, it is indeed the exclusionary nature of the label refugee – beyond exclusion by political interests or legal norms – and its failure to capture the diversity of contemporary displacement processes that underpins the growing popularity of terms such as forced displacement and forced migrant.

From anthropological and sociological literature, Chatty and Marfleet (2013) call for greater conceptual rigour in defining the labels but elide the terms, using the formula refugee studies/forced migration studies throughout their paper without offering a conceptual elaboration of this elision or their equally extensive use of the word displacement. Martin's (2000) overview paper likewise deploys the wider category of forced migration in her review of the evolving humanitarian regime. But again, this is a largely descriptive rather than an analytical account of different categories of forced migrant in additional to refugees. And, as Turton notes, the problem with such accounts is that they rely on the 'artefacts of policy concerns, rather than of empirical observation and sociological analysis', on which a conceptualisation could be developed (2003: 2).

The challenge, as Nassari notes (2009), is the breadth of the field encompassed by terms such as forced migration. In discussing the expanding areas of study and the range of disciplinary approaches that forced migration incorporates, he reflects on the dilemma between limiting the field to retain the essentialised significance of the objects of study, and the value of capturing the diverse and complex experiences of forced migrants more widely defined (Nassari, 2009: 6). However, like Chatty and Marfleet, and Martin, he eschews analysis of the concept.

Colson in her landmark analysis of 'Forced Migration and the Anthropological Response' (2003) also avoids distinguishing between the terms, preferring to discuss 'the study of refugees *and* other forced migrants' (emphasis added) (2003: 1). Whilst acknowledging this wider grouping her review does not, in fact, deal with particular categories of forced migrants but the phenomenon of the displacement process itself and the consequences of being uprooted, irrespective of status or category. Whereas for Hathaway, as we have seen, the driver ('social disenfranchisement') rather than the phenomenon of movement is the categorical determinant, for Colson, shifting the terms of reference from legally defined categories to the patterns and processes of displacement and how these are experienced by the displaced is key. This position is consistent with her life-long contribution to the field. Nevertheless what is missing in her analysis is precisely the conceptual link between the drivers of forced migration and the dynamics of the displacement processes themselves: the latter includes, as Colson highlights, the differential experiences and needs of the diverse groups of people subjected to the phenomenon. I shall suggest how this conjuncture can be addressed below.

Castles (2003), like Colson, and Chatty and Marfleet eschews analysis of the term forced migration, instead taking as given its meaning and adopting an inclusive approach in which refugee flows, asylum seekers, internal displacement and development-induced displacement form a somewhat pragmatic but unexplained collection of categories. Complementing Colson's focus on the lived experience of those who are displaced, Castles stresses that forced migration needs to be analysed as a social process in which human agency and social networks play a major part, notably in a transnational context. In this regard he follows the mainstream sociological discourse on structure and agency in conditioning social relations (Giddens, 1984). Taken together, the contribution of this sociological and anthropological literature, whilst lacking a rigorous conceptualisation of forced migration, highlights important elements of such a conceptualisation which will be explored in the next section.

Predating and standing in contrast to the work cited so far in terms of its analytical focus, Kunz's two seminal papers (1973, 1981) framed refugee flight as an individual decision set within a wider context of different motivations and drivers. Whilst not using terms such as forced migrant, he broadened the concept of refugee beyond the constrained limits of legal and normative definitions. His frequently cited typology offered an analytical tool that had been missing until that point which aimed to provide a fully worked out conceptualisation of the motivations for refugee movements, rather than the drivers and patterns of displacement per se. Moreover his recognition of the agency of refugees and the mediating role of social relations in the decision to flee (and in resettlement) drew attention to crucial variables which subsequently lay neglected by researchers for at least 20 years. The conceptualisation offered in the third part of this chapter draws on Kunz' pioneering work on motivations and agency.

Echoing Colson, Castles and Kunz, Richmond (1988, 1993) and van Hear (1998) also give primacy to the agency of refugees. Their work provides an additional and valuable analytical focus by proposing a continuum of migratory movements embracing a spectrum of descriptive categories of migrants including refugees and forcibly displaced migrants amongst others. In this way Richmond and van Hear contest both the binary between refugees and forced migration, and indeed the binary premised upon the distinction between forced/voluntary and simple 'cause-effect' relationships leading to categorical legal distinctions (such as persecution). They move beyond specific categories on which the dichotomy is based to a schema which, as Richmond puts is, recognises the multi-variate causes and consequences of all migratory movements, including forced displacement (1998). Van Hear (1998) further refines the continuum of movements by adding a spatial dimension.

Richmond and van Hear's work adds conceptual value by systematically disaggregating the many different motives and drivers of migration and displacement, and then re-aggregating them in terms of a typology of 'mixed motives' and spatial outcomes which are mediated by the multiple political, economic and existential factors that underpin displacement. I return to this formulation as well later in the chapter.

Turton (2003a) questions the tendency to use the terms refugee and forced migrants almost as though these were interchangeable categories. Building on the conceptual apparatus of Richmond and van Hear, he offers a nuanced account of the concept of forced migration, accepting the necessary fuzziness of the continuum metaphor, but with two added analytical perspectives. First, he argues that rather than trying to resolve the methodological and ethical problems of constructing separate categories of forcibly displaced people, we should consider, instead, the lived experiences of all displaced people and to see them as ordinary people and purposive actors, embedded in particular (and usually harmful) social and historical circumstances (Turton, 2003a: 15–16). In echoing Colson's preoccupation, the argument is also a moral one: whilst forced migrants make a special claim on our concerns this is because their existence demands that we consider not them but 'us'. In other words, forced migration should be conceptualised around, and is reflected in, the way we create social constructs such as membership, citizenship, social belonging and alienation. The discursive formation of a language of forced migration which is replicated and refined in policy and practice reinforces the dehumanising process which Turton's conceptualisation rejects (2003b: 10). His second and perhaps more pragmatic argument is put in a sequel paper (Turton, 2003a). Here, he considers the structural similarities between many different kinds of displacement. Citing Cernea's work on development-induced displacement, he argues that the distinction between the study of this type of displacement (as a proxy for many forms of forced displacement) and refugee studies evaporates as they share similar empirical, theoretical, methodological and political concerns.

The dominance of anthropological and sociological analysis is countered by Betts. In his exploration of forced migration (2009, 2013), he offers an international relations perspective on those who flee existential threats to their socio-economic well-being or the severe deprivation of their rights. He recognises here the problematic of the millions of people who fall outside the legal and normative label of a refugee by introducing and developing the concept of 'survival migration', to describe and analyse the situations in which such forcibly displaced people find themselves. Included in his term are, for example, those displaced by environmental change, food insecurity and generalised violence, as well as conditions in fragile states that make possible human rights deprivations. In some respects 'survival migration' is a parallel term to the concept of forced displacement. The claim he makes is to substantially expand protection categories that would encompass the diverse economic and social needs and rights of those who are forcibly displaced out with the legal and normative understanding of persecution and the protection of civil and political rights which defines the status of refugee. I return to this argument later.

In conclusion, the limitations of the academic literature in conceptualising forced migration can be summarised as follows. First, much of the literature is based less on theoretical reflection about, and elaborating a coherent conceptualisation of, what constitutes forced migration than on simply asserting the terminology. Whilst recognising that a single analytic category such as refugee is limited, unfortunately, the failure to interrogate the term forced migration has obscured the conceptual potential of the phenomenon. Second, the literature is largely descriptive and based on documenting empirical categories rather than providing an objective analytical construct. Whilst the tension between theory and practice compels us to question the normative and methodological value of an exclusively legal distinction between refugee and forced migrant, it does not of itself answer the challenge of providing a coherent elaboration of the concept. Third, the advocates for the more inclusive terminology have not responded to the charge that the distinction between refugee and forcibly displaced persons or forced migrants merely emerges as a product of political and policy interests. It is not posited as a device to reveal the empirical reality of different forms of displacement and consequential protection needs and rights, In this context the exclusivity of the refugee label serves the interests of both states in limiting access to protection – most noticeably in the push back from 'fortress Europe' (Zetter, 2014: 65–73) and the securitisation of migration (Zetter, 2014a) – and humanitarian actors who may uphold the distinction of a status-based category to target assistance with consequentially harmful effects on equally deserving but excluded categories. Fourth and relatedly, the case for considering a wider conceptualisation of forced migration and forced displacement is still broadly predicated on the assumption that such people need protection, as is the case of refugees. However the key point here is the diversity of protection needs and rights that are not simply contingent on a status-based category such as refugee. Fifth, whilst the need for an interdisciplinary construct of forced migration is implicitly accepted in some of the research literature, mono-disciplinary approaches prevail and this has constrained a more inclusive conceptualisation. Partly the outcome of this narrow disciplinary base, and in sharp contrast to the migration literature, the literature on forced migration has, until recently, tended to underplay both structural conditions and the role of migrant agency that mediate such displacement even in situations where 'force' appears to be the dominant characteristic. Finally, and more prosaically, with its concern for territorial boundaries and legal categories, the literature has frequently underplayed the experience of IDPs as forcibly migrants, numerically far greater than refugees.

As I will argue in the next section, a rigorous conceptualisation embraces a far more comprehensive understanding of the complexity and the multiple and mixed drivers of forced displacement, and a continuum of processes rather than simpler 'cause-effect' explanations. It also provides an important entry point into distinguishing the diversity of protection needs and rights. These conceptual challenges have been profoundly problematic for government policy makers and humanitarian and development actors. A more rigorous conceptualisation also recognises that forced migration paradoxically incorporates compulsion *and* choice as well as agency *and* constraints, as Colson, Castles and Kunz amongst others understood.

Towards a conceptualisation of forced displacement

Against this backcloth of fragmented engagement by practitioners and the discursive but very incomplete account of the concept of forced migration to be found in the research literature, how, then, might we conceptualise the term? The chapter now provides an empirically grounded conceptualisation.

Eschewing the current engagement with agentive and structuralist concepts (see eg de Hass 2014), and drawing on the previous sections, forced migration is conceptualised from two overarching and complementary perspectives – the drivers of forced migration, and the patterns and processes of forced migration.

Drivers and scenarios of forced displacement

Whereas persecution has been established as the archetypal 'driver' of refugees, multiple factors precipitate forced migration and shape and influence each context and situation. Moreover, it is a combination of drivers that most often accounts for the majority of those who are forcibly displaced and renders them highly vulnerable: forced migration is rarely mono-causal, such as persecution in the case of refugees, or a uniquely cause-effect outcome. A conceptualisation of forced displacement must reflect this multi-variate character in a comprehensive way.

A typology of the different drivers comprises six broad scenarios covering contemporary and emerging situations.

1. The existential threats of socio-economic and state fragility – between migration and forced displacement

The impression that voluntary migration and involuntary displacement are two clearly distinct phenomena within a wider framework of human mobility breaks down because increasing numbers of migrants neither leave their countries of origin entirely voluntarily nor enter transit or destination countries by regular means.

Today many millions of international migrants leave their habitual places of residence and their countries because of a multiplicity of reasons which fall into three broad, but often overlapping groups of factors:

- Impoverishment: lack of livelihood opportunities, food insecurity, depletion of natural resources, contested land rights;
- Governance fragility: state and political fragility, together with weak public institutions and the erosion of essential public services;
- Rights deficits: religious or ethnic discrimination, human rights deprivation, low level repression, generalised violence and failure of the rule of law.

Situated between voluntary migration and more recognisable drivers of forced displacement discussed below, this broad grouping of drivers – socio-economic impoverishment and marginalisation, governance fragility, persistent human rights deficits – captures situations where the distinction between these two extremities is most blurred, as Lindley argues, for example, in the case of Somalia (Lindley, 2013). For these reasons, the conceptualisation of this form of forced migration has been problematic. Even so, whilst these drivers of forced migration – sometimes termed the 'globalisation of fragility' (OECD, 2016) – may be less discernable and dramatic than is manifest in overt conflict situations, these structural factors account for an increasing, though hard to document and quantify, volume of forcibly displaced people.

Failing to find a suitable way to conceptualise this form of migration, there has been a mistaken tendency in the literature to locate this complex typology within a 'crisis' frame (Betts, 2013; Lindley, 2014; Martin, Weerasinghe and Taylor, 2014). This seems to juxtapose contradictory dynamics since this is not crisis-like form of forced migration. By contrast, and echoing Lindley (2014), I argue that the conceptualisation of this particular form of forced migration must be contextualised within a wider frame of political, economic and social transformation. It is often associated with long-standing and pre-existing vulnerabilities; it tends to be incremental over long periods and slow onset, not crisis like; and it generally starts with internal displacement that typically expands into international movement. It is thus harder to detect and define than the more familiar crisis/rapid onset processes of forced migration. The 'forced' migratory response to cyclical food insecurity in the Sahel region is one example (Devereux and Edwards, 2004): sustained out-migration from West African states such as Gambia, Mali and Nigeria (where impoverishment and governance fragility prevail for some populations) (Flahaux and de Haas, 2016), and escape from human rights violations in Zimbabwe (de Jager and Musuva, 2016, Betts and Kaytaz, 2009) provide other examples.

Moreover, like most migrants, whether forced or voluntary, there is usually a combination of reasons for leaving their country of origin, not just one of these factors (Castles, de Haas and Miller, 2015). Whilst there may be no obvious or immediate 'force' which precipitates their displacement, equally, the decision to leave is clearly not a voluntary choice amongst competing alternative strategies to deal with vulnerable conditions (Zetter, 2014: 28–43). And in some cases the anticipation that these factors will intensify and lead to potential existential threats, rather than their actuality, precipitates displacement as Kunz showed (1973).

Sharpening our conceptualisation of forced migration in this way shows why this space is highly problematic for displaced people themselves: they are in very vulnerable situations, and lack protection and rights (Zetter, 2014: 18–27). Precisely because the observable drivers of displacement are often indistinct, involuntary migrants in this space often fall through the net of humanitarian engagement and 'status' recognition which brings with it rights protection from their own governments or governments of transit or destination countries. They lack a clearly articulated route, or the access to rights, security and other entitlements, which more precise recognition as refugees would afford.

Highlighting this blurred space between voluntary migration and displacement which is more evidently involuntary recognises and clarifies the existence of a very broad grouping of factors which, whilst not obviously forcing people to leave, nevertheless precipitates a substantial volume of contemporary displacement. Focusing on these varied existential phenomena sharpens our conceptualisation of forced displacement.

A better understanding of how these structural weaknesses can generate conditions of forced migration produces a more robust conceptualisation of the phenomenon. And for humanitarian and development policy makers, this knowledge helps in anticipating and thus promoting policies and actions that could diminish these conditions, such as conflict prevention, respect for international humanitarian law (IHL) and peace building.

2. The nexus of armed conflict, other situations of violence and human rights violations

Armed conflict – intra-state armed conflict with armed groups (so called non-state actors (ANSAs)) and often with state-led forces (the predominant situation), or international armed conflict between states (to a much lesser extent) – plays a crucial role in forcing people to flee, for example, in Colombia, the Democratic Republic of the Congo, Somalia, Iraq and South Sudan (Keen, 2007; Kaldor, 2007). Captured in the phrase 'escape from violence' (Zolberg, Suhrke and Aguayo, 1993), this form of forced migration epitomises the popular conception of the refugee. Often conflict and the violation of international humanitarian law and human rights violations go hand in hand (armed conflict and genocide in Bosnia (Prunier, 1998) and Rwanda (Valenta and Strabac, 2013), for example, and ANSAs and government forces in Syria). Armed conflict and other situations of violence are usually the outcome of, and exacerbated by structural conditions, sometimes termed 'root causes', discussed above in the first typology. Often these factors may themselves also be drivers of forced displacement – for example, post-election violence in Kenya in 2007, inter-ethnic/faith tension in Iraq, Libya and Syria. And, increasingly these drivers are set within a wider global (see eg Duffield, 2001) or neo-liberal and governmentality frame.

Sometimes indiscriminate and generalised, the proliferation and wide array of violations of international humanitarian law, human rights violations, and the structural conditions that propel people to leave their homes, do not generally involve persecution in the legal and normative sense enshrined in international refugee law. Invoking the concept and label of refugee is therefore problematic: IHL and human rights (HR) law may apply in some cases but lack the traction of refugee law.

A better understanding of how the nexus of human rights violations, violence and armed conflict, as well as structural weaknesses in affected countries, can generate conditions of forced migration produces a more robust conceptualisation of the phenomenon.

3. Environmental degradation and climate change

Turning to environmental degradation and climate change, these phenomena are increasingly significant generators of population displacement, but in combination with other factors. There are several characteristics to consider in expanding the concept of forced migration to include these phenomena.

Climate change and environmental degradation provide a context which may precipitate 'slow-onset' displacement. This presents new and unfamiliar challenges in understanding the concept which, as we have seen, is more often deployed in the context of crisis/rapid onset displacement. These challenges are compounded by great uncertainty on the scale, distribution and timing of potential displacement (McAdam, 2010; Piguet, Pécoud and de Guchteneire, 2011).

Next, whilst growing evidence links environmental change and climate change in particular to forced displacement, these phenomena are rarely unique drivers of population displacement but they may produce a 'tipping point'. Like the drivers of forced migration such as state fragility and the nexus of conflict, violence and rights violations, they are one, albeit significant determinant, operating in conjunction with economic, social and political factors, and linked to existing vulnerabilities (Zetter and Morrissey, 2014a, 2014b). Moreover, a counterargument sometimes presented is that migration can be conceptualised as a positive adaptation strategy (Barnett and Webber, 2010), not a negative default when all other options to displacement have been exhausted or denied.

Taken together, these conclusions further contest the ides of causality and indicate that direct causal links can only be proved in exceptional cases. It is conceptually difficult to establish a precise category of environmental or climate migrant; the extent to which displacement is 'forced' is open to debate – the populist term 'climate refugees' is profoundly misleading (Zetter, 2017).

Nevertheless, the volume and consequences will be significant, posing not only conceptual challenges but also, consequentially, for humanitarian, development and human rights actors.

Likewise, while it is plausible to assume that environmental degradation/climate change might lead to violence and conflict over scarce resource (such as water, or grazing land for nomadic pastoral communities, for example) these links have yet to be firmly established. Thus the consequential links between climate change induced conflicts and forced displacement is equally tenuous (Reuveny, 2007; Barnett and Adger, 2007). Policy analysts tend to make such assumptions. For example, a recent USAID publication, whilst acknowledging that climate change is a '"multiplier" that exacerbates current trends, conditions, and hazards' (USAID, 2015: 14), is nonetheless predicated on the premise of the need for 'basic climate-sensitive conflict analysis'. Academics tend to be more guarded. As Forsyth and Schomerus (2013) point out in their review of the literature, most of the research and publications alleging direct, linear causal linkages between environmental change, resource scarcity, and violent conflict, do not engage with pre-existing conditions that precipitate conflict and the political contexts within which resource scarcity exists. They suggest a more nuanced, indirect relationship and call for greater recognition of the adaptive capacity of vulnerable communities and for conflict resolution.

These provisos are not to deny the significance of this typology of forced migration and the potential scale of such displacement: rather they argue for a more nuanced understanding of this driver.

4. Development-induced displacement

Whilst some of the characteristics of forced migration so far discussed help to shape a conceptualisation of the drivers, a workable concept also needs to take into account our long-standing awareness of development-induced displacement (Hansen and Oliver-Smith, 1982; Partridge, 1989; Cernea, 1997, 1999). This is a major driver of dislocation for millions of people each year – some estimates suggest as many as 15 million per annum (Oliver-Smith, 2010). Construction of dams, land set aside for national parks, and most significant of all, urban infrastructure and renewal projects that clear (usually) informal settlements, produce different forms of development-induced displacement. Sometimes eviction takes place because economically powerful interests want land. But, more often, when governments or internationally/multilaterally financed development projects plan comprehensive resettlement policies, affected communities are almost always displaced and worse off as a result of displacement even if there are formal plans for resettlement (Cernea, 1999). Given the drive in most developing countries for economic growth and development, this trend is likely to intensify.

Whether development-induced displacement is forced or not may be debateable; but in virtually all cases, the lack of empowerment, inadequate protection and denial of rights of the dispossessed (notably housing land and property rights) are endemic features which resonate with the conditions of other, more recognisably forcibly displaced populations (Baird and Shoemaker, 2007; Cernea and Mathur, 2008; de Wet, 2006; McDowell and Bennett, 2012).

Yet whilst international human rights and specialist advocacy agencies draw attention to the violation of housing, land and property rights and norms, and invoke the 1998 Guiding Principles, development-induced displacement is low on the agenda of international humanitarian and development actors as well as governments compared with well-developed international humanitarian systems to respond to the people displaced by conflict and disasters, for example. Lack of policy and practice recognition has tended to diminish inclusion of development-induced displacement within a wider conceptualisation of forced migration.

5. Natural disasters

Disasters – precipitated by natural hazards such as floods, cyclones, earthquakes, volcanic eruptions, drought and landslips – are also a major driver of forced migration. Despite the enhancement of resilience and disaster risk reduction strategies under the Hyogo and Sendai Frameworks (discussed in the section on praxis, above), they account for significant greater numbers of forcibly displaced people than either refugees fleeing conflict and violence or those displaced by development – some 19.2 million in 2015, more than twice as many as for conflict and violence, and 203.4 million people in the past eight years, averaging 25.4 million each year (IDMC, 2016).

Exposure to most of the hazards which drive this form of forced displacement is not random. It is overwhelmingly the case that pre-existing vulnerable groups are most exposed to these hazards (Wisner et al., 2003). In other words the greatest impacts of loss and damage and displacement are experienced by the most socio-economic vulnerable people; they have greater exposure to hazards because of where they live (for example, marginal land more exposed to flooding and landslips which force them to move), and they have much more limited economic capacity to minimise risks or to deploy resources to recover from the impacts of the disasters. Underlying these physical and economic vulnerabilities, their socio-economic marginalisation also means they have more limited access to rights that might help protect them (Wisner et al., 2003).

Three significant features of disaster displacement contrast with displacement driven by the other conditions so far reviewed. First, displacement is very largely internal rather than international. Second, unlike the other typologies discussed so far, the substantial majority of those displaced by disasters do eventually return home: displacement is not permanent although the same socio-economic factors that mediate exposure to hazards also play a large role in who returns and when. Third, the rising incidence of extreme weather events alongside slow onset environmental degradation is precipitating the expansion of resettlement programmes which may display the same negative socio-economic impacts as development-induced resettlement, discussed above (Johnson, 2012).

Patterns and processes of forced displacement

Turning from the conceptualisation of forced displacement based on these broadly defined drivers and scenarios, this section turns to the second overarching conceptual characteristic – the processes and patterns of movement that forcibly displaced people follow, in other words, the spatiality of displacement.

Not surprisingly, just as the factors that precipitate forced displacement are both complex and diverse, so too the trajectories that forcibly displaced people follow are often diverse and fluid. The patterns of dislocation are complex and diverse – within countries, across borders, with forward, onward and backward movements from place of origin. By describing these characteristics, we can approach a more nuanced understanding of the concept of forced displacement.

Time-space discontinuities of displacement

Rather than a single event of exodus which tended to characterise our conceptualisation of refugee movements in the past, the factors that propel forced displacement are often episodic, oscillating unpredictably between different conflict phases: acute, de-escalation, escalation and stability. Thus, forcibly displaced people may be in transit or stationary, temporarily settled or temporarily returning, permanently exiled or permanently returning: their trajectory is not necessarily predicated on a fixed destination, or a clear status, or durable solution. The displacement of Somali (Lindley, 2013) and Afghan refugees over recent decades exemplify these temporal patterns. Unlike the concept of the refugee, predicated on the assumption that those with this status depart from a country of origin and remain in a host country until there is a durable solution, the conceptualisation of forced displacement can be refined by recognising the episodic nature of this 'displacement continuum'.

Internal displacement

Most people do not willingly leave their home environments even under life-threatening pressure; still less do they wish to leave their country of origin. They often believe displacement will only be temporary and may thus move locally and adopt self-protection strategies. The ratio of IDPs to refugees displaced by conflict is approximately 2.5:1, far exceeding those who cross international borders. However, it is the latter group, and specifically the refugees among them, who have dominated our conceptual (and policy) apparatus, predicated on a defined legal status. A reframed concept of forced migration would place IDPs as the central (in terms of numbers of people) component. Equally the conditions that lead to internal displacement create a reservoir that inexorably spills across international borders – exemplified by the sustained flow of Colombian refugees to Ecuador and Venezuela (now totalling almost 310,000 refugees alongside 6.3 million IDPs), from the 6.6 million IDPs in Syria alongside 4.8 million refugees and 300,000 refugees from CAR alongside 370,000 IDPs (Zetter and Ruaudel, 2016).

Routes and pathways

The arrival of hundreds of thousands of Syrians, Afghans and Eritreans on Europe's borders in recent years (see e.g., UNHCR, 2016), illustrates how forced displacement is also characterised by the unusual routes and means of travel which people undertake and also by the lack formal travel documents and permissions (see also Bloch, Sigona and Zetter, 2011). They often rely on smugglers to assist them, for example, to negotiate border crossings where they usually enter countries without visas or other official permits, or by clandestine means (Mountz, 2010). Often the terms 'irregular migration' and (pejoratively used but erroneous term 'illegal migrant') are also used to describe this informal process of mobility (Scheel and Squire, 2014). These diverse and complex types of movement challenge assumptions about the 'conventional' refugee journey on which refugee status is implicitly embedded (Ben Ezer and Zetter, 2015). A concept of forced displacement, on the other hand, recognises this diversity and complexity as the norm.

Mixed movements

Another and related feature of forced migration which blurs the distinctions between different categories of people on the move is that multiple drivers produce 'mixed movements' of people who do not fit the defintion of the archetypal refugee. For example, voluntary migrants, putative refugees, former IDPs, other forcibly displaced people, and trafficked and smuggled persons, may often be travelling together, along the same routes and with the same aspirations to gain entry and recognised status usually, though not exclusively, in post-industrialised countries. Since many of those caught up in 'mixed movements' are also considered to be 'irregular migrants', the two descriptors are often used synonymously. Whilst 'irregular migrant' is not a legal status per se, it is increasingly taking on a quasi-legal, and largely negative, connotation by many affected governments, especially in the context of 'mixed movements'.

A concept of forced displacement captures these 'shifting statuses' of mixed and irregular migration and echoes the ambiguity/lack of clarity of the drivers that have led to forced displacement in the first place. As we have seen, it is a combination of drivers that most often accounts for majority of those who are forcibly displaced: forced migration is rarely mono-causal or a unique cause-effect connection.

From voluntary to irregular migrant

Increasing numbers of migrants may leave their country of origin voluntarily as regular migrants (i.e., they are not *prima facie* forcibly displaced) but nevertheless in the course of their journeys are subsequently exposed to situations that endanger their lives, freedom or livelihoods and thus render them vulnerable in the same way as those that have been forcibly displaced. For example, regular migrants may become stranded or trapped and caught in conflict or crisis.

This was the case for 800,000 migrant workers legally resident in Libya but who became forcibly displaced by the collapse of the Gadhafi regime in the so-called Arab Spring (Zetter, 2012: 36–37) and for whom there was no international legal protective apparatus.

From camps to cities

The archetype of refugee exile, the camp, is now in decline despite the desire of many host countries to 'contain' refugees and the belief of humanitarian actors that camps provide better conditions for protection. Camps still exist often as holding/processing centres, for example, in Greece, rather than long-term settlements; but given the unsystematic patterns and processes described above, forcibly displaced people and refugees are not willingly encamped. The majority of these populations now migrate to urban areas where economic opportunities are generally better even if living conditions, the quality of protection and material assistance are substantially inferior.

Urban locations as the destination reshape our conceptualisation of the patterns and processes of forced migration. It highlights the agency of the forced migrant and challenges the containment praxis that has lain behind the humanitarian imperative for many decades (Landau, 2014)

Intractable crises, protracted and permanent displacement

In the past, many refugees eventually returned home, especially in the so-called decade of return of the 1990s – Mozambicans from refuge in Malawi; Angolans refugees from Zambia; Bosnians from temporary protection in Europe; Nicaraguans, El Salvadorans, and Guatemalans from refuge elsewhere in Central America (Harild, Christensen and Zetter, 2015). Return – one of three so-called durable solutions[3] – took place as civil wars abated and the peace building efforts of the international community had traction. Although organised voluntary repatriation took place, the majority returned spontaneously when conditions were right for them.

By contrast, a rather different, but nonetheless distinctive, process is that many contemporary situations of forced displacement are protracted or permanent: on average a refugee is displaced for just over 10 years according to a recent World Bank estimate (World Bank, 2016). Most forcibly displaced people will not find a quick or easy resolution to their situation in which they have been driven from their homes by socio-economic and state fragility and existential threats, and also the nexus of armed conflict, violence and human rights violations. The drivers that give rise to displacement are politically intractable: for example, Somalia (since 1990s), Afghanistan (1980s) and Colombia (1980s) have had displacement scenarios lasting between three and four decades; Syria will likely be the same. And, for many, forced displacement will transition to permanency – as in the case of displacement drivers such as development and post disaster resettlement.

The point here is that protractedness is not just symptomatic. Highlighting the lack of politically feasible and sustainable solutions challenges the underlying precept on which the conceptualisation of refugees and IDPs is based – that the process of displacement is a temporary and crisis phenomenon. It also highlights the potential for protracted displacement to be a driver of onward migration from countries of first asylum. Affected populations see little prospect of return to, and no viable long-term future for themselves in their own countries or in countries hosting millions of other refugees.

Onward trajectories, transit countries and global mobility

In the past, most refugees and others who were displaced were contained in their regions of origin, usually in neighbouring countries – Afghan refugees in Pakistan and Iran, Sudanese refugees in Uganda and Ethiopia, Sierra Leone refugees in Ghana. This is no longer the case: onward trajectories, as noted above, are a salient feature of contemporary forced migration. Transit countries have now entered the vocabulary of displacement; and the arrival of millions of forcibly displaced people in mixed and irregular migration flows at the borders of post-industrial countries testify to the global reach of the phenomenon. These trajectories are underpinned by transnational social networks and diasporic communities as receptors, facilitated by social media, and entrepreneurial agents and smugglers. Onward trajectories and global mobility are a direct consequence of the complex multiple drivers of forced displacement which inevitably create the 'need' for new channels and patterns of mobility.

Conclusions

Using the conceptualisation elaborated above, by the end of 2016, UNHCR estimates that 99.7 million people were forcibly displaced.[4] This is the highest total since World War II; however, beyond this documented total, there are many millions more people who have moved involuntarily but are undocumented in mixed migration flows. Driven by a complex range of factors outlined above, many of those who are forcibly displaced fall outside the established international legal and normative frameworks and labels that define refugees and IDPs, for example, and other formal categories.

This conceptualisation addresses some of the analytical challenges in elaborating an understanding of forced migration. It is not a unifying conception as such, but the conjuncture of two sets of parameters helps to unpack the complexity of forced displacement situations and why they differ greatly. Yet, whilst the scale and protracted nature of forced displacement are unprecedented, many of the characteristics described in the preceding section are not new or unfamiliar per se. But a forced displacement lens offers a way of conceptualising and analysing these contemporary phenomena in a more holistic way.

Although distinctions between different categories of people forcibly on the move are not in reality either categorical or always clear-cut, the concept of forced migration presented here seeks to distinguish between different types of forced migrants. It seeks to capture the episodic nature of this 'displacement continuum', the diversity and complexity of patterns, processes and channels, and the 'shifting statuses' of mixed and irregular migration. It moves beyond unique cause-effect relationships and linear processes of movement. At the same time, the analytical approach highlights the interplay between two structural components of forced migration: the complexity and variety of drivers that lead to forced migration are echoed in the complexity and diversity of mobility trajectories that forcibly displaced people undertake, and vice versa.

By contrast, a categorical conceptualisation which is legally and normatively embedded, such as refugee, distinguishes between different varieties of involuntary/forced migrants that are not, in reality, clear-cut but merge into each other. It is this complexity which the conceptualisation of forced migration presented here seeks to capture. Moreover, given the multi-variate factors that propel forced migration, and the diversity of categories of such people, it is essential to capture this variety beyond the undoubted power of a conceptualisation based on international legal status alone. The conceptualisation of forced migration outlined above emphasises precisely the significance of delinking the legal and status-bound definition of the displaced person (such as a refugee) from the drivers and processes of forced migration. Delinkage recognises that categorical distinctions and exclusive protection needs (implicit in legal and normative instruments such as the 1951 Refugee Convention/1967 Protocol), are often not that clear – there is a spectrum. What is also emphasised in this conceptualisation is the agency of the forced migrant at the micro level set within a wider macro level context of structural and mediating factors.

Conceptualising forced migration from these two perspectives is not merely an academic exercise. It also provides a crucial analytical tool for humanitarian and development practitioners, human rights actors, and the international agencies as a whole by opening up new ways of understanding the vulnerabilities, rights and needs of forced migrants beyond a status-based entitlement such as refugee. Transcending a 'status-based' criterion of eligibility for protection and assistance, international intervention should be predicated on a 'needs-based' and 'rights-based' response to these vulnerabilities, and not a specific legal status.

Conceptualised in this way, forced migration can reveal the diversity of protection situations and gaps (such as rights violations and acute socio-economic deprivation and needs) to which forced migrants are exposed and for which protection must be invoked. Such an approach to protection requires a holistic approach linking humanitarian, migration, human rights and developmental perspectives which a forced migration lens facilitates. Likewise a forced migration lens helps to reveal wider challenges that lie at the core of humanitarian and longer term developmental precepts such as sustainable responses, building resilience, recognising the agency of displaced people and strengthening the nexus between these factors.

Notes

1 The AU definition of a refugee does not only rely on persecution as the determining factor but declares that the term refugee 'shall also apply to every person who, owing to

external aggression, occupation, foreign domination or events seriously disturbing public order in either part or the whole of his country of origin or nationality, is compelled to leave his place of habitual residence in order to seek refuge in another place outside his country of origin or nationality', Article 1.2.

> The Cartagena Declaration (applying to Central and Latin America), which is non-binding, similarly offers a wider definition 'in addition to containing the elements of the 1951 Convention and the 1967 Protocol, includes among refugees persons who have fled their country because their lives, safety or freedom have been threatened by generalised violence, foreign aggression, internal conflicts, massive violation of human rights or other circumstances which have seriously disturbed public order'.
> (Article III.3)

2 *2009 African Union Convention for the Protection and Assistance of Internally Displaced Persons in Africa*, legally binds governments to protect the rights and well-being of people forced to flee their within their own country by conflict, violence, disasters and human rights abuses.
3 The three so-called 'durable' solutions of the UNHCR are return to country of origin, local integration and third country resettlement. While return to country of origin is generally seen as the preferred option by States, in many contemporary situations of displacement, return may not be possible for, nor desired by, displaced people.
4 This total includes an estimated: 17.1 million refugees and 2.8 million claiming asylum under the mandate of the 1951 Refugee Convention/1967 Protocol; 40.3 million internally displaced people (IDPs) under the 1998 Guiding Principles on Internal Displacement; 5.2 million Palestinian refugees receiving protection from UNWRA; 19.2 million displaced by disasters (although there are enormous year to year variations and the eight-year average is 25.4 million annual displacements); and 15 million displaced by development. There are no data for displacement by land grabbing. Sources: UNHCR Global Trends in Forced Displacement 2016 www.unhcr.org/uk/statistics/unhcrstats/5943e8a34/global-trends-forced-displacement-2016.html; UNWRA in Figures 2015, www.unrwa.org/sites/default/files/unrwa_in_figures_2015.pdf; IDMC GRID 2017 www.internal-displacement.org/global-report/grid2017/; Cernea and Mathur (2008) for displacement by development.

Bibliography

Baird IG, Shoemaker B (2007) Unsettling experiences: Internal resettlement and international aid agencies in Laos. *Development and Change* 38: 865–888.
Barnett J, Adger W (2007) Climate change, human security and violent conflict. *Political Geography* 26(6): 639–655.
Barnett J, Webber M (2010) Migration as adaptation: Opportunities and limits. In: McAdam J (ed) *Climate Change and Displacement: Multidisciplinary Perspectives*. Oxford and Portland, OR: Hart Publishing.
Ben Ezer G, Zetter R (2015) Searching for directions journeys into exile: Conceptual and methodological challenges in researching refugee journeys. *Journal of Refugee Studies* 28(3): 297–318.
Betts A (2009) *Forced Migration and Global Politics*. Oxford: Wiley Blackwell.
Betts A (2013) *Survival Migration: Failed Governance and the Crisis of Displacement*. Ithaca, NY: Cornell University Press.
Betts A, Kaytaz E (2009) *National and International Responses to the Zimbabwean Exodus: Implications for the Refugee Protection Regime*. New Issues in Refugee Research, Research Paper No. 175. Geneva: UNHCR.

Bloch A, Sigona N, and Zetter R (2011) Migration routes and strategies of young undocumented migrants in England: A qualitative perspective. *Ethnic and Racial Studies* 34(8): 1286–1302.

Castles S (2003) Towards a sociology of forced migration and social transformation. *Sociology* 37(1): 13–34.

Castles S, de Haas H, and Miller M (2015) *The Age of Migration: International Population Movements in the Modern World*. London: Palgrave Macmillan, 5th Edition.

Cernea M (1997) The risks and reconstruction model for resettling displaced populations. *World Development* 25: 1569–1587.

Cernea M (1999) *The Economics of Involuntary Resettlement: Questions and Challenges*. Washington, DC: World Bank.

Cernea M, Mathur HM (eds) (2008) *Can Compensation Prevent Impoverishment? Reforming Resettlement Though Investments and Benefit Sharing?* New Delhi: Oxford University Press.

Chatty D, Marfleet P (2013) Conceptual problems in forced migration. *Refugee Survey Quarterly* 32(2): 1–13.

Chimni BS (1998) The geopolitics of refugee studies: A view from the south. *Journal of Refugee Studies* 11(4): 350–374.

Chimni BS (2009) The birth of a 'discipline': From refugee to forced migration studies. *Journal of Refugee Studies* 22(1): 11–29.

Colson E (2003) Forced migration and the anthropological response. *Journal of Refugee Studies* 16(1): 1–18.de Jager N, Mususva C (2016) The influx of Zimbabweans into South Africa: A crisis of governance that spills over. *Africa Review* 8(1): 15–30.

de Haas, H. (2014) *'Migration Theory Quo Vadis?'* University of Oxford, International Migration Institute, Working Paper Series, Paper 100, November 2014.

de Wet C (2006) *Development-Induced Displacement: Problems, Policies and People*. Oxford and New York: Berghahn Books.

Devereux S, Edwards J (2004) Climate change and food security. *IDS Bulletin* 35(3): 22–30.

Duffield M (2001) *Global Governance and the New Wars: The Merging of Development and Security*. London: Zed Books.

Flahaux ML, de Haas H (2016) African migration: Trends, patterns, drivers. *Comparative Migration Studies* 4(1): 1–25. Available at: https://comparativemigrationstudies.springeropen.com/articles/10.1186/s40878-015-0015-6.

Forsyth T, Schomerus M (2013) *Climate Change and Conflict: A Systematic Evidence Review*. London School of Economics and Political Science, International Development Department, Justice and Security Research Programme, JSRP Paper 8. Available at: http://eprints.lse.ac.uk/56352/1/JSRP_Paper8_Climate_change_and_conflict_Forsyth_Schomerus_2013.pdf.

Giddens A (1984) *The Construction of Society: Outline of the Theory of Structuration*. Berkeley: University of California Press.

Goodwin-Gill G, McAdam J (2007) *The Refugee in International Law*. Oxford: Oxford University Press, 3rd Edition.

Hammerstad A (2014) *The Rise and Decline of a Global Security Actor: UNHCR, Refugee Protection and Security*. Oxford: Oxford University Press.

Hansen A, Oliver-Smith A (1982) *Involuntary Migration and Resettlement: The Problems and Responses of Dislocated People*. Boulder, CO: Westview Press.

Harild N, Christensen A, and Zetter R (2015) *Sustainable Refugee Return: Triggers, Constraints, and Lessons on Addressing the Development Challenges of Forced Displacement*. World Bank Global Program on Forced Displacement, Cross Cutting Solutions

Area on Fragility Conflict and Violence World Bank Group. Avaialble at: http://wwwwds.worldbank.org/external/default/WDSContentServer/WDSP/IB/2015/09/22/090224b0830f4d16/1_0/Rendered/PDF/Sustainable0re00forced0displacement.pdf.

Hathaway J (2007) Forced migration studies: Could we agree just to 'date'? *Journal of Refugee Studies* 2(3): 349–369.

IDMC (2016) *GRID Global Report on Internal Displacement 2016*. Avaialble at: www.internal-displacement.org/globalreport2016/.

IOM (2013) *Migrants in Crisis Operational Framework Information Sheet*. Geneva: IOM. Available at: www.iom.int/files/live/sites/iom/files/What-We-Do/docs/IOM-MCOF-Infosheet-10March2013-page2.pdf.

Johnson CA (2012) Governing climate displacement: The ethics and politics of human Resettlement. *Environmental Politics* 21: 308–328.

Kaldor M (2007) *New and Old Wars: Organized Violence in a Global Era*. Palo Alto: Stanford University Press, 2nd Edition.

Keen D (2007) *Complex Emergencies*. London: Polity Press.

Kunz E (1973) The refugee in flight: Kinetic models and forms of displacement. *International Migration Review* 7(2): 125–146.

Kunz E (1981) Exile and resettlement: Refugee theory. *International Migration Review* 15(1/2): 42–51.

Landau L (2014) Urban refugees and IDPs. In: Fiddian-Qasmiyeh E, Loescher G, Long K, and Sigona N (eds) *Oxford Handbook of Refugee and Forced Migration Studies*. Oxford: Oxford University Press, 139–150.

Lindley A (2013) Displacement in contested places: Governance, movement and settlement in Somali territories. *Journal of Eastern African Studies* 7(2): 291–313.

Lindley A (2014) *Crisis Migration: Critical Perspectives*. London: Routledge.

Martin S (2000) *Forced Migration and the Evolving Humanitarian Regime*. New Issues in Refugee Research, Working Paper No. 20. Geneva: UNHCR.

Martin S, Weerasinghe S, and Taylor A (eds) (2014) *Humanitarian Crises and Migration: Causes, Consequences and Responses*. London: Routledge.

McAdam J (2006) *The Refugee Convention as a Rights Blueprint for Persons in Need of International Protection*. New Issues in Refugee Research, Research Paper No. 125. Geneva: UNHCR.

McAdam J (ed) (2010) *Climate Change and Displacement: Multidisciplinary Perspectives*. Oxford and Portland, OR: Hart Publishing.

McDowell C, Bennett O (2012) *Displaced: The Human Cost of Development and Resettlement*. New York: Palgrave Macmillan.

Migrants in Countries in Crisis Initiative (MICIC) (2016) *MICIC Guidelines to Protect Migrants in Countries Experiencing Conflict or Natural Disaster*. Geneva: IOM. Available at: http://micicinitiative.iom.int/sites/default/files/document/MICIC_Guidelines_english_web_13_09_2016.pdf.

Mountz A (2010) *Seeking Asylum: Human Smuggling and Bureaucracy at the Border*. Minneapolis, MN: University of Minnesota Press.

Nansen Initiative (2015) *The Nansen Initiative Global Consultation*. Geneva: The Nansen Initiative Global Consultation. Available at: www2.nanseninitiative.org/global-consultations/.

Nassari J (2009) Refugees and forced migrants at the crossroads: Forced migration in a changing world. *Journal of Refugee Studies* 22(1): 1–10.

OECD (2016) *States of Fragility 2016: Understanding Violence*. Paris: OECD.

Oliver-Smith A (2010) *Defying Displacement: Grassroots Resistance and the Critique of Development*. Austin: University of Texas Press.

Partridge W (1989) Involuntary resettlement in development projects. *Journal of Refugee Studies* 2(3): 373–284.

Piguet E, Pécoud A, and de Guchteneire P (eds) (2011) *Migration and Climate Change*. Cambridge: Cambridge University Press and UNESCO Publishing.

Prunier G (1998) *The Rwanda Crisis: History of a Genocide*. London: Hurst.

Reuveny R (2007) Climate change-induced migration and violent conflict. *Political Geography* 26(6): 656–673.

Richmond A (1988) Sociological theories of international migration: The case of refugees. *Current Sociology* 36(2): 7–25.

Richmond A (1993) Reactive migration: Sociological perspectives on refugee movements. *Journal of Refugee Studies* 6(1): 7–24.

Scheel S, Squire V (2014) Forced migrants as illegal migrants. In: Fiddian-Qasmiyeh E, Loescher G, Long K, and Sigona N (eds) *Oxford Handbook of Refugee and Forced Migration Studies*. Oxford: Oxford University Press, 188–199.

Shacknove A (1985) Who is a refugee? *Ethics* 95(2): 274–284.

Turton D (2003a) *Conceptualising Forced Migration*. RSC Working Paper No. 12. Oxford: Refugee Studies Centre, University of Oxford.

Turton D (2003b) *Refugees and 'Other Forced Migrants*. RSC Working Paper No. 13. Oxford: Refugee Studies Centre, University of Oxford.

UNHCR (2016) *Regional Refugee and Migrant Response Plan (RMRP), Eastern Mediterranean and Western Balkans Route January to December 2016*. Geneva: UNHCR. Available at: www.unhcr.org/uk/partners/donors/577220cf7/regional-refugee-migrant-response-plan-europe-january-december-2016-revision.html?query=2015%20med%20crisis.

UNISDR (2005) *Hyogo Framework for Action 2005–2015: Building the Resilience of Nations and Communities to Disasters (HFA)*. Geneva: UNISDR. Available at: www.unisdr.org/files/1037_hyogoframeworkforactionenglish.pdf.

UNISDR (2015) *Sendai Framework for Disaster Risk Reduction 2015–2030*. Geneva: UNISDR. Available at: www.preventionweb.net/files/43291_sendaiframeworkfordrren.pdf.

United Nations (2015) United Nations, Population Division, Department of Economic and Social Affairs (UN DESA) – *Trends in International Migrants Stock: The 2015 Revision* (POP/DB/MIG/Stock/Rev.2015, Table 1). Available at: www.un.org/en/development/desa/population/migration/data/estimates2/docs/MigrationStockDocumentation_2015.pdf.

United Nations (2016) *Outcome of the World Humanitarian Summit*. Report of the Secretary-General. New York: United Nations, A/71/353. Available at: www.worldhumanitariansummit.org/sites/default/files/media/A-71-353%20-%20SG%20Report%20on%20the%20Outcome%20of%20the%20WHS.pdf.

United Nations (2016a) *In Safety and Dignity: Addressing Large Movements of Refugees and Migrants, 19 September High-level Meeting on Addressing Large Movements of Refugees and Migrants*. Report of the Secretary-General. New York: United Nations, A/70/ –.

United Nations (2016b) *Outcome Document for 19 September 2016 High-Level Meeting to Address Large Movements of Refugees and Migrants*. New York: United Nations. Available at: www.un.org/en/development/desa/population/migration/events/ga/documents/2016/1August2016/Outcome_Declaration.pdf.

United Nations General Assembly (2017) *Report of the Special Representative of the Secretary-General on Migration*, A/71/728. New York: United Nations, 3 February 2017. Available at: https://documents-dds-ny.un.org/doc/UNDOC/GEN/N17/002/18/PDF/N1700218.pdf?OpenElement.

UNSDGs (2016) Available at: www.un.org/sustainabledevelopment/blog/2016/01/244-million-international-migrants-living-abroad-worldwide-new-un-statistics-reveal/.

USAID (2015) *Climate Change and Conflict: An Annex to the USAID Climate-Resilient Development Framework*. Washington DC: USAID. Available at: www.usaid.gov/sites/default/files/documents/1866/ClimateChangeConflictAnnex_2015%2002%20 25%2C%20Final%20with%20date%20for%20Web.pdf.

Valenta M, Strabac Z (2013) The dynamics of bosnian refugee migrations in the 1990s, current migration trends and future prospects. *Refugee Survey Quarterly* 32(3): 1–22.

Van Hear N (1998) *New Diasporas: The Mass Exodus, Dispersal and Regrouping of Migrant Communities*. Washington, DC: University of Washington Press.

Wisner B, Blaikie P, Cannon T, and Davis I (2003) *At Risk: Natural Hazards, People's Vulnerability and Disasters*. London: Routledge, 2nd Edition.

World Bank (2016) *Forcibly Displaced: Toward a Development Approach Supporting Refugees, the Internally Displaced, and Their Hosts*. Washington, DC: World Bank. Available at: https://openknowledge.worldbank.org/bitstream/handle/10986/25016/9781464809385.pdf?sequence=2&isAllowed=y.

Zetter R (1991) Labelling refugees: Forming and transforming a bureaucratic identity. *Journal of Refugee Studies* 4(1): 39–62.

Zetter R (2007) More labels, fewer refugees: Remaking the refugee label in an era of globalization. *Journal of Refugee Studies* 20(2): 172–192.

Zetter R (ed) (2012) *IFRC World Disasters Report 2012 Focus on Forced Migration and Displacement*. Geneva: IFRC. Available at: www.ifrc.org/en/publications-and-reports/world-disasters-report/world-disasters-report-2012-focus-on-forced-migration-and-displacement/.

Zetter R (2014) *Protecting Forced Migrants: A State of the Art Report of Concepts, Challenges and Ways Forward*. Monograph for Swiss Federal Commission on Migration (FCM) Art.-Nr. 420.933 E. Bern: Switzerland. Available at: www.ekm.admin.ch/ekm/de/home.html.

Zetter R (2014a) Creating Identities – diminishing protection: Securitising asylum seeking in the Europe. In: Kneebone S, Stevens D, and Baldassar L (eds) *Refugee Protection and the Role of Law: Conflicting Identities*. London: Routledge, 22–35.

Zetter R (2015) *Protection in Crisis: Forced Migration and Protection in a Global Era*, Policy Paper for Transatlantic Council on Migration – Migration Policy Institute. Washington, DC. Available at: http://migrationpolicy.org/research/protection-crisis-forced-migration-and-protection-global-era.

Zetter R (2017) Why they are not refugees – climate change, environmental degradation and population displacement. *Siirtolaisuus-Migration Quarterly* 44(1): 23–28.

Zetter R, Morrissey J (2014a) Environmental displacement and the challenge of rights protection. In: Martin S, Weerasinghe S, and Taylor A (eds) *Humanitarian Crises and Migration: Causes, Consequences and Responses*. London: Routledge, 179–198.

Zetter R, Morrissey J (2014b) The environment-mobility nexus: Reconceptualising the links between environmental stress, mobility and power. In: Fiddian-Qasmiyeh E, Loescher G, Long K, and Sigona N (eds) *Oxford Handbook of Refugee and Forced Migration Studies*. Oxford: Oxford University Press, 342–354.

Zetter R, Ruaudel H (2016) *Refugees' Right to Work and Access to Labor Markets – An Assessment KNOMAD Study* (Volume 2). Available at: www.knomad.org/publications.

Zolberg A, Suhrke A, and Aguayo S (1993) *Escape from Violence: Conflict and the Refugee Crisis in the Developing World*. Oxford: Oxford University Press.

Chapter 3

Why critical forced migration studies has to be post-colonial by nature

Paula Banerjee and Ranabir Samaddar

Introduction

Forced migration is a fairly recent field in pedagogy. It began in the global north after the World War II as refugee studies. As it became clear that modern state formation was often accompanied by large-scale population displacements resulting in large population groups becoming refugees, there was a sudden upsurge in interest on who these people were. When it became apparent that these people were racially and perhaps even by religion different, this population movement came to be recognised as a crisis. What was ignored was the knowledge that population movements happened in all historical periods and not especially during and immediately after World War II. But forced migration in the context of known history of Europe were largely movements of white people so it was never considered as a problem or crisis. But the end of colonialism witnessed partitions that often went hand in hand with hordes of people moving in the global south who were not white. Many of these people had aspirations to move to the global north because they correctly associated their marginality with colonial rule that was often based on divide and rule policies. So countries in the global north marked such movements as crisis that necessitated policies and laws that gave the authority to respective states as to who should be taken and who shunned. Because more people were stopped from entering the northern borders, policies and laws were formulated and the hordes that were moving were homogenised as a faceless, nameless mass and in no way were they to be humanised in the narratives because the moment they appeared as individuals their claims for rights could not be ignored.

This was further accentuated by the fact that studies on refugees were initially hemmed in schools of law. Law dehumanised the field and then came the sociologists and anthropologists who developed narratives that put the onus of migration of refugees on the global south and was more concerned with the development of mechanisms of how to deal with these people as they were also the soft under belly of the large-scale industrialisation that was going on in Europe and the United States and often provided the necessary cheap labour. What was ignored was the post-colonial aspect of the problem of forced migration. Hence a corrective became necessary and the challenge was taken up by a handful of scholar–activists who, through their analysis, corrected the notion that refugees were rootless hordes moving to the global north without any political intervention from the north. In this chapter we argue that to understand the nature of forced migration in the post–World War II period, one has to develop a perspective that is critical of the given knowledge of forced migration. This criticality can be achieved when one uses the lens of post-coloniality. We will argue why critical forced migration studies have to be post-colonial by nature. Our examples are taken largely from the South Asian experience but it could very well be true of other post-colonial regions, such as Africa.

The colonial discourse of identifying populations – India's northeast

Scholars from Africa and Asia through their lived experience came to recognise why the problem of forced migration at least in the present time of history is a post-colonial problem. Only a post-colonial orientation may enable them to understand its complexities, gravity, various dimensions, and the coping strategies that the victims of forced migration take. To understand the phenomenon of forced migration in the twentieth century calls for a more holistic approach to the issue that refugee studies, with its overemphasis on law, could not provide. When around the mid-1990s post-colonial groups began in their own small way forced migration studies, they were of course aware of bonded labour, indentured labour, village to city labour migration and forms of servitude, etc., in short the various forms in which the 'forced' comes into play, and they refused to take up refugee studies as a separate field of research. Forced migration was, it appeared from the beginning, a much more holistic concept. The reason for this realisation was that only with a post-colonial sense of history could one move on from the old, restricted way of looking at things to the broader, more historical, political way of looking at the phenomenon of forced migration. A critical post-colonial approach means a certain way of chronicling and analysing various forms of forced migration, which is to say, being informed by a strong sense of history, awareness of the distinct nature of post-colonial politics and society, and an appreciation of the migrant and the refugee appearing as the subject of history of our time that is marked by the return of the empire.

A post-colonial analysis to begin with gives a different explanation of the notions of security and insecurity of states due to the fact that births of post-colonial nations are often marked by large-scale population movements. For example, the birth of South Asia was accompanied by massive population movements. Population movements bring up questions of security/insecurity frontally. In South Asia one of the major debates on the issue of forced migration is over the question of security, particularly because this notion of security is constantly mediated and created by a notion of difference. The forced in the phrase forced migration results from a sense of difference that leads to security/insecurity of all who are affected by it. Since forced migration brings to the fore the question of difference and how politics deals with it, and since all traditional notions of security are predicated on the inviolability and salience of the concept of difference in order to justify all methods including military methods, to control the phenomena emblematic of difference, the question of whose security are we talking about becomes crucial. The insecurity of the nation, the host communities, or elite groups who control access to resources, or the forced migrants? And what of the fact that someone's security may be another's insecurity? These uncertainties are a product of the post-colonial gaze without which forced migration studies is often reduced to refugee studies. With post-colonial interventions one can say that forced migration studies has come out of the restrictive framework of refugee studies, and has evolved to embrace many other aspects of migration, and has now entered a critical post-colonial phase.

The criticality of the post-colonial is embedded within the history of the colonial. To understand how differences were made that ultimately racialised and then nationalised histories of partition and graded democracies, one needs to look at colonial administration and the creation of differences as was done in the northeast of India in the eighteenth century. The colonial administration had introduced in that period the notion of 'racial difference' between the plains and the hills. The hill people belonged to the 'Mongolian areas', they belonged 'neither historically nor racially' to 'India proper' and its 'backward area' (that is, plains in the northeast); and therefore as one colonial administrator, R.N. Reid, noted, while power would be soon transferred in the country, these people of the 'non-Indian Mongolian areas' should not be made to negotiate with 'alien politicians'. Another administrator J.P. Mills noted the 'sharp cultural distinctions . . . (which) needed little re-emphasis'. The 'languages of the hills with the exception of the Khasis were all Tibeto-Burman'; the indigenous system of self-government was 'vigorously alive' in the hills while it had 'disappeared from the plains', the 'hills were clearly different', 'self-sufficiency was greater, artistic development was higher, squalor and misery rare, and sense of social responsibility . . . high'. And just as Hindusim and Islam covered all aspects of life in the plains, 'Christianity or animism' similarly covered the tribal way of life (Reid, 2001). In the context of what the colonial administration saw as racial, ethnic and cultural differences, the Deputy Commissioner of the Naga[1] Hills, J.H. Hutton recommended the entire hill area between the two countries, India and Burma, to become a crown colony (like Singapore and Swaziland) after the transfer of power. The relation of fidelity between the colonial ruler sticking to indirect rule and the semi-autonomous area and people would be thus retained. There was no case for transforming an excluded area into a partially excluded area, and a partially excluded area to full inclusion. The 'hillmen' did not want Hindu domination; besides they had given unforgettable service to the army during the World War II – particularly in the battles of Kohima and Imphal – by constructing roads, fighting and bringing back the wounded and the stranded from Burma, and the British could not leave them in the lurch.

Yet, as we know, the nationalist pressure proved too strong for retaining such an indirect and graded system of rule. The 1935 Act with respect to Assam had designated the Northeast Frontier Tracts, the Naga Hills District, the Lushai Hills District, and the North Cachar Sub-division of the Cachar District as excluded areas. The Garo Hills District, the Mikir Hills in Nowgong and Sibsagar Districts, and the British portion of the Khasi and Jaintia Hills District other than Shillong Municipality and Cantonment became the partially excluded areas. A special cadre for the frontier area was created in Burma, and India followed suit. The only nagging problem remained the issue of slavery. The Government of India adhered to the League of Nations Slavery Convention (1926). Slavery, practised by many hill communities, therefore, could not be allowed to continue indefinitely. However, control over slavery and human sacrifice was only the beginning of the march towards extending full administrative control and settlement of the area. War became the second occasion. And the third occasion was the argument voiced by Gopinath Bardoloi and the Khasi leader Nichols-Roy, which gained ground after the war ended in that area, that with independence the fruits of self-rule and democratic institutions could no longer be denied to the hill people of that region. By the time the Indian constitution came to be framed, political exclusion of the hill areas (including Manipur and Tripura which had evolved along different historical line) was out of question.

The main recommendation of the Constituent Assembly's sub-committee in Northeast Frontier Tribal and Excluded Areas was that the future of these areas did not lie in absorption, it lay in political and social amalgamation. Thus, distinction (read difference) would remain, but political identity with the Union would also become an accompanying reality. As we all know, with nationalist pressure mounted by Nehru and Kripalani in particular, the concept and history of excluded areas were given summary burial. But more than this, the framing of the constitution and subsequent reorganisation of the region reflected three major developments: (1) the boundary demarcation between India and Burma was complete, dividing people like the Nagas and the Mizos who by that time had started to think of themselves as belonging to distinct nations; (2) the national rule in India had firmly established its toe in these areas, and then hold, largley ending the graded system of rule (except what came as special political grant in form of the sixth schedule); (3) the restructuring of the political-administrative space by creating settled and (hopefully) stable units of political-administrative units in form of states.

The nature of the contentious politics of migration cannot be understood without this preceding history of Indian nationalism and the mirror history of the borderlands. The reason is that this history will persuade us not to take a generalised view of the relationship between migration and security, which is perched on the dominant phenomenon of political borders. Instead, by taking a critical view of the conflicts within the borderlands, we can know the blocks in the scenario, and understand why migration appears in politics as a theme of security, underwritten by a history of continuities and discontinuities through the colonial past and a nationalist presence.

The resource question

The issue of immigration and security is predicated on the question of resources. If we continue with our narrative of northeast India then our story again begins with the colonial trade of tea and timber. Besides the British owned tea estates, gradually other estates came to be owned by various Indian groups and the Assamese groups – in the previous decade about 150 tea estates were owned by about 130 Assamese companies in the Assam valley with the largest tea company having an annual turnover of about Rs. 50 crores. The rest of the Assamese bourgeoisie today consists of contractors, transporters, traders and people engaged in the hotel industry and real estate business, besides engaging in LPG distribution or timber trade. An unofficial estimate puts the number of small tea growers in Assam at 500, of whom 80% are Assamese. In Meghalaya the daily transaction of timber sale outside the state is nearly Rs. 20 lakhs. The share of central grant-in-aid to total revenue receipts in Meghalaya in 1990–1995 has ranged between 55% and 60%. In Arunachal Pradesh it has been between 64% and 70%, and in Nagaland, as high as 87%. Thus while the revenue generating capacity of states in the northeast has been extremely weak, with the entire region lagging behind the rest of the country in industrial growth, power supply, fertiliser consumption, credit flow, communication facilities, and transport network, the political class survives with central aid with which it makes its nation. Besides public rent-seeking activities, private rent-seeking continues unabated – be it in the tea industry, or in local petty trade, or in a barber's shop, in some cases the percentage of the earning given out as rent payment to private parties is as high as 25%.[2] We have thus an absolutely combustible combination: renter state, a parasite political class, massive mass discontent, weak or nil growth, and the absence of any appropriate policy of local development and resource generation and utilisation – with the immigrants being seen as the cause of all miseries of life.

In most parts of northeast India migrant populations were not looked upon kindly and perhaps no history of Assam in the post-colonial period can be written without dealing with the contentious issue of migration. There is a school of thought that argues that British efforts to recruit labourers for tea companies 'took the shape of a well-planned conspiracy' (Bhattacharya, 2001: 33). The British from 1770 decided to raise land revenue so high that it became impossible for a common cultivator to depend on agriculture alone for their livelihood. But the Assamese cultivators were still not interested to work in British companies as wage earners. The British then had to import tea labourers. First they looked towards China. But with the rising cost of labour they wanted to recruit locally. The problem became all the more acute during the boom in tea markets in 1860s. The Assamese were still apathetic to plantation jobs and so the British turned to Bihar, Orissa, Madhya Pradesh, etc. The result of such a policy was that The

Transport of Native Labourers Act of 1863 was passed, opening the floodgates for migrants (Bhattacharya, 2001).

Government officials such as Hiranya Kumar Bhattacharya are of the opinion that most of Assam's woes began with these migrants. There are others who may not hold such extreme views but still blame British policies for much of Assam's problems today. They feel that although the British were responsible for making Assam a multi-ethnic state, their policies kept the hill and the plains people apart. The Inner Line Regulations were introduced ostensibly 'to discourage unnecessary interference with and economic exploitation of the tribal people'; in reality [it was used] 'to exclude all contact, between them and the inhabitants of the plains' (cited in Barpujari, 1998: 5). Such a policy adversely affected the development of the tribal people. When Sir Robert Reid, the Governor of Assam (1939–1942) prepared his note on the *Future of the Present Excluded, Partially Excluded and Tribal Areas of Assam*, he stressed the differences between the people of the administrative areas of the Hills and Plains ethnologically, linguistically and culturally. He noted that over the excluded areas the British had at best 'the most shadowy control' (Reid, 1942: 295). According to historians such as H.K. Barpujari, this may have alienated the hill people, who were largely tribal, and the plains people.

Immigrants from neighbouring districts of Sylhet, Mymensing and Rangpur were populating the plains. The Bengalis were fast replacing the Assamese in the officialdom. Bengali had to be made the language of the court in place of Persian, as there were numerous Bengalis in the administration; and when a Persian scribe went on leave, it was extremely expensive and difficult to replace them (Barpujari, 1975). The Bengalis also became indispensable because only they could teach in the newly established government schools. They continued to occupy most of the white collar jobs, much to the resentment of the Assamese. In other sectors such as trade, both wholesale and retail, the Marwaris enjoyed a monopoly. Beside trade, they acted as moneylenders and agents of tea garden managements. According to some social scientists, the 'immigrants occupied in an organized way waste lands, grazings and forest reserves' (Barpujari, 1998: 37). By 1931, most of the wasteland in the Brahmaputra valley was occupied by the settlers. Many felt that in their hunger for land the immigrants encroached on government land and land belonging to the local people. By 1941 the immigrants penetrated the then Lakhimpur district. After Saadullah became the Premier of Assam for the second time in August 1942, it is alleged that he attempted a systematic settlement of East Bengal Muslim peasants in Assam (Saikia et al., 2003).

According to the Assamese, the situation after 1947 became worse. Between 1958 and 1961 the number of Hindu refugees from East Pakistan rose from 487,000 to 600,000 (Barpujari, 1998). At that time there were also inflows of migrants in search of work and other economic opportunities (Saikia et al., 2003). It is alleged that during 1971 a large number of East Pakistanis fled to Assam, and many of them did not return to their places of origin even after the formation of Bangladesh. Sentiments regarding 'foreigners' started hardening after 1972. In

1979 during a bi-election about one-sixth of the voters were declared foreigners by courts. The All Assam Students Union (AASU) declared 'no revision, no election', meaning without a revision of the voter list no election could be held in Assam. They demanded detection, deletion and deportation of foreigners. They had support from organisations such as All Asom Gana Sangram Parishad (AAGSP) and Asom Sahitya Sabha. Violent clashes occurred all over Assam. The movement dragged on with the political parties divided in their opinion. For the next few years, communal riots recurred in a number of areas and violence spread across communities. Even the moderate Assamese opinion was moved by a 'genuine fear that unending immigration across the border will reduce the indigenous people into a minority and the fate of Assam will be the same as that of Sikkim and Tripura' (Barpujari, 1998: 65).

Fear of immigrants did not stop with Assam. It spread to other parts of northeast India as well. Trouble with 'foreigners' started in the Mizo Hills much later and according to some had a direct impact on relations between India and China. Initially the Mizos were more concerned with their ethnic kin left in Burma. For that purpose the members of the hill tribes of Burma borderlands were allowed to enter India without any passport, 'provided they did not proceed beyond 25 miles' from the land border (Pakem, 1992: 106–7). Hence most of the immigrants came to Mizo hills from Burma. However, even before that, the Nepalese had settled in this area. The Nepalese or the Gurkhas, as they were known, came to the region from the beginning of the nineteenth century. But according to official records their settlements began in 1891 'after permanent forts were constructed in Aizawl and Lunglei' (Pradhan, 2004: 58). Gurkha settlers continued to remain in Mizoram until 1980, when their identity question cropped up. Initially the state of Mizoram agreed to confer some citizenship benefits to Gurkhas who had settled before 1950, but that notice was later rescinded. Some social scientists of Mizoram, who might even be sympathetic to the case of the Gurkhas, still consider them as 'illegal immigrants' (Sangkima, 2004a).

The case of the Chins was even more bizarre. Historically, people inhabiting the Mizo hills were considered part of the Kuki-Chin tribes. Thus the Chin people had close connections with the Mizo people. But in the majoritarian Mizo discourse, when in the early 1970s the Burmese government started taking actions against the Mizos, apparently even the Chin people did not give them refuge and became belligerents. Hence these Mizos living in Myanmar had to move back to Mizoram (Sangkima, 2004b). When in 1988 a military regime, the State Peace and Development Council (SPDC), came to power after brutally crushing the pro-democracy movement the Chins faced enormous problems. The predominantly Buddhist SPDC embarked on a campaign to 'Burmanize' the ethnic minorities in the country, and a large number of Chins have come to India to escape the religious, cultural and political persecution in their state, where the majority of the population is Christian. When the initial influx of refugees came to India, the government set up camps for them, but the camps were closed in 1995 as ties improved between India and Burma. Since then, the

Chin people have been scattered all over Mizoram state and in the absence of any humanitarian support have been surviving by doing whatever work they can find. In early 2003 the number of Burmese in Mizoram was estimated to be at least 50,000 (Refugees International, 2004). According to human rights activists the way the Chins 'were treated by the Mizoram government and the local people discourage them from claiming their refugee status' (Hre Mang, 2000: 63).

The point then is that if migration and the consequential presence of immigrants is an issue related to resources such as land or money, it is an issue related equally to nationalised politics, citizenship and the search for a self-sufficing identity. On the one hand, this is linked to a process of collective violence and collective politics in which every nationhood is submerged and which it summons everyday while on the other hand, this requirement of a self-sufficing identity is a gross caricature of what Antonio Gramsci called the 'national-popular' that can democratise internal relations. The insecurity that immigration raises everywhere is the proof that there is very often a thin difference between democracy and xenophobia. A polity with little effort can pass from one to another. In this build-up of an 'organic mass' – a mentality – immigration is the sign of the closure – at the same time all that signify that closure, namely borders, boundaries, collective violence, insecurity, in short contentious politics.

Decolonisation, partition and the making of borders

Another issue where scholars of migration from the global north and those from the south take their different paths is over the question of partition. According to scholars of the south, the twentieth century will be remembered as a century of partitions. Partition leads to forced migration – refugee flows and flows of other types. Partition also makes the question of return crucial. Do partition refugees have right to return? If they have the right to return, then what is the period they will enjoy the right? Also, will there be certain conditions placed upon return, in as much as we know that there may be forced return. Partition is the prism in which the stakes in the study of forced migration become sharper. But there is a danger also. Partition scholars take post-partition migration to be a unique process, and ignore the possibility that post-partition migration can be built on lines of historical continuity, and it is important to find out the continuities and discontinuities in the process and if necessary take a comparative approach. Do we study, for instance, the nature of forced migration in Europe in their century of religious wars, and compare that with what happened in India when the great religious war broke out in the second half of the forties of the last century? Do we compare the subjectivity evoked in Bertold Brecht's *Mother Courage* and that invoked in Sadat Husain Manto's *Toba Tek Singh*? We are perhaps still to appreciate the stakes in studying partition as a major marker in forced migration studies. Partition of the Ottoman Empire, Germany, Palestine and Korea in the last century, or the Indian partition – these are only some of the major events to shape the story of forced migration.

Partition creates histories of population movements embedded in histories of hatred that encourages ruling elites to progressively make partitioned borders more rigid. When the British divided South Asia, they did it largely on paper. The ruling class have made those borders rigid due to power considerations. Only by making the borders static and rigid can the state hope to control their respective populations. These rigid borders go against the social, cultural and economic traditions of the region. We are still grappling with studies of the border and producing western imitations only because we have not been able to formulate a South Asian concept of borders. To us the borders remain 'rimlands' difficult to govern and western hegemony even in the realm of ideas has made it imperative that for the purposes of 'sovereignty' that we convert the borders into watertight lines. A close study of Indian efforts for total demarcation of borders will show that even our best efforts cannot be considered as a success story. Such rigid demarcation will work against topography, economy, kinship networks and any other linkages. In an effort to serve the political demands of the received theory of sovereignty we are breaking 'utilitarian complementarities' and denying the history of the region.

If one looks at the history of migration between India, Bangladesh and Myanmar one understands how partitions create contentious histories. In most of northeast India today there is tremendous antipathy towards migrants, particularly from Bangladesh and Myanmar. In any given month there are a number of reports in newspapers from northeast India about the expulsion of migrants from one or other of the northeastern states. A random survey of some leading newspapers from northeast India in the month of August in 2003 portrayed that almost every day there were news stories that highlighted how migration in the northeast was a security hazard. Typically there were news on how Bangladeshi dacoits had penetrated Tripura; they were described as 'clad in lungi and armed with country made guns [as they] raided the houses'.[3] Other news items included information on how efforts were made to evict refugees. One such news item quoted the Home Minister of Mizoram stating that:

> We guess there could be at least 30,000 Myanmar nationals illegally staying in Mizoram. Anybody found staying illegally would be deported or their applications for asylum might be taken up. The decision to intensify a drive to detect illegal settlers from neighbouring Myanmar follows an anti-foreigners uprising by local groups in the hill state of Mizoram.[4]

There were other news items showing how migrations had led to the increase of police or security forces at the borders. They reported on how the Mizoram government had decided to deploy more police personnel at the Mizoram-Myanmar border hamlet of Zokhawthar even as the mass exodus of the Myanmarese nationals continued and 4,110 people including 2,074 women had crossed the border river Tiau till 3 p.m. Monday. Police said that one additional section of second battalion of Indian Reserve Police would soon be deployed at border to check illegal infiltration from Myanmar.[5]

Such discourses clearly show that migration has become a security issue. It also portrays how what is considered threatening is not just the political status of a foreigner but also her/his ethnicity and religion. But perhaps a more important question in the context of this chapter is how securitising migration has affected the vulnerable sections of the society including minorities, stateless people and women, and such a discourse is sadly lacking from most of the available written sources. However, a reading of traditional sources point to at least one corrective and that is migration into this region cannot be treated as an aberration. It has taken place over centuries and for most of that time it was accepted as natural. For slightly over the last 50 years it has been recognised as a security issue but with little understanding as to what kind of insecurities are created by securitising migration. That such securitisation affects a large number of women is hardly ever recognised in mainstream discourses thereby blurring the gender dimensions of treating migration as an issue of national security. In the subsequent sections we address the question of whose security is affected by securitising migration in northeast India. These histories of partition-induced migration also demonstrate the indelible link between the figure of the citizen and the alien. Partitioned independence is always Janus faced. The citizen exists in the alien as the savage form. Citizen is articulate; the alien is inaudible, silent. To understand this life world of visibility and shadow, forced migration studies will have to adopt the strategy of interrogating alterity.

Partition, hatred, conflict over resources, multiplication of borders all go on to make the category of the internally displaced, who are not quite refugees but can be more vulnerable. The southern discourses on forced migration have popularised this category of forced migrants that refugee studies have long ignored. Partition and post-coloniality in much of the global south have given rise to the question of development-induced IDPs. In India we cannot exaggerate the importance of this issue, apart from the fact that the IDP issue has been of singular significance to forced migration studies. While there is some truth in the observation that IDPs are 'another' governmental category and a creation of the policy world, we think that by focusing on the IDPs we are now able to link issues of nation, sovereignty, economy, globalisation, social violence, developmental issues, etc. in a more meaningful way. Recognition of the rights of the IDPs is the collective product of decades of struggles of population groups trying to survive. It is strange that very few key scholars in refugee studies care to see displacement in a broad light or do substantial research on IDP issues. Also this is a situation where old forms of refugee status determination do not make much sense in this new situation. Old guarantees of asylum likewise do not make sense in the light of preventing strategies like *Fortress Europe*. Also, how does one distinguish between a classic refugee, a person escaping hunger and in search of work by any means and anyhow, and say, trafficked labour in servitude? Rights are indivisible.

In this situation a more dialogic relationship is necessary, also we have to struggle for minimising – if we cannot do away altogether – the hold of security-related thinking, and the myriad of restricting provisions and practices in matters of recognising and protecting the rights of the victims of forced migration. Institutions have their vested interests and their domains. To try to reduce them is the need of the hour. To do so we have to begin with working out and formulating the consequences of the theoretical recognition that population flows are massive and mixed. The reality of these mixed and massive flows questions old polarities. They need to be recognised in their variety, plurality and amorphous nature – and this is possible only when we have a more federal way of looking at things, not from an institutional-pyramid point of view from the top, but from the point of understanding how it works on the ground. We shall then be able to challenge the customary distinction between refugee studies and forced migration studies, and episodic violence and structural violence in terms of protection policies and institutions. This is possible only when we consider forced migration studies not as an isolated discipline or a subject, defined by some strange esoteric rules, but as a field marked by lines of power and flight paths of various subjectivities. To work with that awareness we require not only a sense of rights and responsibilities, but some sort of political awareness of the way in which the migrant appears in our civilised societies as *abnormal*. Interrogating the production of abnormality in the figure of the migrant has to be the main research concern. All these are additionally relevant when we recognise the current time as one of the return of primitive accumulation when footloose labour becomes the ubiquitous figure of abnormality in the society of the settled and the propertied.

Trafficking, gender and the post-colonial narrative of migration

Perhaps even more vulnerable than the footloose labour or IDPs among the forced migrants are trafficked people. While the global north concerns itself with the differences between trafficking and smuggling, the global south is concerned with the criminalising of the trafficked. Though liberal South Asian laws and constitution guarantee people's right to be protected from exploitation and thereby prohibits trafficking, no amount of liberal and humanitarian legislation has been able to stop this form of servitude or semi-servitude of large groups of women. One has to realise that it is not merely a question of more or less governance but a continuance of erosion of women's physical, economic and social security by the patriarchal mode of national security that holds sway in our world. Violence faced by the trafficked women is the worst form of violence faced perhaps both by women as a social category and by the category of forcefully displaced people.

Women from Bangladesh are largely trafficked to India. From India they might then be taken to Pakistan or the Middle East. In research by Sanlaap in two red light areas of West Bengal, it was revealed that most of these women migrate from one place to another: 90% of the red light areas that they have identified as places that they have worked in are situated in the states that border Bangladesh. Most of these are either in northeast India or in West Bengal. In one particular red light area, named Changrabandha, about a third of women said that they have come from Bangladesh. In Dinbazar, many of the sex workers have said that their mothers came from Bangladesh. The report clearly states, 'The rate of trafficking in Changrabandha is remarkably higher than Dinbazar. The red-light area of Changrabandha is adjacent to Bangladesh border and women are trafficked through this border like any other commodity'.[6]

Trafficking often assumes worse forms when it is related to statelessness as is evident from the literature of forced migration from South Asia. We can discuss here the case of the Rohingya women who are stateless. These women are Muslims and are considered 'resident foreigners', even in their homeland. Their subordinate status within their own community discourages them from procuring education or working outside their homes. The state authorities and the army habitually sexually abuse them. Sayeeda, an 18-year-old Rohingya girl, who has had some education, was of the opinion that the state machinery used rape as a way to push women out of Myanmar.[7] Forced relocation especially without compensation is also used to push women out of Myanmar (Images Asia, 1999). These women are first taken to Bangladesh. But after the UNHCR repatriation programme started in Bangladesh, new arrivals were no longer admitted to UNHCR camps. They were often pushed across the borders to India and then to Pakistan (see Banerjee, 2003 for a more detailed analysis). Women, in this process of displacement, are abused sexually and otherwise before, during and after displacement. In any stage of displacement they are soft targets for traffickers. The government of Pakistan has largely ignored the issue of trafficking of Rohingya women. Besides the risk of being sold, Rohingya women become victims of slavery through debt bondage and their undocumented status makes them vulnerable to arrest and imprisonment (Ghosal, 2000). In the jails of West Bengal, there are over a hundred Rohingya men and women who are held in bondage indefinitely as the nation knows not how to deal with them since they are stateless. Imprisoned in Baharampur jail, 70-year old Manadma Begum can neither express herself nor can she understand why she is being incarcerated for so long.[8] Her language sets her apart from the Bangladeshi inmates who are much larger in number. Parvin Bibi, a 20 year old Rohingya woman in the Dum Dum jail, claims that she is from the Chittagong Hill Tracts and sheds tears saying that she should be treated as a Bangladeshi as her husband is a Bangladeshi national. But the police inform us that such is not the case as when she was caught she had claimed that she is a Rohingya.[9] When we asked Parveen Bibi why she originally called herself a Rohingya, she said that she was told that it would fetch a lighter jail term. Nurbahar Bibi, a Rohingya from the Cox's Bazar, talks to us despondently as she has lost all her hopes. Her Bangladeshi husband has been pushed back, and she has no access to the man who had brought her here, so even if she is released where would she go?[10]

Trafficking finds little space in traditional security discourse yet it is one mode of migration that actually leads to physical insecurity of a region. Equating trafficking with sex slavery has given rise to many unforeseen security hazards. One such hazard is the marking of the female subject as nothing but victim. Indeed as Kapur writes:

> the Third World victim subject has come to represent the more victimized subject; that is, the real or authentic victim subject. Feminist politics in the international human rights arena, as well as in parts of the Third World, have promoted this image of the authentic victim subject (2002: 2).

The states have appropriated this image of silent female victim as the true representation of trafficked women. This image has also served the states well because now the state policy makers are able to argue that a police regime has to be imposed on the borders to protect these silent victims. Although such a regime is imposed for the protection of women, women are the most marginalised. The perception of threat derives from women's sexuality and mobility because mobility ordains women's sexuality as uncontrolled. Since migration and trafficking follow the same routes the two categories collapse. With the criminalisation of trafficking, migration is also criminalised. Trafficked women and undocumented migrant women therefore become a threat to the purity of the national borders. So to protect women's sexuality, a police regime is imposed that have to protect the women from the consequences of their own uncontrolled sexuality otherwise that will affect national security. This leads to criminalisation of any form of undocumented migration across the border.

Concluding observations

How does one stop criminalisation of migrants? In the colonial times all those who were considered as racially different were marked as aliens. The post-colonial states have inherited that practice. To legitimise their control of resources they have tried to marginalise anyone who is considered as a threat. Migrants are a visible threat to their control of resources. Running parallel to this thought process of control in the former colonies there is the popular practice of dialogue. There is an interesting story on this Indian notion of dialogue. It was said that when the Parsis first came to India, the Indian monarch would not let them settle in India. But before turning them away he invited them to a dialogue. He filled a glass with milk and told the leader of the Parsis that India is like a glass full of milk. There is no place for anyone. The leader of the Parsi delegate then took a spoon full of sugar and dissolved it in the milk. He said that the Parsis were like the sugar. They would seamlessly assimilate and make the state more inclusive and therefore a better place for all. To address the issue of forced migration, it is important to strengthen this tradition of dialogue. Dialogue is ethics. The ethical practices of care and protection to the extent they are there in the legal mechanisms for protection of the displaced persons are like a double-edged sword. They strengthen the principles of humanitarianism, which we need in our individual and collectives lives. Yet when applied, they tend to reduce the persons they seek to protect and care for to being objects of care and charity. Also, people may say, perhaps rightly, that whatever protection people have got is not due to the principles of care and hospitality, but through struggle for rights. How is basic rightlessness removed? Derrida (2000) argued in a profound way that while the principle of care and hospitality is unavoidable, we care only to the extent self-care allows. Thus there is always a limit to the care that these international legal mechanisms offer. At times a great power will bomb a country, create refugees, displace millions, and then the so-called international community will invoke the principles of care to rush aid in those bombed out countries, and help the displaced within the limits set by the big power. That is why people in war-ravaged countries sometimes despise the humanitarian workers, many of whom are inspired with the noblest values, yet get represented as the ones who have come to supply artificial legs in the evening after their legs have been cut off in the morning on the order of a tyrant.

Humanitarianism is an ideology that works like a machine. We begin with sentiments, we create institutions to give effect to those sentiments, and then we legitimise those institutions with an overarching ideology of care, which often glosses over the injustices of the entire process through which persons have been reduced to being objects of care and protection (Samaddar, 2004). Hence we often hear the question of agency. And in any case a large number of the displaced millions on earth, possibly the majority of the displaced persons, do not depend on these legal arrangements. Care operates in the lives of the millions in a different way.

We can see this paradox even in the legal and administrative mechanisms for the protection of the displaced in India. There is no one single arrangement. Care of the displaced due to violence is organised along one line, or set of lines, while care of the displaced due to developmental activities runs along another set, while again the care of the displaced due to natural disasters is organised in a different set of ways (Banerjee et al., 2006). There are similarities in these three cases, yet the principle of care operates in a differential way. Humanitarianism in the nineteenth century was for the destitute, the abnormal, the poor in the colonies, etc. Now it is for the displaced and the migrant, the abnormal subject of our time.

Yet we cannot do away with the principle of care. Federalisation of care is important. Likewise important is the task of making dialogic the principles of care and protection. This requires the insertion of the principle of justice, which will bring back the issues of claims and rights. We thus cannot avoid the contradiction between care and rights; only a sense of justice can make us more caring. The evolution of the jurisprudence on disability rights in India shows how a sense of justice can lead to a more caring approach (Kannabiran, 2012). Discourse on migration and justice is another one of the post-colonial concerns coming out from the global south.

Notes

1. Reid R (2001) A Note on the Future of the Present Excluded, Partially Excluded and Tribal Areas of Assam, and Mills JP A Note on the Future of the Hill Tribes of Assam and the Adjoining Hills in a Self-Governing India. In: Fuji Takeshi (ed.)(2001) *Mirrors of the Colonial State – The Frontier Areas between North East India and Burma.* New Delhi: Manohar Publishers.
2. These figures are from the various reports of the Comptroller and Auditor General of India (CAG) with respect to these states, reproduced in Gurudas Das (1998) Liberalization and Internal Periphery – Understanding the Implications for India's Northeast. In: Gurudas Das, Purkayastha R.K.(eds.) *Liberalisation and India's North East.* New Delhi: Commonwealth Publishers, 146–149.
3. "B'deshi dacoits penetrate security cover in Khowai," in *Tripura Observer,* 21 August 2003.
4. "Myanmar refugees in Mizoram face eviction,"*Shillong Times,* 8 August 2003.
5. "Mizoram to deploy more cops on Myanmar border,"*Assam Tribune,* 14 August 2003.
6. Project:Linkage, *A Situational Analysis on Trafficking and Prostitution in Dinbazaar (Jalpaiguri) and Changrabandha (Behar)*, A Sanlaap Initiative *Cooch* Report, supported by Gana Unnayan Parshad and Human Development Centre (unpublished) p. 18.
7. Interview with the author on 20 September 1998, in Dhaka
8. Manadma Begum in Baharampur Correctional Home 2014, Personal Communication.28 November.
9. Parveen Bibi in Dumdum Correctional Home 2014. Personal Communication.28 October.
10. Nurbahar Bibi in Baharampur Correctional Home 2014. Personal Communication. 8 November.

Bibliography

Banerjee P (2003) Refugee women and the fundamental inadequacies in institutional responses in South Asia. In: Joshva R (ed) *Refugees and Their Right to Communicate: South Asian Perspectives.* London: World Association for Christian Communication, Section 4(b).

Banerjee P, Samaddar R, Guhathakurta M, Begum S, Acharya J, and Hans A et.al. (2006) *Voices of the Internally Displaced in South Asia.* Kolkata: Mahanirban Calcutta Research Group.

Barpujari HK (ed) (1975) *Political History of Assam.* vol. 1. Guwahati: Government of Assam.

Barpujari HK (1998) *North-East India: Problems, Policies & Prospects.* Guwahati and New Delhi: Spectrum Publishers.

Bhattacharya HK (2001) *The Silent Invasion: Assam Versus Infiltration.* Guwahati and New Delhi: Spectrum Publishers.

Derrida J (2000) *Of Hospitality.* Stanford, CA: Stanford University Press.

Ghosal S (2000) Stateless and oppressed from Burma: Rohingya women. *Refugee Watch* 10 and 11(3): 15.

Gurudas Das (1998) Liberalization and internal periphery – understanding the implications for India's Northeast. In: Das Gurudas, Purkayastha RK (eds) *Liberalisation and India's North East.* New Delhi: Commonwealth Publishers, 146–149.

Hre Mang JH (2000) *Report of the Chin Refugees in Mizoram State of India*. New Delhi: Other Media Communications.
Images Asia (1999) *Trafficked from Hell to Hadis*. Unpublished report. Images Asia.
Kalpana K (2012) *Tools of Justice: Non Discrimination and the Indian Constitution*. New Delhi: Routledge.
Kapur R (2002) The tragedy of victimization rhetoric: Resurrecting the "native" subject in international/post-colonial feminist legal politics. *Harvard Human Rights Journal* 15(2): 1–37.
Pakem B (1992) *India-Burma Relations*. New Delhi: Omsons Publications.
Pradhan KL (2004) Settlement of Gorkhas. In: Sangkima E (ed) *Cross Border Migration: Mizoram*. New Delhi: Shipra Publications, 55–70.
Refugees International Bulletin (2004) *Between a Rock and a Hard Place: Burmese Chin Refugees in India*, 23 July 2004.
Reid R (1942) *History of the Frontier Areas Bordering Assam, 1883–1941*. Shillong: The Society for Northeast Hill Regions.
Reid R (2001) A note on the future of the present excluded, partially excluded and tribal areas of Assam. In: Mushirul H and Nakazato N (ed) *The Unfinished Agenda: Nation Building in South-Asia*. New Delhi: Manohar, 203–205.
Saikia A, Goswami H, and Goswami A (2003) *Population Growth in Assam, 1951–1991: With Focus on Migration*. New Delhi: Akansha Publishing House.
Samaddar R (2004) *The Politics of Dialogue: Living Under the Geopolitical Histories of War and Peace*. Aldershot, UK: Ashgate Publications.
Sangkima E (ed) (2004a) *Cross Border Migration: Mizoram*. New Delhi: Shipra Publications.
Sangkima E (2004b) Myanmarese in Mizoram since the beginning of the twentieth century A.D. to the present. In: Sangkima E (ed) *Cross Border Migration: Mizoram*. New Delhi: Shipra Publications, 71–94.
Sanlaap A (2003) *Project: Linkage, a Situational Analysis on Trafficking and Prostitution in Dinbazaar (Jalpaiguri) and Changrabandha (Cooch Behar)*. Kolkata: Sanlaap.

Chapter 4

Securitising the Mediterranean?
Cross-border migration practices in Greece

Eftihia Voutira

Introduction

The great French historian Fernand Braudel has famously identified the Mediterranean as the seedbed of western civilization by isolating the significance and interconnections between the ancient worlds of Greeks and Romans and the interactions between Christianity and Islam. The Mediterranean, he argued, was not simply a body of water separating nation-states, but rather a multitude of interconnected land masses and bodies of water, without borders. It is ironic to note that today, contemporary public discourse almost exclusively identifies the Mediterranean space as a territorial border with northern Europe. As a result, the main policy response at the European Union level has been the introduction of policing migration aimed at securing the EU's external, maritime borders rather than seeing it as a landlocked basin framed in political terms in Roman times, labelled 'mare nostrum'.

This chapter focuses on a bio-political approach to forced migration with an emphasis on Greece. It argues that the recent European obsession with security has distorted the space, environment and political economy of the Mediterranean region. Using Greece as a case study I seek to identify the varieties of human rights violations in the context of international law and the lack of global responsibilities concerning 'asylum at sea', a key issue in forced migration research.

The Mediterranean as a conceptual category

We know since Braudel's grandiose analysis of the Mediterranean that it is much more than 'a sea'. References to its ancient and contemporary relevance extend from the original ecological/cultural Braudelian universe to the recognition that the Mediterranean is in the last hundred years colonizing most other seas (e.g., the Baltic Sea is referred to as 'The Mediterranean of the North'). While it is also perceived and transformed through mass culture into a vacationland (Club Med) for the global elites, it is currently most appreciated as a household term (Mediterranean diet, which is good for the heart and the soul!).

Securitising the Mediterranean? 61

The evolution of the category of the Mediterranean in an academic context can be most prominently identified in the work of German 19th-century geographers such as Karl Ritter, who was one of the first to identify the historical significance of the environmental component in the creation of 'high culture' (Ritter, 1881).

On the European cultural level, the journey to the Mediterranean – including North Africa – became identified as a rite of passage among the 19th-century intellectual elites.[1]

It was only in the 19th century, with the disciplinary emergence of geography as an academic field, that the Mediterranean became associated with the German cultural and economic expansion and the interwar competitive *Lebensraum* distinguishing, thus, the European (German) economic interests from the British Southeast Asian presence and the French colonial expansion to the Maghreb. These geopolitical arrangements lasted through World War II when the emergence of fascism in Italy (Mussolini), Spain (Franco) and Germany (Hitler) necessitated a politically relevant conceptual vision.

As argued by more recent critics of the Braudelian paradigm (Harris, 2006; Horden and Purcell, 2000, 2006), the Mediterranean is more than 'a sea' with historical land masses and this discovery led to the emergence of a new academic field, the Anthropology of the Mediterranean (Abulafia, 2006; Ben-Yehoyada, 2014; Chambers, 2008; Davis, 1977; Kinoshita, 2009; Morin, 1999; Morris, 2003). British anthropology became fascinated with the discovery of a non-European '*other*' in its own backyard, characterized by a unique value system of honour and shame (e.g., Herzfeld, 1991, 1987, 1985).

Contrary to those large-scale intellectual schemes, and vast territorial distances, the focus of this chapter will be on a narrow strip of water that separates the island of Lesbos from the shores of Izmir (see Figure 4.1 and Table 4.1). My argument is that the depth of history and signification of this narrow strip of water – not more than 10 kilometres distance from shore to shore – is so drenched with history, social memories and historical significations that it is no accident that it warranted a visit from the Pope himself at the height of the refugee crisis in July 2015.

Figure 4.1 The narrow strip of water that separates the Greek island of Lesbos from Izmir, Turkey.

The civil war in Syria beginning in 2011 has caused a humanitarian crisis, with one of the biggest refugee flows in this century. As of July 2015, nearly 4 million Syrian refugees were registered or awaiting registration in Egypt, Lebanon, Iraq, Jordan and Turkey (UNHCR, 2015). The humanitarian situation has continued to deteriorate, and by the end of 2016 the total number of forcibly displaced people in Syria had reached 12 million (UNHCR, 2017). Turkey established an open-border policy at the onset of the crisis, welcoming more than 1.8 million registered Syrian refugees. By the end of 2016 Turkey hosted more refugees than any other country in the world – nearly 3 million – with most coming from Syria (UNHCR, 2017). According to the Disaster and Emergency Management Authority of the Republic of Turkey (AFAD),[2] 264,637 Syrian refugees are currently sheltered in 25 camps in 10 provinces of Turkey while nearly 1.5 million non-camp Syrian refugees are living dispersed among communities throughout the country. The non-camp refugees are scattered around various locations, intensely concentrated in the south and southeastern provinces of Turkey such as Hatay, Kilis, Gaziantep, Kahramanmaraş, Şanlıurfa, Adana and Mardin, where their network of relatives and friends had already settled.

The history of this border crossing

There is a long history of crossing the border between Turkey and Greece. As argued by Hirschon (2003), who presents a comprehensive reappraisal of the 1923 Compulsory Population Exchange between Greece and Turkey, the purpose and its long-term consequences were to solidify the Greek and Turkish borders respectively.[3] It remains a mystery among contemporary observers of the post-2016 refugee crisis in the island of Lesbos as to why the existing local population maintains a surprisingly open and hospitable attitude towards the mass arrival of newcomers from the East.

Different accounts (e.g., Papataxiarchis, 2016) and researchers addressing the issue of 'mixed migration flows' in the eastern Mediterranean (Crawley and Skleparis, 2017; Kumin, 2014) argue on the basis of their own data from the 'field' and further explored below, that various humanitarian interventions in the different hot spots on the island of Lesbos represent different theatres of engagement among the various actors that find themselves in the 'field', including international NGOs, a variety of volunteers and key international figures, such as the Pope and celebrities, and UNHCR supporters (e.g., Angelina Jolie, Susan Sarandon, Vanessa Redgrave).[4] The presence of international NGOs and multiple volunteers has been received with various degrees of suspicion, not least because of their massive and indiscriminate presence.[5] There is little doubt that the presence and visibility of NGOs remains a key issue in all situations of 'humanitarian emergencies'.[6]

Following from all the media attention, the migrant crisis in Greece has launched an international concern for global recognition.[7] One of the important realizations of this current visibility of the refugees in Lesbos is the fact that most rescues for which the Greek rescue team received the Nansen Award take place closer to the shore rather than 'at sea'.[8] This re-conceptualization of 'asylum at sea' as a result of changing practices and new refugee realities puts the burden of the proof on new actors, whose daily survival has for years depended on the sea: the local fishermen. According to most accounts they remain the unknown heroes of these tragedies since they are the first to risk their own means of livelihood in the interest of saving lives. As represented in the famous artistic creations of Ai Weiwei exhibited at the centre of continental Europe (Berlin, Vienna), the red life jackets are only the relics of the survivors.[9] Certainly such powerful reconceptualizations of survivors and surviving at sea represent a serious challenge to the way international law has to date defined asylum at sea.[10]

International obligations and asylum at sea

Asylum at sea is an important chapter in international law, yet since the late 1970s the issue has been transformed into a major humanitarian challenge, involving rescue at sea and, by extension, refugee protection (Goodwin-Gill, 2016, 2017; Kessler, 2016; Phillips and Starup, 2014). In the past, when the numbers were relatively small, it was possible to have refugee claims processed in the next convenient port of the rescuing ship. The Vietnam War, which resulted in large numbers of people travelling by boat, changed this (Grant, 2011).

Historically, in the early 1980s UNHCR brokered an agreement whereby coastal states would allow 'boat people' to come ashore if Western states agreed to resettle these people within 90 days of their disembarkation. Yet, this smooth proposal did not work as states demanded settlement provisions to be put in place prior to disembarkation. Ship owners bore the cost of making a rescue.

Throughout the 1980s refusals to respond to distress calls rose to high numbers. Efforts to find a solution to the refugee boat crisis from Vietnam in the mid-1980s diminished. In the 1990s a new upsurge of people taking to the sea to reach places of safety imposed a counter-measure of tighter controls at the borders and ports of entry, while resulting in the lucrative business of people-smuggling. From the standpoint of forced migration research, a major issue concerns the practice of lumping all arrivals in the category of economic migrants. On the other hand, pressuring states and UNHCR to uphold humanitarian practices has long been ineffective. In the case of the European Union and recent practices of asylum at sea, while there are talks of general responsibility sharing arrangements for the protection of refugees rescued at sea, the practice seems to lag behind and, hence, the international outcry about deaths in the Mediterranean (Ayre, 2016; Bigo, 2002; Laczko et al., 2016; Moreno-Lax and Papastavridis, 2017; McMahon and Sigona, 2016).

Normalization is worse than the crisis?

As of May 2017, Greece, according to the international community, is no longer 'a humanitarian priority'. This simple statement has serious implications for the day-to-day management of people stranded and left behind in the hotspots of the Aegean islands. The practice most commonly sees Syrians fast-tracked over Afghans, Iraqis, Bangladeshis and countries with low application success rates, fuelling tensions within camps that sometimes spill over into violence. 'Greek authorities, with EU support, should ensure asylum seekers have meaningful access to a fair and efficient asylum procedure based on individual claims, not nationality', a spokesperson for Human Rights Watch said, urging Greece to end the policy of containment on its islands and transfer asylum seekers to the mainland, where children can be enrolled in school and adults can work.

Table 4.1 Arrivals and Fatalities in the Mediterranean Sea, 2014–2017

	2014	2015	2016	2017 (until 03/05)
Arrivals (Europe)	219,000	1,004,356	363,348	44,209
Deaths (in the Mediterranean)	3,279	3,771	5,079 (+ incidents that have not been fully accounted for)	1,096 (1,009 of these in the Central Mediterranean route)
Arrivals (Greece)	n.a.	853,650	173,561	5,316
Deaths (Eastern Mediterranean route)	33	805	434	37

Source: Data from the International Organization for Migration (IOM).[11]

Image 4.1 Local responses and the legacy of the past.
Source: Papataxiarchis, E. (2016: 3).

I started this chapter by referring to the 1923 forcible exchange of populations between Greece and Turkey. The most visible and famous local inhabitants that captured the western European imagination have been 'the grannies'. This elderly community found a role for itself trying to be 'useful' in the context of the local crisis. For most Greek people, these pictures made sense since the majority of modern Greek children are brought up in an educational environment (national curriculum) that promotes the image of Asia Minor refugees as a major national resource in modern Greek state development (Voutira, 2014, 2016; Voutira and Harrell-Bond, 2000).

The grandmothers depicted in Image 4.1 are an example of the survival of long-term memory transmitted through family and educational lore. Their own engagement is an instance of the desire to participate in what was seen as the moral obligation to their own family experiences since they see themselves as 'survivors' of the Asia Minor catastrophe (Hirschon, 1989). Their picture became viral in the social media and created new demands for such human interest stories among the internet audience.

What is evident from this discussion is the relevance of local history and its significance for living memory, which allows for an ongoing inter-generational engagement with different members of the international and local community. Papataxiarchis introduces the concept of *e-volunteers*. He argues that,

> the groundedness of local professional humanitarians, although totally necessary, is surpassed by some foreign freelance 'volunteers' who seem to place humanitarian action on the ground in the surface of an e-career. These e-volunteers pursue their careers with words, photos and all kinds of signifiers, before a global audience on the internet. Their strategy is largely performative: their actions are meant to be placed on a visual register that becomes available to everyone, primarily through social media, thus attracting large audiences of 'followers' and the necessary resources to keep on travelling (to other humanitarian emergencies).
>
> (Papataxiarchis, 2016: 8)

Lesbos as a case study for understanding the 2015 refugee crisis in the Eastern Mediterranean

An important methodological issue concerning the refugee crisis of 2015 concerns the data documenting the crisis. Different international organizations document the crisis in their reports, focusing on three main routes: eastern Mediterranean, central Mediterranean and western Mediterranean. These routes connect western European countries with the Mediterranean periphery.

The perception of the crisis is discussed and articulated in different social media, including Twitter, Facebook and YouTube. All of these accounts are predicated on immediacy and urgency focusing on the magnitude and intensity of events reported (Collyer, 2010). As such, they do not merely document, they also mobilize public interest. A paradigmatic example is the touching and tragic photo of the young Syrian boy found dead on the seashore in Turkey in September 2015.[12] People in Lesbos continued to refer to this image as part of their own continuous perception of the refugee crisis on the island. Therefore, it is difficult to decipher the image from the emotions generated by it. One key theoretical point here concerns the perception of the historical experience of the newcomers as part of 'our own' refugees. The significance of this perception cannot be overestimated. It concerns the positive attitude of welcoming newcomers by sea. The paradox of the contemporary refugee crisis in Lesbos refers primarily to the realization that the newcomers by sea are themselves confronted with an inherent paradox of 'denying' local hospitality in the interest of finding sanctuary elsewhere in northern Europe.[13]

On Lesbos refugees are housed in camps such as Moria refugee camp. In fact, the site of Moria is a 'hot spot' according to the new FRONTEX terminology, which challenges the imagination as there are no specific buildings or even durable tents in demarcating a site as a 'hot spot'. There are only make-shift constructions visible on Facebook postings and local media pictures protesting the 'foreign invasion'. Protesters argue that the Moria site epitomises,

> The ongoing tragedy in the 'Hot Spot' solution . . . which mirrors the failure of Europe to protect refugees and the violence of the border regime on which European migration policies are based. Screening and registration are priority, peoples' lives are not . . . We demand the immediate end of hotspot procedures and the instant withdrawal of Frontex personnel. The EU has to immediately put an end to the slowing-down of registration procedures produced by Frontex which is life-threatening. We denounce the procedure of 'speeding up returns' in the strongest possible terms. We call for the opening of land borders so that people on the move do not have to risk, and at times lose, their lives. We demand widespread humanitarian aid provisions to sufficiently address the pressing needs of those who arrive on the Greek islands and a dignified welcoming of refugees by offering protection.[14]

The Moria site was identified at the peak of the crisis as a convenient steppingstone to a more permanent establishment. However, as it often happens, the border crossers ended up staying there up to 6 months, receiving minimum hygiene and medical treatment. These types of long-term emergency constructions are a common phenomenon in forced migration literature, as identified by Harrell-Bond's classic study *Imposing Aid* (1986), despite the usage of the concept of emergency, which assumes a short-term response like the notion of the *refugee crisis*. We know from forced migration research that in the 21st century, the management of the 'undesirables' (Agier, 2011) involves a long-term process predicated on hiding or warehousing them, in ways that follow the principle of 'out of sight/out of mind'.

The legacy of the 'Greek refugee past'?

Libby Tata Arcel has written a personal account of the trauma in three generations of Greek Asia Minor refugees with the ominous title *With Persecution in the Soul*. Her account involves the re-engagement with the long-term past of the great-grandmother, who began her journey on the Turkish side of the Aegean, in search of the family history and the lived experience of flight through the eyes of the individual. The author confesses to her audience that:

> As a clinical psychologist in Denmark I began doing therapy with refugees from many parts of the world that had found refuge in Denmark during a time when the Danish society had begun addressing seriously human rights issues . . . Contrary to what is happening today, Denmark offered asylum generously to those that needed it . . . The Danish health services were found unprepared vis-á-vis the physical and mental problems of these newcomers.
> (Tata Arcel, 2014: 25)

The author is a Denmark trained psychologist who ended up working with refugees in Denmark for at least 20 years and in the process comes to terms with her own family history and biography, which she describes as a Greek Asia Minor refugee. The book offers an account, a theory of trauma not as an individual psychological phenomenon but as a collective trauma which impacts on the whole society. She uses the personal narratives to explore biographical, historical and psychoanalytic evidence, in order to understand the theme of loss and change. Her narrative provides the background to understanding the transmission of inter-generational trauma and in this respect it is relevant in explaining the dynamics of what I have called 'Greek exceptionalism', in trying to interpret the positive attitude of the local population in Lesbos in the 2015 refugee crisis.

Her work is also relevant in appreciating the manner in which history repeats itself. For example, we learn that Asia Minor refugees in Moria (in 1923) were asked for passports, being treated as foreigners in their own land. Equally, history repeats itself in daily observations of human rights monitoring, established by the University of the Aegean in Lesbos: 'The shores are full of refugees in distress. Women and children are famished, without water, without food'.[15] The theme of exploitation of refugees by the locals is also common in the literature and articulated in the local press as a critique of the way locals exploit refugees by 'kneading bread with stones to feed the unwanted newcomers' (Tata Arcell, 2014).

In a totally different vein, Peter Loizos's analysis concerning the long-term impact of the refugee experience on types of livelihood and health issues in Cyprus suggests a different approach to the literature on trauma. Loizos's long-term engagement with forced migration and refugee issues introduces an important critique of the whole mental health and refugees literature. The title of Loizos's book *Iron in the Soul* is an imaginative counter theory to the trauma literature. As he says:

> It may help to think of the experience of displacement and its negative memories as being like a splinter of iron which has been trapped inside the now-healed flesh and causes no difficulty until inadvertently pressed, when there will [be] sharp reactive pain. It would seem to be the case that as time goes by, more and more refugees spend more and more time with their refugee identity 'switched off'. If something happens to 'switch it on' then the sense of grievance returns to the surface in full strength – the iron is still in both the heart and soul.
>
> (Loizos, 2008: 186)

Loizos's insightful hypothesis may be used as a corrective device and a sobering strategy against all the media emotion generating discourses, which are meant to mobilize the readers. The introduction of Loizos's hypothesis as a corrective device in the case of long-term inter-generational trauma suggested by Tata Arcel is not meant as an either/or choice. It is introduced as an alternative, anthropological approach to understand how communities cope with the experience of displacement physically, mentally, emotionally and socially. The metaphor of the iron splinter represents the sobering mechanism itself, without undermining the long-term survival strategies refugees invent – often despite themselves – as livelihood strategies. It would be interesting to observe in future generations of research on the survivors of the Syrian refugees which of the two disciplinary models will contribute more to forced migration research.

Back to Braudel

Braudel has argued that there are three types of history/historical times relative to the historical phenomena.

1. The first type is called the history of event, which Braudel calls *microhistory* (*histoire evenementiélle*). This is the history known to traditional historiography because it narrates events that have occurred in the past and includes famous figures as actors in these events.
2. The second type of history is called *conjuncture*. This history involves larger time spans, as it covers 20 to 50 yearperiods. Braudel's example is the history of inflation, a 'business cycle'.
3. The third type of history is the history of the *longue durée (history of long duration)*. This time span expands more than 600 or 700 years. This is Braudel's major contribution to cultural history, in than he refers to the rising of a civilization, which takes a long duration to identify as a historical phenomenon.

Relative to the *conjuncture*, structural history, or the history of the longue durée, inquires into whole centuries at a time. It functions along the border between the moving and the immobile, and because of the long-standing stability of its values, it appears unchanging compared with all the histories which flow and work themselves out more swiftly, and which in the final analysis gravitate around it (Braudel, 1982: 74).

These three types of history in many ways summarize the Braudelian paradigm of historiography that has captured the imagination of scholars for more than a century. In more contemporary terms one can argue that this kaleidoscopic account of history has elements of a cinematographic vision of the 'past', which we are relentlessly attempting to capture in the present; and an anthropological perspective in an erstwhile *ethnographic present*, which has in the past been the hallmark of anthropology as a discipline (Gellner, 1987: 88–107).

Concluding remarks

In the preceding sections of this chapter I have addressed both the mobility and the immobility of the eastern Mediterranean space. In an anti-Braudelian manner I have focused on very concrete and temporal events at the expense of large-scale historical narratives. Bringing the global to communicate with the local represents a major epistemological challenge. What I have tried to point out is the sense in which the living history and the locally developed livelihood strategies – including fishing, olive cultivating and, more recently, tourism and humanitarian aid volunteerism – have brought in a series of new actors that are creating their own living memories of the recent forced migration crisis in the eastern Mediterranean.

The case of Greece and the focus on Lesbos is one instance of the mobility Braudel talks about. The temporalities the Braudelian account refers to is very different from the perception of the forced migration crisis times this chapter has addressed. The rhythms of the latter are dictated by different priorities and, therefore, impossible to be narrated in an analytical framework. The experience of refugee reception in Greece has elements of boom-and-bust cycles of late capitalism, which is a way of appreciating the resilience and endurance of hospitality patterns, still observed in the Aegean island case of the recent past I have described on the level of microhistory.

Most issues identified in the field of forced migration are evident in the eastern Mediterranean. What is not evident is the inherent paradox of willing hosts and uninterested guests who remain with eyes fixed on the European North, which continues to cultivate and generate expectations for this transit, forced migrant population. The current Greek policy response is to disperse these forced migrants from the Aegean islands to mainland Greece. After the closure of the Balkan route, forced migrants who find themselves in Greece will be forced to accept Greek hospitality given locally. The next important step is to observe the future emerging patterns of family unification and relocation within Europe. To date, international organizations, like IOM, pursue a policy of 'voluntary' return to the countries of origin. These countries include Iraq and Afghanistan. It remains to be seen if Syria will also be included in this 'safe country' list in the near future.

Notes

1. The famous BBC Television series *Brideshead Revisited* documents such explorations to the Mediterranean and North Africa (www.imdb.com/title/tt0083390/). Similarly, Bernardo Bertolucci's famous film *The Sheltering Sky* documents these North–South encounters, feeding the European collective cultural imagination (www.imdb.com/title/tt0100594/).
2. Disaster and Emergency Management Authority of the Republic of Turkey (AFAD) is the coordinating institution for managing refugee camps in Turkey and all related services, including the provision of shelter, food, health care, security, social activities, education, worship, translation, communication and banking, with the support of relevant ministries, public institutions, and organizations.
3. This agreement is also the bone of contention in the post-2017 threats by the so-called Sultan Erdogan who continues to violate the Turkey-EU agreement and challenges the existing eastern borders of the Greek state.
4. Pullella, P., & Tagaris, K. (2016, April 16). Pope returns with 12 refugees after visit to Greek island. Reuters. Retrieved from www.reuters.com/article/us-europe-migrants-pope-lesbos-idUSKCN0XD09D (accessed April 2017).

    Press Release (no authors stated) (2016, March 16). UNHCR Special Envoy Angelina Jolie Pitt visits Greece. UNHCR. Retrieved from www.unhcr.org/news/press/2016/3/56e94bd96/unhcr-special-envoy-angelina-jolie-pitt-visits-greece.html (accessed April 2017).

    Xie, Q. (2015, December 19). Actress Susan Sarandon welcomes refugees to Lesbos as she vows to spend her Christmas holiday on the Greek island listening to the migrants' stories. Daily Mail Online. Retrieved from www.dailymail.co.uk/news/article-3367172/Actress-Susan-Sarandon-welcomes-refugees-Lesbos-vows-spend-Christmas-holiday-Greek-island-listening-migrants-stories.html (accessed April 2017).

    www.unhcr.gr/nea/artikel/4e048db2778662dbecf0567bb000f43d/a-different-visit.html (accessed April 2017).
5. Helen Nianias. 'Refugees in Lesbos: Are there too many NGOs on the island?'.*The Guardian*, 5 January 2016.
6. Gunter, J. (2016, February 1). Migrant crisis: Greek volunteers welcome Nobel nomination. BBC News. Retrieved from www.bbc.com/news/world-europe-35460012 (accessed April 2017).
7. 'Over 500,000 signatures back Greek islanders for Nobel peace prize'. http://news.yahoo.com/over-500-000-signatures-back-greek-islanders-nobel-213813999.html (accessed April 2017).
8. Press Release (no authors stated) (2016, October 3). Greek heroes honoured at 2016 UNHCR Nansen Refugee Award ceremony. UNHCR. Retrieved from http://www.unhcr.org/news/press/2016/10/57f2be864/greek-heroes-honoured-2016-unhcr-nansen-refugee-award-ceremony.html (accessed April 2017).
9. Sierzputowski, K. (2016, February 16). Ai Weiwei Wraps the Columns of Berlin's Konzerthaus with 14,000 Salvaged Refugee Life Vests. Colossal. Retrieved from http://www.thisiscolossal.com/2016/02/ai-weiwei-konzerthaus-refugee-life-vests/ (accessed April 2017). https://news.artnet.com/art-world/ai-weiwei-refugee-jacket-installation-vienna-557324 (accessed April 2017).
10. See, for instance, www.unhcr.org/excom/exconc/3ae68c435c/protection-asylum-seekers-sea.html (accessed April 2017) and multiple human rights critics of the inhumanity practised by states, including human rights violations on a grand scale (for example, www.amnesty.org/en/documents/ASA12/2576/2015/en/).
11. International Organization for Migration Press Release (2016) Mediterranean Migrant Arrivals and Deaths, 2016. Available at: www.iom.int/news/mediterranean-migrant-arrivals-top-363348-2016-deaths-sea-5079 (accessed 8.6.2017).

International Organization for Migration Press Release (2017) Mediterranean Migrant Arrivals and Deaths, January–May 2017. Available at: www.iom.int/news/mediterranean-migrant-arrivals-44209-deaths-1096 (accessed 8.6.2017).
12 Death of Alan Kurdi (2017, July 12). In Wikipedia, The Free Encyclopedia. Retrieved July 13, 2017. Retrieved from https://en.wikipedia.org/wik/Death_of_Alan_Kurdi (accessed July 2017).
13 In a UNHCR survey of 245 Syrian refugees, the unfathomable 90.8% of them wishes to seek asylum elsewhere in the European Union.
14 Maravas, I. (2017, June 17). Asfyktika gemati i Moria. Apochi ergazomenon kai miosi simvasiouchon (Moria Suffocating. Employee abstentions and diminishing contractee numbers). Era Aegean. Retrieved from http://www.era-aegean.gr/?p=29303 (Accessed July 2017).
15 Observatory of the Refugee and Migration Crisis in the Aegean: http://refugeeobservatory.aegean.gr/en/about-observatory (accessed November 2017).

Bibliography

Abulafia D (2006) Mediterraneans. In: Harris WV (ed) *Rethinking the Mediterranean*. Oxford: Oxford University Press, 64–93.
Agier M (2011) *Managing the Undesirables: Refugee Camps and Humanitarian Government*. Cambridge: Polity Press.
Ayre KL (2016) Europe, don't copy Australia. *Forced Migration Review* 51: 77.
Ben-Yehoyada N (2014) Mediterranean modernity? In: Horden P, Kinoshita S (eds) *A Companion to Mediterranean History*. Oxford: Wiley Blackwell, 107–121.
Bigo D (2002) Security and immigration: Toward a critique of the governmentality of unease. *Alternatives: Global, Local, Political* 27(1): 63–92.
Braudel F (1982) *On History*. Chicago, IL: University of Chicago Press.
Chambers I (2008) *Mediterranean Crossings: The Politics of an Interrupted Modernity*. Durham, NC: Duke University Press.
Collyer M (2010) Stranded migrants and the fragmented journey. *Journal of Refugee Studies* 23(3): 273–293.
Crawley H, Skleparis D (2017) Refugees, migrants, neither, both: Categorical fetishism and the politics of bounding in Europe's 'migration crisis'. *Journal of Ethnic and Migration Studies* 44(1): 48–64.
Davis J (1977) *People of the Mediterranean: An Essay in Comparative Social Anthropology*. London: Routledge.
Gellner E (1987) *Culture, Identity and Politics*. Cambridge: Cambridge University Press.
Goodwin-Gill GS (2016) Legal and practical issues raised by the movement of people across the Mediterranean. *Forced Migration Review* 51: 82–84.
Goodwin-Gill GS (2017) Setting the scene: Refugees, asylum seekers, and migrants at sea – the need for a long-term, protection-centred vision. In: Moreno-Lax V, Papastavridis E (eds) *'Boat Refugees' and Migrants at Sea: A Comprehensive Approach*. Leiden: Brill Nijhoff, 17–31.
Grant S (2011) 'Identity unknown': Migrant deaths at sea. *Forced Migration Review* 38: 43.
Harrell-Bond B (1986) *Imposing Aid: Emergency Assistance to Refugees*. Oxford: Oxford University Press.
Harris WV (ed) (2006) *Rethinking the Mediterranean*. Oxford: Oxford University Press.
Herzfeld M (1985) Gender pragmatics: Agency, speech, and bride-theft in a Cretan mountain village. *Anthropology* 9(1–2): 25–44.

Herzfeld M (1987) 'As in your own house': Hospitality, ethnography, and the stereotype of Mediterranean society. In: Gilmore DD (ed) *Honor and Shame and the Unity of the Mediterranean*. Washington, DC: American Anthropological Association, 75–89.

Herzfeld M (1991) *A Place in History: Social and Monumental Time in a Cretan Town*. Princeton: Princeton University Press.

Hirschon R (1989) *Heirs of the Greek Catastrophe: The Social Life of Asia Minor Refugees in Piraeus*. Oxford: Berghahn Books.

Hirschon R (2003) *Crossing the Aegean: An Appraisal of the 1923 Compulsory Population Exchange Between Greece and Turkey*. Oxford: Berghahn Books.

Horden P, Purcell N (2000) *The Corrupting Sea: A Study of Mediterranean History*. Oxford: Wiley Blackwell.

Horden P, Purcell N (2006) The Mediterranean and the 'New Thalassology'. *The American Historical Review* 111(3): 22–740.

International Organization for Migration Press Release (2016) *Mediterranean Migrant Arrivals and Deaths*. Available at: www.iom.int/news/mediterranean-migrant-arrivals-top-363348-2016-deaths-sea-5079 [Accessed 8.6.2017].

International Organization for Migration Press Release (2017) *Mediterranean Migrant Arrivals and Deaths*, January–May 2017. Available at: www.iom.int/news/mediterranean-migrant-arrivals-44209-deaths-1096 [Accessed 8.6.2017].

Kessler S (2016) Safety, rescue at sea and legal access. *Forced Migration Review* 51: 28–29.

Kinoshita S (2009) Medieval mediterranean literature. *PMLA* 124(2): 600–608.

Kumin J (2014) The challenge of mixed migration by sea. *Forced Migration Review* 45: 49–51.

Laczko F, Singleton A, Brian T, and Rango M (2016) Migrant arrivals and deaths in the Mediterranean: What do the data really tell us? *Forced Migration Review* 51: 30–31.

Loizos P (2008) *Iron in the Soul: Displacement, Livelihood and Health in Cyprus*. Oxford: Berghahn Books.

McMahon S, Sigona N (2016) *Boat Migration Across the Central Mediterranean: Drivers, Experiences and Responses*. MEDMIG Research Brief No.3. Available at: www.medmig.info/research-brief-03-Boat-migration-across-the- Central-Mediterranean [Accessed 1.6.2017].

Moreno-Lax V, Papastavridis E (eds) (2017) *'Boat Refugees' and Migrants at Sea: A Comprehensive Approach*. Leiden: Brill Nijhoff.

Morin E (1999) Penser la Méditerranée et méditerranéiser la pensée. *Confluences Méditerranée* 28: 33–47.

Morris I (2003) Mediterraneanization. *Mediterranean Historical Review* 18(2): 30–55.

Observatory of the Refugee and Migration Crisis in the Aegean (2017) Available at: http://refugeeobservatory.aegean.gr/en/about-observatory [Accessed 28.11.2017].

Papataxiarchis E (2016) Being 'there': At the front line of the 'European refugee crisis' – part 2. *Anthropology Today* 32(3): 3–7.

Phillips M, Starup K (2014) Protection challenges of mobility. *Forced Migration Review* 47: 27–30.

Ritter, C. (1817). *Die Erdkunde im Verhältniss zur Natur und zur Geschichte der Menschen, oder allgemeine vergleichende Geographie, als sichere Grundlage des Studiums und Unterrichts in physikalischen und historischen Wissenschaften*, vol. I. Berlin: G. Reimer.

Tata Arcell L (2014) Με το Διωγμό στην Ψυχή: Το τραύμα της Μικρασιατικής καταστροφής σε τρεις γενιές. Αθήνα: Κέδρος.

UNHCR (2015) Press Release, July 2015. Available at: www.unhcr.org/uk/news/press/2015/7/559d67d46/unhcr-total-number-syrian-refugees-exceeds-four-million-first-time.html (accessed 1.6.2017).

UNHCR (2017) *Global Trends: Forced Displacement in 2016*. Geneva: UNHCR.
Voutira E (2014) Cultures of 'security' and refugee insecurities [in Greek]. In: E. Πατσαταξιάρχης, Πολιτικες της Καθημερινότητας, εκδ. Αλεξάνδρεια. Αθήνα, 235–260.
Voutira E (2016) *Understanding Greek Exceptionalism*. Paper delivered at the 15th International Association for the Study of Forced Migration conference, 12–15 July 2016, Poznan, Poland.
Voutira E, Harrell-Bond B (2000) Successful refugee settlement: Are past experiences relevant? In: Cernea C, Macdowell C (eds) *Reconstructing Livelihoods*. Washington, DC: World Bank, 56–76.

Chapter 5

Protracted displacement
Living on the edge

Jennifer Hyndman and Wenona Giles

Protracted refugee situations – a global phenomenon

The vast majority of people who have been displaced long term outside their countries of origin – some 86% of the world's refugees – live in the global South. Currently, there are more than 30 recognized crises of indefinite exile (Long, 2011). In 2017, at least two-thirds of the world's 21 million refugees live in extended exile. As of March 2016, Syrians who fled their country in March 2011 and have been displaced for five years officially meet UNHCR's definition of a 'protracted refugee situation' (PRS).

PRS is a concept invented by UNHCR around 2000 that refers to refugees in long-term and intractable exile exceeding five years[1] in which: 'lives may not be at risk, but . . . basic rights and essential economic, social, and psychological needs remain unfulfilled after years in exile' (UNHCR, 2004). To its credit, the concept renders often 'forgotten' groups of refugees as legible objects of policy concern for intergovernmental organizations responsible for their plight. To the extent that invisible and silent refugee disasters can be listed and prioritized for action, PRS can be a useful tool. And yet, the term PRS also has its shortcomings: it merges multiple, distinct, and politically complicated conditions of displacement into a neat category called 'PRS'; it flattens a multitude of geography, history, and context dramatically, creating few if any tools to address these diverse situations. For example, Somalia's civil war, and the various international interventions to 'save' it, over the last 25 years have little in common with Afghanistan's sequential layers of Cold War geopolitics, Taliban government, and post-September 2001 NATO interventions. And yet these are both the longest-standing protracted refugee situations (PRS), excluding Palestinians. Long notes:

> The very fact of protracted displacement is evidence that existing approaches to 'solving' displacement have failed. Voluntary return, local integration and resettlement – the traditional 'durable solutions' – are not accessible for those trapped in protracted displacement. . . .[2] One question which must be asked, however, is whether the very language of 'solutions' is in

fact creating – rather than confronting – the apparent impasse in protracted displacement crisis.

(2011: 8)

Conflict situations in refugee source countries often have little in common with one another, each defined contextually by the history and geopolitics of place and the violence linked to displacement. Hence, the concept of PRS does a kind of epistemic violence to the geopolitics that created displacement and the material conditions of extended exile many people face. PRS is a definitional term, not a very valuable analytical one. Long (2011: 5) adds that 'there is no single experience of "protracted displacement"'; instead, the context of people who have been displaced is often fluid, and understanding this environment is key to defining possible ways forward. No two situations of extended exile will be the same. PRS remains part of the dominant international relations discourse that analyzes the international refugee regime, a set of approaches that privilege perspectives of state security and international organizations, not necessarily those of refugees or other actors (Brun and Fabos, 2015; Dona, 2015). What links these PRS sites are various forms of globalization: militarized, economic, and cultural.

In a thoughtful and important scholarly intervention in a special issue on refugees' relation to home in exile, Dona, Brun, Fabos, and other authors address this gap. Under the rubric of 'Making Home in Limbo', the authors analyze the transnational processes that produce refugee homes and lifeworlds. Dona (2015) especially calls for a re-examination of the term 'protracted refugee situation', which she calls an obsolete category for defining the political displacement of the Karen who have been living along the Thai-Burma border for over two decades. She finds 'prolonged conditions of displacement' (Dona, 2015: 68) more fitting and respectful of people living with temporary and precarious status for so long. Brun and Fabos (2015: 6) introduce their special issue by critiquing the policy context of 'protracted displacement', outlining how refugees experience 'constellations of home' that occur at various scales and in different locations.

Questions of emotion, subjectivity, apprehension, and recognition may seem abstract in reference to people whose lives have been dramatically affected by war, human rights violations, and the like. Yet, if these same people – called refugees – do not register with the wider world as 'people-like-us' and equivalent political subjects whose marginalized lives and livelihoods matter, change in their situation is likely to remain elusive. Policy categories associated with extended displacement – such as 'PRS', 'crisis' and 'emergency' – may also have the unintended effect of depoliticizing the conditions of long-term displacement, rendering them more technical problems that can be 'fixed' with the right salve. More research is required to ascertain the impact of PRS as a discourse and approach to extended exile. Here we are concerned that it is a state-centric and unpeopled discourse. This chapter outlines what scholars have said about PRS, or using alternate language, protracted refugee displacement. We then trace the shortcomings of current approaches that frame the problem as one to be solved by the international refugee regime. The geopolitical shift from the Cold War to the so-called war on terror, and the accompanying strategies used by wealthier governments to exclude refugees from countries are touched upon as part of this critique. Finally, we show how protracted displacement is not easily 'solved' in Kenya, along its border with Somalia, where humanitarian space comes up against counterinsurgency efforts and the 'war on terror', and where national security trumps refugee protection.

The debut of PRS

The earliest published use of the term 'protracted refugee situations', or 'PRS', dates back to 2000 when Arafat Jamal, a UNHCR staff member, analyzed the problem of protracted exile among Sudanese refugees in Kakuma, Kenya.[3] Jamal eloquently states that:

> UNHCR's mandate to protect refugees is absolute, but the financial means with which it is expected to do so are relative. When a hapless refugee population remains in exile and without resolution to their plight, the resource issue becomes especially acute.
>
> (2000: 3)

He proposes that UNHCR depart from an approach of 'minimum emergency standards' as a benchmark for progress, and focus instead on the idea of 'essential human needs'.[4] This, he argues, would provide a more holistic picture of the resources required in long-term camps.[5] And yet, there are more embodied, human-centred ways to understand extended exile. Catherine-Lune Grayson-Courtemanche's (2017) ethnography of Somalian refugee youth living in the same camp years later shows similar characterizations. In the words of 18-year-old Amran, a Somalian refugee:

> When I was in Grade 6, my refugee classmates started going abroad. I wanted to go, I was wondering why I had to stay here. We were called for a [resettlement] process, but nothing happened. Now, all the students I learned with in primary school are gone. I have no friends here. I really want to go. I know I can't study here. I want to go to a good university.
>
> (cited in Grayson-Courtemanche, 2015: 127)

Without school, impatience sets in:

> Without the right to work or move freely, and given the unlikeliness of naturalization, Kakuma cannot be a place where young people want to put down roots.
>
> (cited in Grayson-Courtemanche, 2015: 127).

The greatest consequence of protracted displacement is the lack of a guarantor, or government, to ensure the basic needs for refugees are met (Milner and Loescher, 2011). Most of these refugees are *prima facie*, and are normally designated on a group basis and in greater numbers than Convention refugees (Hyndman and Nylund, 1998; Rutinwa, 2002). The Convention Refugee definition, in contrast, applies to those *individuals* who submit to a refugee status determination (RSD) process supervised by the UNHCR to determine their eligibility. The Convention Refugee definition, ensconced in the 1951 Convention Relating to Refugees, focuses on five grounds of persecution (race, religion, nationality, membership in a social group, and/or political opinion) for people seeking sanctuary outside their countries of origin. While some resettlement countries will accept a handful of refugees with *prima facie* status, the norm is that an individual RSD is required.

By 2016, there are more than 20 million refugees, roughly three quarters of whom live in conditions of protracted displacement. In 2010, four out of five refugees hosted in global South countries were designated as *prima facie* refugees (UNHCR, 2012). This is significant for two reasons: first, a Convention refugee essentially has permission to reside, work, and live in the country that grants the status, sometimes on a permanent basis. And second, since Convention status is the exception and not the rule, the vast majority of the world's refugees with *prima facie* status do not have access to the entitlements outlined in the 1951 Refugee Convention. *Prima facie* status guarantees little more than protection from *refoulement* (forced return) and enough food, water, shelter, and medicine to survive. *Prima facie* refugees constitute the vast majority of protracted refugees, hence changing their status to 'permanent residents' or 'Convention Refugees' would invoke major positive change in the lives of most refugees in extended exile.

A majority of the world's refugees are displaced by conflict, persecution, or other human rights abuses. They endure a habitus of 'permanent temporariness' (Bailey et al., 2002) in conditions of extended displacement for years. Bailey and the team of geographers who conceived the term 'permanent temporariness', use it to describe the plight of Salvadoran migrants in the United States who received only temporary protection one year at a time, for years, never knowing for sure if it would be renewed and yet unable to leave the country. And yet the term is apt for refugee camps and settlements in other parts of the world, as well, especially for those in conditions of prolonged displacement. Camps that were meant to be emergency stopgap measures to ensure human survival, have developed into permanent, if officially temporary, cities. People living in long-term camp situations develop intricate livelihoods and lives, based on a mixture of rations, remittances, small businesses, and access to education. Others live in or move to urban areas nearby or to other countries that tolerate migrants and refugees who want to settle, work, and live in cities, where the informal economy is bigger and where higher education opportunities may be better. Later in this chapter, we ground these hypothetical scenarios in more detail based on our research with Somalian refugees in Kenya.

People defined as refugees would rather be something else, almost anything else (Kumsa, 2006): residents, permanent residents, even citizens. However, as Malkki notes, those called 'refugees stop being specific persons and become pure victims in general . . . Humanitarian practices tend to silence refugees' (1996: 378). In a similar vein, with reference to internally displaced persons[6] (IDPs), Seshadri describes that the very naming of displaced persons 'as a universal category, a global epistemological unit' (2008: 32) leads to their further depoliticization and loss of public status.

Why study 'protracted refugee situations'?

Analyzing the fate of refugees who have seen no marked change in their legal status in more than five years, or possibly more than two or three decades, is a sobering deed. That the clear majority of the world's more than 20 million refugees, including Palestinians, live in extended exile is reason enough to study why and how the supposedly temporary spaces and status they endure continues. As space for seeking asylum shrinks in the global North, supposedly temporary forms of accommodation in the global South expand. Acute humanitarian crises capture world attention, bringing the plight of the displaced to light. However, once the 'emergency' or 'crisis' is over and people-at-risk have been fed, housed, and triaged for medical care, world attention wanes and the displaced disappear from view. When humanitarian subjects cease to be at risk of dying, their subjectivity slips to a more abject status (Butler, 1993; Spivak, 1988; Ramadan, 2012; Redfield, 2005).

Temporary refugee protection in 'regions of origin' is clearly not a short-term prospect. It is the new normal. In the liminal spaces of transit countries, forms of detention and deterrence proliferate while readmission agreements and safe third country policies ensure that uninvited migrants, including asylum seekers, are returned to where they came from (Mountz, 2011). Access to asylum in safe countries that grant permanent legal status or allow access to housing, jobs, and schools for migrants (like South Africa) is increasingly difficult. Our goal in this chapter is not to take down the 'international refugee regime' by criticizing its ineffectiveness. Rather, we take apart the accepted language of 'solutions' and policies and rethink them in new ways that might allow us to imagine different futures, politics, and policies. Analyzing protracted displacement, as we prefer to call it, or 'protracted refugee situations' (PRS) in UN parlance, is a useful starting point.

The state of research on refugees in protracted conditions

A great deal has been written about protracted refugee situations, largely in a policy context in which displaced persons are outside their countries of origin and have few prospects of repatriation, resettlement abroad, or local integration into a host community. Although PRS is a construct of the UNHCR, this organization also indicates its recognition that each context of protracted displacement is distinct and cannot be solved with a 'one size fits all' approach (UNHCR, 2009).

Many scholars and policy makers have observed that the end of the Cold War has fundamentally changed the position of refugees in global politics (Hyndman, 2000). Crisp (2003) notes that protracted 'refugeehood' persists because of declining international attention towards refugees who have become marginal to major power interests. In turn, these sites of displacement have been neglected and poorly funded, while border technologies in the global North have been fortified and well-resourced. Durieux (2009), a senior UNHCR director for many years, goes further and contends that the reluctance of host states towards local integration is a major factor in the degradation of standards in refugee settlements, and refugees being

> unable to break free from enforced reliance on external assistance. What this attitude reflects, however, is essentially a deep mistrust in an international system of responsibility-sharing that has all too often failed to deliver fairness.
>
> (Durieux, 2009: 61)

The mistrust and lack of fairness Durieux identifies supersede other explanations and proposals to 'fix' the problem of long-term exile for refugees. Insights from international relations and contemporary critical geopolitics on PRS have helped to trace the exclusionary cartographies that repel asylum seekers at the borders of many countries in the global North. Humanitarian, development, and security agendas intersect and affect those in exilic refugee spaces, as much of the literature on 'protracted refugee situations' has aptly argued (Loescher and Milner, 2005a; Adelman, 2008; Loescher et al., 2008; Milner and Loescher, 2011; Betts and Loescher, 2011). Loescher and Milner both argue for more 'comprehensive approaches' that engage regions of origin and overseas resettlement actors (Loescher and Milner, 2005b; Loescher and Milner, 2003).

The debut of PRS and its UN proponents are part of a more practical and policy-oriented approach to 'fixing' long-term displacement. For example, the 'UNHCR Policy on Alternatives to Camps' (2014) is directed mainly at UNHCR staff who plan, design, and deliver humanitarian activities in the field and those who develop tools and training that support such activities. It tacitly acknowledges that most refugees are stuck in conditions of prolonged displacement, and that camps are sites that are the least respectful of their rights and freedoms (UNHCR, 2014). Ultimately UNHCR must persuade host governments to assist refugees outside of camps, not just its own staff.

As Hovil (2014) explains, refugee camps are an expression of the salient narrative that refugees are outsiders, foreigners, or security threats that merit close scrutiny until they can return home. She notes that camps have provided a visible tool for raising funds and managing humanitarian demands for the UNHCR.

Citing research showing that refugees who have managed to leave the camp context and live in more urban areas feel more secure and have engaged in the local economy, Hovil (2014) illustrates that far from being passive victims, they have taken control of their lives, often without any external assistance. Our own research shows the same, and demonstrates a tension between agency and perceived victimhood among displaced and contained Somalians in Kenya and Afghans in Iran, wherein ingenuity, volition, and aspirations remain intact if truncated (Hyndman and Giles, 2017). The conversation needs to shift beyond technical fixes, such as the UNHCR's 'durable solutions' or 'PRS' so that the international refugee regime might be re-imagined in new ways.

Excluding displaced people: linking global geopolitics of exclusion and PRS

Our analysis of protracted displacement points to the asylum politics and border policies in the global North as connected to the intransigence of extended exile among refugees in the global South. This is not a technical issue to be solved. Rather, a political consensus that refugees should be protected in their 'regions of origin', not in the global North, prevails. This has led to the externalization of asylum and general 'pushback' against uninvited migration. Unsurprisingly, the decision to accept a claim and process an asylum seeker arriving at one's border in the global North is not the same as deciding to provide refugee food rations in a far-away camp. Asylum seekers approaching borders in the global North are often seen as unwanted visitors and are 'securitized', that is, rendered a threat, and then treated as such. As we describe in the paragraphs that follow, refugees who stay put in the global South are produced and depicted in the global North as the 'deserving' refugees who warrant humanitarian assistance, such as food, housing, and basic medicine (Hyndman and Giles, 2011). The externalization of asylum – that is, the movement of refugee determination processes offshore, away from a destination country's own borders – is a geopolitical constellation of biometric requirements, readmission agreements, airline liaison officers, visa regulations, and interdiction practices that have very material effects on asylum seekers, including their criminalization.

Not all asylum seekers are refugees, and some will fail to meet the criteria states set. Yet, states are not enthusiastic about doing this work of adjudicating claims through expensive and required legal processes within their own borders. Assessing such claims is costly and time-consuming, and so most global North states take pre-emptive measures to prevent or *preclude* asylum seekers from making a claim in the first place (Hyndman and Mountz, 2008). Asylum seekers are kept away from borders as much as possible. After introducing a new asylum regime in December 2012, Canada saw a precipitous drop in asylum claims to the country: from 20,500 in 2012 to 10,400 in 2013, even while the number of asylum claims globally rose 28%. Despite international legal obligations to hear claims if asylum seekers manage to enter a country, there is no regulation of preclusion and refusing entry to potentially unwanted others through biometric regimes, visa requirements, and shared databases among global North countries. These exclusionary practices contribute to long-term displacement in sites within the global South by foreclosing on pathways to secure legal status and economic independence.

Many scholars have analyzed PRS in detail, both across political and regional contexts and from sectoral or thematic perspectives (Loescher et al., 2008). As we have argued elsewhere, the material conditions and depictions of refugees as immobile and passive in places of extended exile have contributed to a *feminization of asylum* (Hyndman and Giles, 2011). By this we mean that refugees perceived to be passive, waiting, or stuck in extended exile may well be perceived as feminized refugees, worthy of aid and assistance, but also far away from the borders of the global North. As those same bodies move towards such borders, they become far more threatening and subject to processes of 'securitization' which portray migrants, including refugees, as threats to national security.

Securitization is a process of social construction that moves an area of regular politics into the area of security by employing a discursive rhetoric of emergency, threat, and danger aimed at justifying the adoption of extraordinary measures. Campesi (2011: 2) contends that securitization is a process whereby a political or social problem becomes read through a 'security prism'. As migrants and asylum seekers, including refugees, approach borders in the global North they are no longer read as passive, stuck, and deserving of assistance. Quite the opposite.

Maintaining refugees facing extended exile in their 'regions of origin' keeps donor states feeling more secure, even if people caught in these conditions become less secure.

Insurgency meets humanitarianism in the Dadaab refugee camps of Northeastern Kenya

'Permanent temporary solutions' is how Bono described the Dadaab refugee camps when he visited on 12 April 2016 (Bono, 2016). News reports repeated that term over and over – as if it was a new concept – but it is not. Dadaab camp refugees have been 'discovered' many times over by many celebrities who have all tried to help, but still the refugees remain. Amina arrived in Ifo camp from Somalia in Dadaab in 1994 as a young girl with her parents from Kismayo, a port town in southern Somalia that had been a battleground for various political factions.[7] When UN peacekeeping troops left that region in 1994, Amina's family decided it was time for them to leave also. Now, at 22, she has a primary school education from a school in the camps that was followed by marriage when she was 13 years old. Two of Amina's three children are now in primary school in the camps, and she is pregnant with a fourth child. Unlike her parents, she sees the benefit of girls completing high school. Indeed, some of her own friends have managed to go to university, but this is now a distant dream for Amina. She nonetheless takes literacy classes at a non-governmental organization (NGO) in Ifo camp where she lives, and is hoping that both her sons and daughters will complete high school, and help the family to prosper, either in the camps or when they all return to Somalia. Amina's husband finished high school in the Dadaab camps and teaches at a high school in Ifo camp, where he is paid the equivalent 'incentive wage' of about $120 a month.[8] He hopes to return with Amina and the children to Mogadishu in Somalia, and continue to teach there, despite the fact that he has no real accreditation, but rather a number of certificates for short courses that have been offered by NGOs over the years.

Three Dadaab camps sprawl across the northeastern Kenyan scrub desert for about 20 kilometres.[9] In recent years, transport from one camp to another has become limited, expensive, and dangerous. So Amina hardly ever travels beyond Ifo camp, almost 6 kilometres away from the town of Dadaab. She does not have the money for a *matatu* [bus] transport or taxi, and her husband is afraid for her safety beyond the limits of the camp. Amina's daily life is busy in Ifo, where the family has a mud brick hut in a small compound, surrounded by a fence of thorn branches from an acacia tree. After sending two of her children to school, she cooks some of the family's food rations, along with other vegetables paid for by her husband's salary, over an open fire, saving some of the prepared food to sell in Ifo camp market. She combines the money she makes from selling food in the market with her husband's salary, rationed food aid (oil, grain, salt, and pulses such as beans) that a neighbour helps her collect with his donkey cart from the food distribution centre in Ifo camp every two weeks, and the remittance of a hundred dollars that her aunt sends her from Toronto every few months. Together, this enables the family to scrape by. But Amina knows that some of the camp residents are in much more dire straits than her family, especially families led by a sole parent or no parent at all, and there are many in that situation due to the combination of the civil wars, droughts, and related poor health conditions in Somalia and in the Dadaab camps.

The violence in the Dadaab camps is ever present and threatening. It wasn't always this way. Now no one is certain who might be working for Al-Shabaab ['the Youth'], the brutal terrorist group that has been very active in Somalia, as well as Kenya. International UN and NGO staff members are well protected as they move around the camps during the day, always travelling with armed guards and in convoys. At night they are housed in highly protected compounds, mostly outside the camps, near Dadaab town. Amina continuously fears for the safety of her family. Her husband's plan to return may come into effect much sooner than expected, as the Kenyan government has started to close camps in Dadaab. However, in 2016, Human Rights Watch reported that Somalia's civil war continues to take a heavy toll on civilians and that 'Kenyan, and Ethiopian forces, and Somali forces against Al-Shabaab, as well as clan-fighting, resulted in significant civilian displacement' throughout Somalia, where citizens face eviction from and destruction of their homes, without access to basic survival (Human Rights Watch, 2016). Security conditions in south-central Somalia are so precarious that anyone returning to the country may end up going back into asylum. It is ironic, then, that Kenya has for some time declared refugees in the camps a threat to its own national security.

Somalian refugees began settling in Ifo, the first of three initial Dadaab-based camps in 1992. These camps were designed to house 90,000 people. In 2011, 150,000 new refugees joined the camps, leading to the development of five camps that housed more than 500,000 people at that time. With the closing of the camps, there are currently about 270,100 people in three camps; of these, 249,144 (92% of the total) are nationals of Somalia (UNHCR, 2017a, 2017b). Tens of thousands of people have been born in the camps, and call Kenya – not Somalia – home. Thousands more Somalians have been resettled to countries like the United States, Canada, Sweden, and Australia, and many more dream of a 'better life' through resettlement elsewhere, or *buufis*[10] (Horst, 2006). As has been illustrated elsewhere (Rawlence, 2016; Horst, 2006; Hyndman, 2000; Giles, 2012), lives and livelihoods are truncated in camps due to people's lack of mobility, permission to work, and establish a more permanent home. Kakuma camp in north-western Kenya houses Sudanese refugees and is currently starting to swell with non-Somalian refugees from the closure of the Dadaab camps. Grayson-Courtmanche's (2015; 2017) ethnography of Kakuma presents stories and narratives of Somalian refugee youth living there. Her in-depth description and incisive analysis of their immobility, their hopes and disappointment, and the violence inherent in camp life is sobering. She cites one young Somalian man who finished high school there, who calls Kakuma an 'open-air jail'.

Conclusion

Amina and her family hope to escape camp life in Dadaab one day. Livelihoods are meager, and security for her family is always in question. UNHCR contends that 'humanitarian action cannot remove the causes of displacement, but it can and should mitigate the consequences' (2012: 28), even if humanitarian action is only palliative. In the current global context, the flawed, if imperfect humanitarian enterprise of providing lives-saving aid during a disaster or emergency help to people at risk of dying remains relevant and essential. However, once people find safety and health is secure, providing humanitarian aid for years at a time – as in the Dadaab camps of Kenya – is highly problematic.

Humanitarian aid to people stuck in extended exile is palliative, nothing more. It may relieve hunger and physical suffering, but does nothing to address the long-term protection and socio-economic development needs and desires of people. In the case of Kenya, security concerns trump humanitarian ones, and Somalian refugees are at risk of being returned to a country that lacks its own security, infrastructure, and resources to meet the needs of people. Further research is essential to examine how the state-centric discourse of 'durable solutions' and 'protracted refugee situations' persists, despite the failure of this language and these arrangements in the 21st century. Current terminology must be re-examined – 'refugees', 'populations', even 'newcomers' all point to 'others' (i.e., not 'us'). What language and practices allow 'them' to become part of 'us', at which point we may be willing to rethink the wisdom of 'parking' them (Agier, 2011: 182) in 'regions of origin' for years, if not decades, at a time?

Notes

1 The United States Committee for Refugees and Immigrants (USCRI) defines protracted displacement slightly differently, as an exile for 10 years or longer (Adelman, 2008). USCRI also includes Palestinian refugees in its statistics, a move that dissolves the artificial separation between this group and all others.
2 Most people located in a long-term encampment are there because they cannot return to a war-torn homeland; they are ineligible for formal resettlement in the country in which the camp is located; and because they do not meet the requirements of a global North country for resettlement.
3 In December 2001, a ministerial meeting on PRS in Africa was convened by UNHCR in Geneva. This was followed by published studies on PRS undertaken and commissioned by UNHCR's Evaluation and Policy Analysis Unit (Crisp, 2003).
4 Even palliative aid is precarious. And yet UN agencies are the sum of their parts, funded by donor and member countries. In December 2014, the UN World Food Programme announced major cuts to food aid for Somali refugees in Kenyan camps and to Syrians refugees in Jordan. Despite demonstrated need, donor funds were insufficient to maintain essential support (Cumming-Bruce and Gladstone, 2014). Less than two weeks later, after a major international donors' conference, food aid resumed to the Syrians (Reuters, 2014). Humanitarian assistance is always contingent on the support of governments in the global North and the geopolitics of the host country. Recently in Kenya, food aid has been reduced in the Dadaab camps, which the government is closing.
5 When refugees live in camps for years on end, 'refugee warehousing' is another term used to describe the plight of waiting in confined quarters (USCRI, 2008). Warehousing, however, connotes a 'warehouser', and there is rarely if ever a single actor or factor that keeps all refugees in long-term limbo.
6 Internally displaced people are defined as those forced to flee their homes, ending up displaced within their own countries, unlike refugees who have crossed borders to safety.
7 The case study of Amina, while fictional, is based on a number of interviews with various refugees and throughout many visits to Dadaab between 1994 and 2016. It is thus a composite case study.
8 This wage is about 10 times less than what a Kenyan would earn for the same job. Refugees are limited to these jobs, as well as other jobs in the informal sectors because they cannot access work permits in Kenya.
9 Until recently, there were five camps, but as of May 2017, the Kambioos refugee camp had closed and its buildings were handed over to the government of Kenya. The Ifo 2 East camp is in the process of closing in the very near future.
10 As Cindy Horst explains,

> The Somali word buufis is commonly used in the Kenyan refugee camps of Dadaab, referring to a person's dream of resettlement. It is an ambiguous phenomenon, bringing hope and remittances into the camps but also removing investments from the region and, when the dream cannot be reached, sometimes having adverse psychological effects.
>
> (Horst, 2006a)

Bibliography

Adelman H (2008) Protracted refugee situations and the right of return. *Metropolis World Bulletin* October, 8: 16–19.
Agier M (2011) [Flammarion:2008]). *Managing the Undesirables: Refugee Camps and Humanitarian Government* (D. Fernbach, Trans.) Cambridge: Polity Press.
Bailey A, Wright R, Mountz A, Miyares I (2002) (Re)producing Salvadoran transnational geographies. *Annals of the Association of American Geographers*, 92(1): 125–144.
BBC (2016) *Kenya Announces Dadaab Refugee Camp Will Close by November* [Online]. Available at: www.bbc.com/news/world-africa-36418604 [Accessed 1.8.2016].
Betts A, Loescher G (eds) (2011) *Refugees in International Relations*. Oxford: Oxford University Press.
Bono (2016) The permanent temporary solution. *New York Times*, 12 April 2016.
Brun C, Fabos A (2015) Making homes in limbo? A conceptual framework. *Refuge* 31(1): 5–17.
Butler J (1993) *Bodies That Matter: On the Discursive Limits of 'Sex'*. New York: Routledge.
Campesi G (2011) *The Arab Spring and the Crisis of the European Border Regime: Manufacturing Emergency in the Lampedusa Crisis*. San Domenico di Fiesole: European University Institute Working Papers.
Crisp J (2003) *No Solutions in Sight: The Problem of Protracted Refugee Situations in Africa*, Working Paper 75 [Online]. Available at: www.unhcr.org/3e2d66c34.html [Accessed 12.10.2013].
Cumming-Bruce N, Gladstone R (2014) U.N. cuts food aid to refugees from Syria. *The New York Times*, 1 December 2014.
Dona G (2015) Making homes in limbo: Embodied virtual "homes" in prolonged conditions of displacement. *Refuge* 31(1): 67–73.
Durieux JF (2009) A regime at a loss? *Forced Migration Review* 33: 60–61.
Giles,W (2010) Livelihood and Afghan workers in Iran. In: Barber P, Lem W (eds) *Class, Contention and a World in Motion*. Oxford: Berghahn Press, 23–40.
Giles W (2012) Humanitarian and livelihood approaches: A view from the Dadaab refugee camps in Kenya. In: *Confronting Capital: Critique and Engagement in Anthropology*. New York and London: Routledge, 208–221.
Grayson-Courtemanche CL (2015) *Growing Up in Exile: An Ethnography of Somali Youth Raised in Kakuma Refugee Camp, Kenya*. Unpublished Ph.D dissertation. Montreal: Department of Anthropology, Universite de Montreal.
Grayson-Courtemanche C-L (2017) *Children of the Camp: The Lives of Somali Youth Raised in Kakuma Refugee Camp, Kenya*. New York and Oxford: Berghahn Books.
Haddad E (2008) The external dimension of EU refugee policy: A new approach to asylum? *Government and Opposition* 43(2): 190–205.
Horst C (2006) *Abstract for Buufis Amongst Somalis in Dadaab: The Transnational and Historical Logics Behind Resettlement Dreams* [Online]. Available at: www.prio.org/Publications/Publication/?x=323 [Accessed 1.8.2016].
Horst C (2008b) [2006]. *Transnational Nomads: How Somalis Cope with Refugee Life in the Dadaab Camps of Kenya*. New York and Oxford: Berghahn Books.
Hovil L (2014) With camps limiting many refugees, the UNHCR's policy change is welcome. *The Guardian*.
Human Rights Watch (2016) *Somalia: Events of 2015* [Online]. Available at: www.hrw.org/world-report/2016/country-chapters/somalia [Accessed 26.5.2017].

Huysman J (2006) *The Politics of Insecurity: Fear, Migration and Asylum in the EU*. New York and London: Routledge.

Hyndman J (2000) *Managing Displacement: Refugees and the Politics of Humanitarianism*. Minneapolis, MN: University of Minnesota Press.

Hyndman J, Giles W (2011) Waiting for what? the feminization of refugees in protracted situations. *Gender, Place and Culture* 18(3): 361–379.

Hyndman J, Giles W (2017) *Refugees in Extended Exile: Living on the Edge*. Abingdon-on-Thames: Routledge.

Hyndman J, Mountz A (2008) Another brick in the wall? neo-refoulement and the externalization of asylum by Australia and Europe. *Government and Opposition: An International Journal of Comparative Politics* 43(2): 249–269.

Hyndman J, Nylund BV (1998) UNHCR and the status of prima facie refugee status in Kenya. *International Journal of Refugee Law* 10(1): 21–48.

Jamal A (2000) *Minimum Standards and Essential Needs in a Protracted Refugee Situation: A Review of the UNHCR Programme in Kakuma, Kenya*. Geneva: s.n.

Kumsa M (2006) "No! I'm not a refugee!" be-longing among young Oromos in Toronto. *Journal of Refugee Studies* 19(2): 230–255.

Loescher G, Milner J (2003) The missing link: The need for comprehensive engagement in regions of refugee origin. *Inernational Affairs* 79(3): 519–617.

Loescher G, Milner J (2005a) Protracted refugee situations: Domestic and security implications. In: *IISS Adelphi Paper 375*. London: Routledge.

Loescher G, Milner J (2005b) The long road home: Protracted refugee. *Survival* 47(2).

Loescher G, Milner J (2006) Burma: Refugees and regional relations. *World Today* 62(7).

Loescher G, Milner J, Newman E, and Troeller G (eds) (2008) *Protracted Refugee Situations: Political, Human Rights and Security Implications*. Geneva: United Nations University Press.

Long K (2011) *Permanent Crises? Unlocking The Protracted Displacement of Refugees and Internally Displaced Persons, Policy Overview* [Online]. Available at: https://www.rsc.ox.ac.uk/publications/permanent-crises-unlocking-the-protracted-displacement-of-refugees-and-internally-displaced-persons.

Malkki L (1996) Speechless emissaries: Refugee, humanitarianism, and dehistoricization. *Cultural Anthropology* 11(3): 377–404.

Milner J (2009) *Refugees, the State and the Politics of Asylum in Africa*. Basingstoke: Palgrave MacMillan.

Milner J, Loescher G (2011) *Responding to Protracted Refugee Situations: Lessons from a Decade of Discussion – Forced Migration Policy Briefing 6*. Oxford: Refugee Studies Centre and Oxford Department of International Development, Oxford University.

Mountz A (2011) The enforcement archipelago: Detention, haunting, and asylum on islands. *Political Geography* 30(3): 118–128.

Ramadan A (2012) Spatialising the refugee camp. *Transactions of the Institute of British Geographers* 38(1): 65–77.

Rawlence B (2016) *City of Thorns: Nine Lives in the World's Largest Refugee Camp*. New York: Picador.

Redfield P (2005) Doctors, borders, and life in crisis. *Cultural Anthropology* 20(3): 328–361.

Reuters (2014) UN resumes food aid for Syrian refugees. *Al-Jazeera*, 10 December 2014.

Rutinwa B (2002) *Prima Facie Status and Refugee Protection*. s.l.:UNHCR EPAU.

Seshadri KR (2008) When home is a camp: Global sovereignty, biopolitics and internally displaced persons. *Social Text* 94(1): 29–58.

Spivak G (1988) Can the subaltern speak? In: Nelson C, Grossberg L (eds) *Marxism and the Interpretation of Culture*. Urbana: University of Illinois Press.

U.S. Committee for Refugees and Immigrants (USCRI) (2008) *World Refugee Survey 2008* [Online]. Available at: http://www.refworld.org/docid/485f50d9ad.html [Accessed 27.5.2018].

UN News Centre (2016) *Kenya Assures Head of UN Refugee Agency That Rights Obligations Will Be Followed for Somali Returns* [Online]. Available at: https://news.un.org/en/story/2016/06/531932-kenya-assures-head-un-refugee-agency-rights-obligations-will-be-followed-somali [Accessed 22.6.2018].

UNHCR (2004) *Protracted Refugee Situations* [Online]. Available at: http://www.unhcr.org/excom/standcom/40c982172/protracted-refugee-situations.html?query=protracted refugee situations [Accessed 22.6.2018].

UNHCR (2009) *Excom Conclusion on Protracted Refugee Situations, No. 109 (LXI)* [Online]. Available at: www.unhcr.org/4b332bca9.html [Accessed 29.3.2012].

UNHCR (2012) *The State of the World's Refugees: In Search of Solidarity*. Oxford: Oxford University Press.

UNHCR (2014) *UNHCR Policy on Alternatives to Camps, UNHCR/HCP/2014/9* [Online]. Available at: www.unhcr.org/5422b8f09.html [Accessed 18.12.2014].

UNHCR (2016) *Camp Population Statistics by Country of Origin, Sex and Age Group* [Online]. Available at: http://reliefweb.int/sites/reliefweb.int/files/resources/KakumaCampPopulation_20160111.pdf [Accessed 1.8.2016].

UNHCR (2017a) *Refugees in the Horn of Africa: Somali Displacement Crisis*. Kenya, Dadaab [Online]. Available at: https://data2.unhcr.org/en/situations/horn?id=3 [Accessed 22.6.2018].

UNHCR (2017b) *UNHCR Dadaab. Camp Population Statistics: By Country of Origin, Sex and Age Group* [Online]. Available at: https://reliefweb.int/sites/reliefweb.int/files/resources/REG_H04CampPopulationbyCoOSexAgeGroup%28Final%29January2017.pdf [Accessed 22.6.2018].

Walters W (2008) Putting the migration-security complex in its place. In: Amoore L, de Goede M (eds) *Risk and the War on Terror*. London and New York: Routledge, 158–177.

Zolberg A, Suhrke A, and Aguayo S (1989) *Escape from Violence: Conflict and the Refugee Crisis in the Developing World*. Oxford: Oxford University Press.

Chapter 6

Deportation and forced return

Nassim Majidi and Liza Schuster

Introduction

Since the end of the last century, there has been an increasing drive by states to forcibly remove people without permission to remain (Anderson, Gibney and Paoletti, 2013; Coutin, 2015). This drive is part of a growing restrictionism towards migration and migrants, regardless of whether the numbers of asylum seekers increased or decreased. Whereas for a number of decades, deportation was an exceptional weapon of migration control, by the end of the 1990s it had become normalized (Bloch and Schuster, 2005; Schuster, 2005) and the following decade has seen the dismantling of many of the protections that had been put in place in order to reduce the deportation gap – the difference between the number of people with removal orders and those actually forcibly removed (Gibney, 2008; Paoletti, 2010).

Persons liable to being forcibly returned from the territory of one state to another today include, depending on the expelling state: visa overstayers, undocumented migrants, the children of those without papers, foreign nationals convicted of crimes and, perhaps most controversially, persons whose asylum claims have been rejected. The primary focus of this chapter is on the removal of those who start their journeys as forced migrants. For reason of space and of disciplinary choices this chapter is embedded in the forced migration literature. We will therefore not deal with the forced removal of foreign national criminals, overstayers or those who have been naturalized but deprived of their citizenship.

Deportation, acknowledged to be a brutal, expensive and ineffective state practice (Schuster, 2005; Gibney and Hansen, 2003; Collyer, 2012) is variously referred to as expulsion, forced return, removal and involuntary repatriation. The use of terms such as administrative removal further confuses the issue and makes the assemblage of comparable data very difficult. We begin with an outline of the different terms used, and by whom. Following a review of the literature on forced return, we survey current deportation practices globally and explore the function of forced return for states. We have a particular emphasis on Afghanistan and Somalia as the authors work in these areas and given ongoing conflict, forced removal to both is controversial. In the final section, we focus on the impact of forced return, including what happens post-deportation.

What is deportation?

Under normal circumstances, citizens may not be removed from, or denied entry to, the territory of their own state (Universal Declaration of Human Rights, Art. 12), though states may withdraw citizenship from naturalized citizens in order to deport them (unless doing so would render them stateless). In particular, states are prohibited by law from returning people to the frontiers of territories where his life or freedom would be threatened on account of his race, religion, nationality, membership of a particular social group or political opinion (Art.33, Geneva Convention Relating to the Status of Refugees). This principle of *non-refoulement* is enshrined in European law and in the laws of its member states.

Terminologies on forced returns and forms of expulsion have varied from state to state (Goodwin-Gill, 1983). Traditionally, in the United States, deportation was used to refer to those who were refused at the first point of entry, and sent home. With time, deportations have grown to include those having already been granted access, but who may have been visa overstayers, failed asylum seekers, criminals, or foreign nationals – aliens – whose rights have been revoked. The terminology remains varied: in the United Kingdom, the preferred administrative term is 'removal', while under international law 'expulsion' is used (Henckaert, 1995).

The word 'expulsion' is commonly used to describe that exercise of state power which secures the removal, either 'voluntarily', under threat of forcible removal, or forcibly, of an alien from the territory of a state (Goodwin-Gill, 1983: 201). Deportation is usually understood as the physical removal of a migrant from the territory of one state to another, against his/her will, but as implied by Goodwin-Gill (1983), people may be forced to return by means other than physical compulsion (Collyer et al., 2009). While many of those liable to forced removal might not be understood to be *forced* migrants, deportation or forced return itself is a form of forced migration (Gibney, 2013).

In Europe, the practice is referred to officially as forced return or removal and is governed by the European Returns Directive, as well as the national laws of individual Member States, which specify who is liable to forced return and under what conditions. Deportation is used by lawyers and policy-makers in the UK to refer to the forced removal of foreign national criminals (see Paoletti, 2010 for discussion of the confusion between removal and deportation), while in France for example, it refers to the deportation of Jews by the Vichy regime. As such, the term deportation carries significant historical weight and so is also the preferred term of anti-deportation activists and lawyers in the Anglophone world, while laws and regulations prefer forced return or removal. In this chapter, we use the terms interchangeably.

In a contribution to a *Journal of Ethnic and Racial Studies* Special Issue on *Deportation, Anxiety, Justice*, Susan Bibler Coutin noted the differences between deportation and other forms of migration:

> Deportation is forcible rather than voluntary, the decision to deport is in the hands of the state rather than that of individual migrants, the direction

of movement is from so-called receiving country to sending country and definitions of origin and membership are disrupted by the act of removal. Indeed, even to refer to deportation as a form of migration challenges common understandings of this term.

(2015: 672)

However, as Coutin notes, in reading deportation as a form of forced migration, we call further into question the original assumptions of migration scholarship, including the neat split between forced and voluntary, the presumption that migration was a single unidirectional event, and the absence of the state. Deportation involves physical, psychological and emotional compulsion (Khosravi, 2016) at the hands of the state. In terms of direction of movement, return may be to a country that is wholly unfamiliar, if, for example, one is an Afghan who was born and grew up in exile in Iran or Pakistan. Deportation is not always the end of the migration journey, not always a return to home: migration is multidirectional, including for those deported, many of whom leave again and more than once (Schuster and Majidi, 2013).

Deportation may describe the removal of an individual or family, as well as groups ranging from a handful of people by commercial flights from Europe to dozens by chartered boats, buses and trucks to various countries of origin (Schuster and Majidi, 2013: 2015).[1] It can also refer to the mass deportations of thousands of families herded across borders into neighbouring territories, whether from Kenya to Somalia (Majidi, 2017a) or Iran or Pakistan to Afghanistan (Human Rights Watch, 2017). Finally, the concept of force is a flexible one. Some people who are classed as voluntary returnees may in fact feel that they have no choice but to return, and hence feel that their return has been forced upon them.

Deportation scholarship

In arguing that deportation is a form of forced migration, Gibney (2013) queried why it had received so little attention from migration scholars. In the last decades of the 20th century there were a handful studies, but coinciding with the increased interest from states in deporting, there has been a steady growth in the literature on the subject through the 2000s. Academic literature on deportation initially focused on the earlier stages of the process, exploring the difficulties of removing rejected asylum seekers (Noll, 1997, 1999; Phuong, 2005; Ellermann, 2005), resistance against deportation (Nyers, 2003), and the dangers and injustices of the deportation experience (Fekete, 2005; Kanstroom, 2007). This critical view of the practice of forced return has continued, with scholars such as Fischer (2015) and DeBono, Rönnqvist and Magnusson (2015) drawing attention to the psychological damage inflicted on those awaiting deportation.

However, in the early 2000s, as the practice of deportation became normalized (Bloch and Schuster, 2005; Schuster, 2005), this focus was complemented by a growing body of literature on the place of deportation in the states anti-migration arsenal (Ellermann, 2009) and increasingly on the theoretical and practical implications of that normalization (Bloch and Schuster, 2005) or what Gibney and Hansen (2003) have referred to as the 'deportation turn' (see also De Genova and Peutz, 2010).

De Genova (2002) has explained how deportability, the condition of being liable to forced return, creates an exploitable, oppressable, vulnerable workforce that serves the interest of globalized, capitalist economies (see also Bloch and McKay, 2016). De Genova uses the concept of deportability to refer to the protracted possibility of being deported, which produces 'practical, materially consequential, and deeply interiorized modes of being' (De Genova and Peutz, 2010: 14). Underlining the negative impact of the threat of deportation, others describe it as part of the state's apparatus to marginalize, terrify, exclude and expose (Bloch and McKay, 2016; Jones et al., 2017). In this view, deportation works on the deportable to make them compliant and exploitable.

Others have written on how deportation works for governing elites to reinforce the value and significance of national citizenship, underlining the distinction between citizen and non-citizen, since the former cannot be deported (Anderson, Gibney and Paoletti, 2013: 2; Walters, 2016). And yet, as underlined by scholars working in this field, deportation also underlines the fuzziness of that distinction and the binding ties between citizen and non-citizen, which make deportation so brutal for those effected, including citizens. In 2017, the Dutch authorities forcibly removed a 60-year-old man from his wife of 40+ years to Afghanistan after 20 years. She had become a Dutch citizen and was in need of his care. They were left to fend for themselves separately, without family support or any source of income.[2]

As deportation studies have multiplied, the focus has shifted to include more studies on what happens post-deportation (Peutz, 2006, 2010; Brotherton, 2008; Ruben, Van Houte and Davids, 2009; Khosravi, 2009; Schuster and Majidi, 2013, 2015), though the work on what happens to forced migrants returned against their will is still limited, and that on forced return within the global south even more so. There are of course practical reasons, besides ethnocentricity, why there are so few studies conducted in refugee-generating countries.[3] Nonetheless, scholarly attention to these inevitably brutal state practices and their consequences are particularly important, as there is no evidence that they will either decrease or become more humane (if that were possible), largely because, as Gibney (2013) says, deportation carried out by the liberal state is largely seen as legitimate and just.

There are two other significant gaps in the literature to date. First is an ethnography of policy-making, which makes visible the calculations of those who devise the policies to be implemented. Ellermann (2006) is one of the very few scholars working on the implementation of these policies by street-level bureaucrats but not from an ethnographic perspective. Second, since the sharply insightful overview by Chimni in 2004, there has been no further critical analysis of the role of the international community in implementing and legitimizing forced return, accepting it as part of repatriation, one of its three durable solutions, the other two being local integration and resettlement.

History of deportation and forced returns[4]

Deportatio, under the Romans, referred to a forced exile within the empire, often to an island. The evolution from a citizen's to a foreign national's expulsion is a rather recent phenomenon. Return refers to the process of going back to one's country of citizenship – if return is voluntary – and increasingly, the process of *sending* back people to their country of citizenship – when return is forced. This shift – from going to sending, from voluntary to forced – has happened gradually, yet is accelerating as part of a discourse on solutions. Deportation is therefore closely linked to return migration. Return migration policies are increasingly used by states to manage migration. The assumption is that populations on the move, be it refugees, failed asylum seekers or migrants, can return to their home country, voluntarily or by force, to resume their lives in societies of origin. The aim is return to what is assumed to be a natural order in the international system.

Return or repatriation has traditionally been seen as the end of the migration cycle, including or especially for refugees (Black and Koser, 1999), the point at which a host state's responsibility to refugees ends. As Anderson, Gibney and Paoletti (2013) have argued: deportation is an exercise of state authority that aims definitively to end the relationship of responsibility between the state and the non-citizen by forcing the non-citizen beyond the sphere of the state's authority. The emphasis on return, in particular for refugees who were forced to leave their homes, assumes a natural order, that the right place is home, that somehow return is the best and most desirable outcome. Malkki (1995) has challenged the assumption that return serves to restore a natural 'national' order by returning people to where they belong, showing that refugees in exile were not necessarily an anomaly or uprooted, but may have created a home elsewhere. However difficult the situation in their new home, conditions in the country of origin may make return and reintegration impossible and therefore refugees (and non-refugees) may be reluctant to end their relationship with the receiving state.

However, the inability or unwillingness of many forced migrants to return to their countries of origin or habitual residence has led to an increased emphasis on forcing them to return. Chimni (2004) tracks the steps that paved the way for this shift. The focus of the states of the Global North, expressed through UNHCR policy, moved from an emphasis on *resettlement* (1945–85), essential for those who could not return home and who would provide a much-needed supplement to the North's post-war depleted national labour forces, to *repatriation* (1986–1998), the preferred durable solution for states in the Global North unable to halt the arrival of refugees from the Global South. As described by Chimni, that second phase saw a shift from *voluntary* to *forced* repatriation, in spite of arguments such as Malkki's (1995) and Harrell-Bond's (1989) that there was no research to suggest that repatriation was possible or appropriate for most refugees. Chimni suggests that an idealized image of repatriation, of return, was used to legitimize what were in effect forced returns, as many refugees did not in fact volunteer to return, having created new homes in exile.

Next came a shift towards *safe return* in the early 1990s following the Yugoslav wars as states took advantage of the absence of any reference to *voluntary* return in the Geneva Convention (Hathaway, cited in Chimni, 2004). As Chimni notes it merely called upon state parties to ensure safe return so that it is left to the state alone to decide when there has been a sufficient change in the circumstances in the country of origin to warrant invoking the cessation clause (Art.1c, 1951 Refugee Convention). In other words, the subjective perceptions of the state authorities are substituted for the experience of the refugee in making the decision that it is time to leave (Chimni, 2004).

Chimni (2004) makes clear that state humanitarian responses to the arrival and presence of refugees are always politically driven. This is particularly evident from Chimni's (2004) description of the acceptance by UNHCR[5] that under a doctrine of *imposed return*, refugees may be sent back to less than optimal conditions in their home country against their will because it is happening anyway, because in the era of mass movements the doctrine of individual expression of free will to return has been less relevant and less used and because imposed return has become necessary because of pressure from host states and a lack of money to care for refugees (McNamara, cited in Chimni, 2004: 10–11). The hosts who were forcibly and massively returning refugees at the time were largely in the Global South (Sudan, Zaire, Tanzania), and they were doing so in the face of resistance by states in the Global North to share the responsibility and the introduction of increasingly restrictive measures to prevent the arrival of refugees on European shores (it was at this time plans for processing centres in the region and in North Africa were mooted). In other words, the Global North did not have any moral authority to condemn these forced returns, which anyway worked in their interests.

Mass involuntary repatriation has a history as a weapon of weak states. Such states, who host far larger populations of refugees than states in the Global North, have used the threat of mass returns to exert pressure on the neighbouring state of origin (frequently an even weaker state) or on donor states in order to leverage further resources or pursue a particular agenda. For example, Afghanistan's neighbours Iran and Pakistan have, over the last 40 years, each hosted more than 2 million Afghans. At regular intervals, these states threaten and do push back thousands of people daily (Turton and Marsden, 2002; Human Rights Watch, 2017).

At the end of 2014, tensions between Afghanistan and Pakistan deteriorated as the latter accused its neighbour of sheltering the perpetrators of the attack on the Army Public School in Peshawar that killed 145 people, including 132 children. Pakistan punished Afghan refugees by extending their residence permits for only 6 months, then 3 months (instead of the 18–36 months as they had previously), and stepping up abuses and harassment so that there were three times as many returns in 2015 (181,000) compared with 2014 (61,000). In 2016, when the Salma Dam,[6] financed by India with a promise of a further $1 billion in aid, was inaugurated, Pakistan was furious and Afghan refugees felt the brunt of it (Bjelica, 2016). In June during clashes on the border, a Pakistani Army Major was killed. That month, the numbers being returned daily reached 4,000–5,000, with more than 600,000 Afghans returned from Pakistan in the space of 6 months (347,000 with refugee cards and 247,000 undocumented) (Human Rights Watch, 2017).[7]

Kenya has hosted Somali refugees since the 1990s, most in the Dadaab camps, which by 2011 had a population of half a million (Lindley and Hammond, 2014). Originally, Kenya accepted Somalis fleeing civil war and the collapse of the state in 1991 as *prime facie* refugees, and again in the wake of the 2011 famine in Somalia, on the understanding that their stay would be temporary and UNHCR would take care of them. In 1993, 170,000 Somalis were repatriated, but due to ongoing insecurity, drought and famine, many continued to be displaced and by the early 2000s, repatriations had dwindled to a few hundred per year. However, this period saw the growth of Al-Shabaab, a radical Wahabist movement, in Somalia, and in 2011 they allegedly began a series of deadly attacks in Kenya. In response, Kenya began to push for repatriations from the enormous Dadaab camp. They began deporting urban refugees in 2014 and announcing that 'hosting refugees has to come to an end'. In 2013, UNHCR, Kenya and Somalia signed an agreement on the 'voluntary repatriation' of Somali refugees, but given the continued instability in Somalia, the refugees were not easy to convince.[8] In 2016, the Kenyan government threatened to close the Dadaab camp complex by year's end, de facto forcibly returning all of its population to Somalia. The vast majority of Somali refugees to date still do not want to return, and those who have returned lack the necessary information and networks to facilitate their reintegration, pointing to a failed return process (Majidi, 2017a).

In Europe, though the numbers are significantly smaller (of both refugees and those forcibly returned), the drive to deport is increasing and the justification used is the preservation of the asylum system, i.e., without the threat of deportation the system would be overwhelmed by fraudulent claims. The deterrent effect of deportation is treated as a given (in spite of a complete absence of any research data to that effect) and is used to justify the increase in returns and the introduction of measures to reduce the deportation gap. The 2015 EU Action Plan on Return (European Commission, 2015: 453 final) argued that

> One of the most effective ways to address irregular migration is the systematic return, either voluntary or forced, of those who do not or no longer have the right to remain in Europe. Fewer people that do not need international protection might risk their lives and waste their money to reach the EU if they know they will be returned home swiftly.

At the same time, acknowledging that voluntary returns are more effective (i.e., those who return voluntarily are more likely to remain in their countries of origin) than forced returns, the document also states that the appeal of voluntary return schemes also depends on how credible the prospect of forced return is (European Commission, 2015: 3). There appears to be some truth in this. In the course of multiple flights to Kabul via Istanbul (between 2015 and 2017), Schuster met and spoke with dozens of such young men and a handful of families who described the pressure they had been subjected to in Norway and Turkey in particular (see Khosravi, 2016 on Sweden), including being told that if they did not sign a document stating that they agreed to return, they would be physically removed, or not allowed to leave detention. They explained they had signed the voluntary return paper because they were told they had no choice, and this way they would be able to access some support on return. Such returns are more properly described as soft deportations (Leerkes, Van Os and Boersema, 2017) and usually require fewer or no escorts, so are considerably cheaper, even when a return or reintegration package is included.

However, while the threat of hard deportations may increase the uptake of soft deportations, undocumented migration continues apace and many of those deported re-migrate (Schuster and Majidi, 2013), leading us to question the justifiability and utility of deportation, and with De Bono (2016) to argue that this presentation of returns as a necessary element of the solution to the refugee crisis is problematic because it is based on misconceptions about the experience of those returned, because there is no evidence to support the core deterrent argument and because so little is known about what happens post-deportation.

Nonetheless, EU states are determined to close the deportation gap (Gibney and Hansen, 2003; Paoletti, 2010), that is, the gap between the number of people subject to deportation orders and those the state actually manages to deport, because of a range of constraints (Gibney and Hansen, 2003). The deportation of those with established networks, who can offer support to the person targeted, is extremely difficult, while it is much easier to deport those already in detention. The practice of detaining those who *may* be liable to deportation works in two ways – it makes the person targeted for forced return physically available, and it inhibits the creation and maintenance of networks which might interfere with the process of removal (Tyler, 2017). However, objections to removal and to the violent restraints used have also been voiced by strangers, passengers on commercial flights used to forcibly return individuals, resulting in a move towards collective forced removals using charter flights from EU member states. This is an expensive option and difficult to enforce without the cooperation of the countries of origin who have to accept the return of their citizens, as we will see in the next section.

Constraints on forced return

It seems that only 40% of migrants who have been given an order to leave the EU, actually leave (Andrijasevic, 2010). Removal orders may not be carried out for a number of reasons, one of the most important being legal and human rights constraints. While mass returns occur largely in the global south, a body of legal instruments, and of lawyers and migrant and human rights organisations make it more difficult to decide from one day to the next to expel large numbers of people from countries in the Global North. Even when the courts have decided an individual is not a refugee and does not meet the refugee criteria, removal may not be possible. Protection may be granted to asylum seekers based on rights guaranteed by the European Convention on Human Rights and Fundamental Freedoms. For example, the Prohibition on Torture (Art.3) and the right to Family and Private Life (Art.8) has protected those whose asylum claims have been rejected, but who have managed to build families, and whose rights would be infringed should the claimant be removed. Others are also exempt from deportation, including unaccompanied minors, who may not be removed until their 18th birthday; female headed-households from certain countries where they would be at risk; and those whose return would not be considered reasonable for example those with certain health conditions that cannot be adequately treated in the sending state. However, the law is not always respected, and individuals with family connections, such as the Afghan man referred at the beginning of the chapter, have been forcibly returned.

It is at the street level that the true costs of deportation – the coercive uprooting of individuals from their communities, families and workplaces – become most visible (Rosenberger and Winkler, 2014; Tyler, 2017). Supporters of those facing deportation work to make forced return difficult through lobbying and campaigning, and their demands to stop forced returns are often framed around the human costs to the community. As Ellermann (2015) notes, this reframing of deportation in humanitarian terms threatens to undermine the legitimacy of bureaucratic decisions by reintroducing the deportee as a classmate, work colleague, girlfriend, friend and human being – counteracting the dehumanizing narratives of failed asylum seeker.

Aside from the constraints in EU states, there is also the lack of cooperation with countries of origin, which make returns difficult. There is little cooperation from some states in verifying the nationality of those to be deported (De Bono, 2016). For some states, there is little benefit to be gained from facilitating the forced return of their citizens, in particular when their families rely on remittances. It is often overlooked the extent to which asylum seekers and refugees remit and help to support and sustain families at home, and therefore the consequences for those families post-deportation. In 2015, with an upturn in refugee arrivals, European policy-makers began to apply pressure not only to rejected asylum seekers but also to transit and origin states to prevent irregular migration and facilitate returns (European Commission, 2015: 453 final). The Commission warned Member States that effective returns require political will and prioritisation and that the implementation of EU Return Directive, by the Member States leaves room for improvement (European Commission, 2015: 15).

A major step forward in terms of restricting arrivals and facilitating returns was the EU-Turkey deal, signed in 2016, whereby, in exchange for €3 billion (later doubled) and the easing of visa restrictions for Turkish citizens, the Turkish authorities agreed to take back those who had transited Turkey to Greece and to prevent others from doing the same (there was also to be a resettlement programme for Syrians from Turkey to the EU, so that for every Syrian arriving irregularly into Greece who Turkey took back, the EU would resettle one) (Tunaboyla and Alpes, 2017). However, such a strategy only works if the transit country does not get stuck with those returned. Turkey currently hosts 3 million refugees, most of whom are from Syria, but there are also significant numbers from Afghanistan.

In 2016, Afghanistan had the highest number of civilian casualties since 2001 (UNAMA, 2017), the Taliban was in control of more than 50% of the country, there were major attacks by Daesh/ISIS and the Al Haqani network and a concerted effort by the EU states to push Afghan refugees back into Afghanistan. The appointment of a new Refugee Minister in 2015, Syed Alemi Balkhi, was a barrier to this intention, since he explicitly stated it was not safe to return people to Afghanistan and did his best to resist. EU states complained bitterly about the lack of cooperation, arguing that countries that refused to cooperate should not expect as much from donor states. Although it is a country still in conflict, the EU Member States took advantage of the Brussels Donor conference in October 2016 to apply significant pressure on the Afghan government, warning President Ghani that further aid could not be guaranteed unless an agreement (the *Joint Way Forward*) was signed in which the Afghan government promised to issue travel documents, assist with identification and accept returns.[9]

The number of people being deported from Europe to Afghanistan is relatively low, certainly by comparison with forced returns from those whose host the majority of the world's forced migrants. However, the plan to operationalize the *Joint Way Forward* foresees a total of 10,000 returns in 2017: 5,000 voluntary returns and 5,000 forced (Bjelica and Ruttig, 2017). This would mean a more than 10-fold increase since 2016, which, UNAMA noted, had seen an overall the highest total civilian casualties recorded since 2009 when UNAMA began systematic documentation (UNAMA, 2017). The Afghan government, in spite of President Ghani's statements, is being forced to accept these returns. In June 2017, both Minister Balkhi and his Deputy Minister pleaded in vain with EU MS to suspend deportations, pointing to the attacks that month that cost more than 150 lives in the capital alone, and the challenges of coping with returns from Pakistan and Iran.

This raises the question of *missing* constraints. In spite of constraints just listed – legal, social and international – states push ahead with forced returns that are illegal, whether it is Pakistan harassing documented refugees, the Netherlands abusing Art.1F of the 1951 Refugee Convention to refuse asylum to innocent men, Germany deporting a man with severe schizophrenia, or Norway separating families. Even though migration tribunals recognize that those applying for asylum have well-founded fears of persecution, they deport on the basis of the possibility of safe internal relocation, for example, that those being returned will be safe in Kabul, ignoring UNHCR guidelines that stress the importance of social networks. In recent years, a growing number of legal and migration scholars have been arguing for the need for a post-deportation monitoring process as a way of avoiding these miscarriages of justice.

The arguments for the necessity of monitoring in deportation situations is built on three rights-based principles and protection safeguards: first, that deportation can constitute *refoulement*; second, due to the risk of harm when they return to their country of origin; third, the lack of assistance, institutional support and social protection upon return (Bowerman, 2017; Alpes et al., 2017). Without monitoring, redress for errors (which may be fatal) is highly unlikely. On the other hand, the absence of monitoring makes it harder to prove that states have *refouled* and are in breach of their obligations.

The impact of deportation

Although the literature on what happens post-deportation is growing, as noted previously, the work on what happens to rejected asylum seekers, particularly those from countries still in conflict, is very limited. Nonetheless, some work has been done. The LOS country catalogue (2017: 5), using country of origin and human rights organisations reports lists 27 countries, most of whom penalize undocumented exit with arrest and detention. There were also details of beating and harassment by police, in particular where claiming asylum is considered as treason.

However, being desk based, the catalogue focused largely on what happened in the short term. Little is known about the impact of deportation on rejected asylum seekers in the longer term, on women, on children or on the families of those returned (whether in the country of origin or the receiving country). Schuster and Majidi's work in Afghanistan (2013, 2015) points to a number of problems encountered, including being targeted as contaminated because of time spent in the West, and being stigmatized for failure, especially when the flight was financed by selling or mortgaging family property. One consequence that became abundantly clear, was that in contrast to those who had genuinely chosen to return, the overwhelming majority of those who were returned against their will left again. It was also clear that aside from the physical risks to those deported and to their families, the failed investments in migration to Europe – because asylum seekers do work and earn money and support families at home – was a huge burden for many of the families. Nonetheless, some people make large profits from deportation.

The impact of deportation on psychosocial well-being is increasingly being reported in the scholarly literature, with empirical evidence on the effects of detention, deportability and deportation. De Bono, Rönnqvist and Magnusson (2015) discuss the effects of deportability – or living in limbo in the country of destination – on migrants' psychosocial well-being. The psychological effects of detention and deportation are experienced in the countries of reception as well as of return, leading to a layering of harms to mental health that often go unaddressed and untreated upon return. In *Enduring Uncertainty*, Hasselberg (2016) discusses the emotional and psychological impact of an uncertain status, of deportability and deportation in the receiving country. In line with Dow's previous work (2007), she reviews the lived experiences of deportation orders. A common thread in their accounts was the element of psychological damage, psychological torture (Hasselberg, 2016) and changes in behaviour caused by the deportation order. Whether returned or not, the living conditions under uncertainty and exclusion has an impact on psychological well-being.

The requirements for psychosocial well-being, as presented by De Bono, Rönnqvist and Magnusson (2015), include (1) agency, autonomy and control, (2) participation and involvement, (3) social relationships and networks and (4) safety. Ruben, Van Houte and Davids (2009) further discuss the impact of previous migration phases on psychosocial embeddedness, of which psychological well-being is one of the core elements. The authors argue that the layering of trauma during migration stages creates further instability. The symptoms they identify are depression, phobias and schizophrenia. Elsewhere Majidi (2017b) has shown that a common marker among deported migrants is the inability to negotiate their post-return lives, and to regain a sense of home. The lack of preparedness in forced returns, the loss of control and networks, can put deportees in a state of psychosocial instability that leads to them feeling lost upon return.

The business of deportation

Deportations are not only part of an administrative component of migration and immigration systems, they are also big business (Walters, 2002, 2016; De Genova, 2010).[10] The delegation of state authority (Guiraudon and Lahav, 2000) has seen the involvement of other 'local, private and transnational actors' (Andreas and Snyder, 2000: 6), in particular private sector actors. The privatization and outsourcing of migration management has been discussed in the literature with the pioneering work of Lahav (1998), De Genova and Peutz (2010) and Menz (2011). What were once key state functions are being delegated to private companies for a fee: from running detention facilities or removal centres in the UK, transporting deportees on commercial flights, using private security contractors to escort deportees, or relying on construction companies in countries of origin to build reception or reintegration facilities.

The problem with the shifting of state tasks to private companies is precisely the introduction of a profit motive for deportations. Such a motive creates incentives to treat people as targets, as means to a profit goal. Moreover, given the lack of oversight and monitoring it is inevitable that there will be casualties. In 2010, Jimmy Mubenga was removed from a British Airways flight at London Heathrow Airport by a private security firm – G4S – whose custody officers' treatment of Mr. Mubenga on board the plane led to a heart attack and subsequent death. Although medical records of the death clarified the cause of death (chokehold and compression of the chest, despite being handcuffed and seated with his seatbelt on), all G4S duty officers were cleared of charges during the trial. Gammeltoft-Hansen (2013) predicted that the investigation would not yield any results as such cases outsource questions of liability. While grassroots mobilization targets the government to appeal or block deportation measures, private companies' actions are hidden from public view, implying less liability and accountability to the treatment of migrants and deportees. From private chartered flights to foreign security personnel, the amount of public information is still limited and warrants greater attention to the norms regulating such a deportation industry.

Conclusion: reflections on an inhumane and illiberal practice

Although, as we have argued, deportation has become normalized, and the pressure to increase the number forcibly returned has increased, it is a blunt instrument and the effects are felt by many more than those physically removed. When return contains an element of coercion and force it cannot be considered a durable solution – in particular when individuals are sent to states still in conflict, with the economic and social consequences that entails. The rationale presented by policy makers is that return migration, combined with other measures, will deter irregular migration, send a strong message to traffickers and smugglers, preserve the asylum space against asylum shopping and enforce international and national laws. Academics have been testing assumptions but cannot keep up with the policy world: return has been happening, whether assisted or unassisted, but its effects are under-explored. What do we know of the impacts of return migration policies and programmes? What happens to people, institutions and states in the wake of massive returns home? What happens after return to conflict and post-conflict settings? Return is proposed as inherently positive; as a concept, it is paired with other concepts such as reintegration, assuming that return is meant to be linked to a process of economic, social and cultural insertion back home. What are the consequences when the process of return fails? To date, studies indicate that reintegration rarely follows forced return and that re-migration is the most likely consequence (Schuster and Majidi, 2013).

Notes

1 Walters (2016) has argued for greater attention to be paid to the practices and spaces involved in the transport of people being forcibly removed, and in particular for a critical analysis of the policies and practices involved.
2 The man was refused asylum on the basis of his employment in Afghanistan's Communist government in the 1980s/1990s. Letters from the Afghan government insisting that he was not guilty or suspected of any crime were ignored. In 1999 the Dutch government drafted a report, which stated, quite simply, that all Afghan officers who had worked for the secret services and/or a liaison organisation in the eighties and the nineties, during the time that Afghanistan was considered a Soviet satellite state, were in fact war criminals. The consequence of this report was that if a refugee from Afghanistan had worked for the secret service as an officer, he (or she, but mostly he) would get an 1F-status and would be excluded from asylum and all social rights. Any

proof and/or piece of evidence from individual Afghan asylum seekers that they have been falsely accused and do not fall under 1F, was and is still today not accepted. This resulted in a situation where hundreds of Afghans were denied a status as refugees (EDAL, 2017).
3 A significant practical reason is that rejected asylum seekers and refugees are frequently being returned to states in conflict, and research institutions rely increasingly on (risk averse) insurance companies to make the decision on whether it is safe to conduct research in those environments. Where they agree, it is frequently under security conditions that make research impractical, if not impossible.
4 We have focused on the history of forced return due to space limitations and because deportation historically involved a very wide range of people.
5 Specifically, Dennis McNamara, the Director of UNHCRs Division of International Protection (DIP), in September 1996 (Chimni, 2004: 10–11).
6 Another dam, in Herat Province, which threatens the water supply to Iran, may be behind the sharp increase in forced returns from that country in 2016 to 435,000, with a further 600,000 promised for 2017.
7 This case is particularly complex as UNHCR were accused of complicity in Pakistan's mass re-foulement, encouraging people to return by increasing the cash support to each returnee from $200 to $400 (HRW, 2017), and the reaction of the Afghan President which was to encourage further returns with wholly unrealistic promises of land, homes and jobs 'as many as 30 million people live in Afghanistan and that the return of two or three million more people would not have such a bad impact on the current situation in the country' (Ghani, cited in Bjelica, 2016).
8 A joint return intention survey conducted by the International Organization for Migration (IOM) and UNHCR Kenya revealed that only 2.6% of refugees in Dadaab intended to return to Somalia in 2014.
9 Ministers Balkhi (Refugees and Repatriation), Iklil (Finance), Zakhi (National Security Council) and Rabbani (Foreign Affairs) each stood up before Parliament and explained that the Europeans had threatened them with cancelling future aid if they failed to sign.
10 The involvement of transportation companies in deportation and mass expulsions has a long history. Walters (2002), for example, highlights the participation of train companies under the Nazi regime and the use of shipping companies in England's transportation of a criminal class to New South Wales and, as noted above, the contemporary use of the airline industry to deport unwanted aliens and refused asylum seekers back to countries of origin worldwide.

Bibliography

Alpes J, Blondel C, Preiss N, et al (2017) Post-deportation risks for failed asylum seekers. *Forced Migration Review* 54: 76.

Anderson B, Gibney M, and Paoletti E (eds) (2013) *The Social, Political and Historical Contours of Deportation*. New York: Springer.

Andreas P, Snyder T (2000) *The Wall Around the West: State Borders and Immigration Controls in North America and Europe*. London: Rowman & Littlefield.

Andrijasevic R (2010) From exception to excess: Detention and deportations across the mediterranean space. In: De Genova N, Peutz N (eds) *The Deportation Regime: Sovereignty, Space, and the Freedom of Movement*. Durham, NC: Duke University Press, 147–165.

Bjelica J (2016) Caught up in regional tensions? The mass return of Afghan refugees from Pakistan. *Afghanistan Analysts Network*. Available at: www.afghanistan-analysts.org/caught-up-in-regional-tensions-the-mass-return-of-afghan-refugees-from-pakistan/.

Bjelica J, Ruttig T (2017) Voluntary and forced returns to Afghanistan in 2016/17: Trends, statistics and experiences. *Afghanistan Analysts Network*. Available at: www.afghanistan-analysts.org/voluntary-and-forced-returns-to-afghanistan-in-201617-trends-statistics-and-experiences/.

Black R, Koser K (1999) The end of the refugee cycle? In: Black R, Koser K (eds) *The End of the Refugee Cycle?* Oxford: Berghahn, 1–19.

Bloch A, McKay S (2016) *Living on the Margins: Undocumented Migrants in a Global City*. Bristol: Policy Press.

Bloch A, Schuster L (2005) At the extremes of exclusion: Deportation, detention and dispersal. *Ethnic and Racial Studies* 28(3): 491–512.

Bowerman E (2017) Risks encountered after forced removal: the return experiences of young Afghans. *Forced Migration Review* 54: 78–80.

Brotherton D (2008) Exiling New Yorkers. In: Brotherton D, Katsemenas P (eds) *Keeping Out the Other: Immigration Control in the New Millennium*. New York: Columbia University Press, 161–178.

Chimni BS (2004) From resettlement to involuntary repatriation: Towards a critical history of durable solutions to refugee problems. *Refugee Survey Quarterly* 23(3): 55–73.

Collyer M (2012) Deportation and the micropolitics of exclusion: The rise of removals from the UK to Sri Lanka. *Geopolitics* 17(2): 276–292.

Collyer M, Wimalasena P, Ansar N, and Khan A (2009) *Return Migrants in Sri Lanka*. London: Institute for Public Policy Research.

Coutin S (2015) Deportation studies: Origins, themes and direction. *Journal of Ethnic and Migration Studies* 41(4): 671–681.

De Bono D (2016) Returning and deporting irregular migrants: Not a solution to the 'refugee crisis'. *Human Geography* 9(2): 101–112.

De Bono D, Rönnqvist S, and Magnusson K (2015) *Humane and Dignifed? Migrants Experiences of Living in a State of Deportability in Sweden*. Malmö: Malmö University.

De Genova N (2002) Migrant illegality and deportability in everyday life. *Annual Review of Anthropology* 31(1): 419–447.

De Genova N, Peutz N (2010) *The Deportation Regime*. Durham, NC: Duke University Press.

Dow M (2007) Designed to punish: Immigrant detention and deportation. *Social Research: An International Quarterly* 74(2): 533–546.

EDAL (2017) Strategic litigation as a tool to help the Afghan 1Fers in the Netherlands. *European Database of Asylum Law*. Available at: www.asylumlawdatabase.eu/en/journal/strategic-litigation-tool-help-afghan-1fers-netherlands.

Ellermann A (2005) Coercive capacity and the politics of implementation: Deportation in Germany and the United States. *Comparative Political Studies* 38(10): 1219–1244.

Ellermann A (2006) Street level democracy: How immigration bureaucrats manage public opposition. *West European Politics* 29(2): 293–309.

Ellermann A (2009) *States Against Migrants: Deportation in Germany and the United States*. Cambridge: Cambridge University Press.

Ellermann A (2015) Do policy legacies matter? past and present guest workers recruitment in Germany. *Journal of Ethnic and Migration Studies* 41(8): 1235–1253.

European Commission (2015) *EU Action Plan on Return* (COM) 473 Final. Brussels: European Commission.

Fekete L (2005) The deportation machine: Europe, asylum and human rights. *Race & Class* 47(1): 64–78.

Fekete L, Webber F (2010) Foreign nationals, enemy penology and the criminal justice system. *Race and Class* 51(4): 1–25.

Fischer N (2015) The management of anxiety: An ethnographical outlook on self-mutilations in a French immigration detention centre. *Journal of Ethnic and Migration Studies* 41(4): 599–616.

Gammeltoft-Hansen T (2013) The rise of the private border guard: Accountability and responsibility in the migration control industry. In: Gammeltoft-Hansen T, Nyberg Sorensen N (eds) *The Migration Industry and the Commercialization of International Migration*. Abingdon: Routledge, 128–151.

Gibney M (2008) Asylum and the expansion of deportation in the United Kingdom. *Government and Opposition* 43(2): 146–167.

Gibney M (2013) Is deportation a form of forced migration? *Refugee Survey Quarterly* 32(2): 116–129.

Gibney M, Hansen R (2003) *Deportation and the Liberal State: The Forcible Return of Asylum Seekers and Unlawful Migrants in Canada, Germany and the United Kingdom*. UNHCR Evaluation and Policy Analysis Unit. Geneva: UNHCR

Goodwin-Gill G (1983) *The Refugee in International Law*. Oxford: Clarendon Press.

Guiraudon V, Lahav G (2000) A reappraisal of the state sovereignty debate: The case of migration control. *Comparative Political Studies* 33(2): 163–195.

Harrell-Bond B (1989) Repatriation: Under what conditions is it the most desirable solution for refugees? An agenda for research. *African Studies Review* 32: 41–69.

Hasselberger I (2016) *Enduring Uncertainty: Deportation, Punishment and Everyday Life*. Oxford: Berghahn.

Henckaerts JM (1995) *Mass Expulsion in Modern International Law and Practice*. Leiden: Martinus Nijhoff Publishers.

Human Rights Watch (2017) *Pakistan Coercion, UN Complicity: The Mass Forced Return of Afghan Refugees*. Human Rights Watch. Available at: www.hrw.org/report/2017/02/13/pakistan-coercion-un-complicity/mass-forced-return-afghan-refugees.

International Organization for Migration (IOM) / UNHCR (2014), *Joint return intention survey report 2014*, Kenya.

Jones H, Gunaratnam Y, Bhattacharyya G, Dhaliwal S, Forkery K, Jackson E, et al (2017) *Go Home? The Politics of Immigration Controversies*. Manchester: Manchester University Press.

Kanstroom D (2007) *Deportation Nation: Outsiders in American History*. Cambridge, MA: Harvard University Press.

Khosravi S (2009) Sweden: Detention and deportation of asylum seekers. *Race & Class* 50(4): 38–56.

Khosravi S (2016) Deportation as a way of life for young Afghan men. *Detaining the Immigrant Other: Global and Transnational Issues* 169.

Lahav G (1998) Immigration and the state: The devolution and privatisation of immigration control in the EU. *Journal of Ethnic and Migration Studies* 24(4): 675.

Leerkes A, Van Os R, and Boersema E (2017) What drives 'soft deportation'? Understanding the rise in assisted voluntary return among rejected asylum seekers in the Netherlands. *Population, Space and Place* dx. doi.org/10.1002/psp.2059. Available at: https://www.academia.edu/35242701/What_drives_soft_deportation_Understanding_the_rise_in_Assisted_Voluntary_Return_among_rejected_asylum_seekers_in_the_Netherlands.

Lindley A, Hammond L (2014) Histories and contemporary challenges of crisis and mobility in Somalia. In: Lindley A (ed) *Crisis and Migration: Critical Perspectives*. Abingdon: Routledge.

LOS (2017) *Post Deportation Risks: A Country Catalogue of Existing References*. Rotterdam: Stichting LOS.

Majidi N (2017a) Uninformed decisions and missing networks: The return of refugees from Kenya to Somalia. *Espace, Populations, Sociétés* 2017(1). doi:10.4000/eps.7098

Majidi N (2017b) Deportees lost at home: Post-deportation outcomes in Afghanistan. In: Khosravi S (ed) *After Deportation: Ethnographic perspectives*, Global Ethics Series. Basingstoke: Palgrave Macmillan.

Malkki L (1995) Refugees and exile: From refugee studies to the national order of things. *Annual Review of Anthropology* 24: 495–523.

Mathieu L (2006) *La double peine: Histoire dune lutte inachevée*. Paris: la Dispute.

Menz G (2011) Neo-liberalism, privatization and the outsourcing of migration management: A five-country comparison. *Competition and Change* 15(2): 116–135.

Noll G (1997) The non-admission and return of protection seekers in Germany. *International Journal of Refugee Law* 9(3): 415–452.

Noll G (1999) Rejected asylum seekers: The problem of return. *International Migration* 37(1): 267–288.

Nyers P (2003) Abject cosmopolitanism: The politics of protection in the anti-deportation movement. *Third World Quarterly* 24(6): 1069–1093.

Paoletti E (2010) *Deportation, Non-Deportability and Ideas of Membership*. Refugee Studies Centre Working Paper Series No. 65. Oxford: Refugee Studies Centre.

Peutz N (2006) Embarking on an anthropology of removal. *Current Anthropology* 47(2): 217–241.

Peutz N (2010) "Criminal Alien" deportees in Somaliland: An ethnography of removal. In: Peutz N, De Genova N (eds) *The Deportation Regime: Sovereignty, Space and the Freedom Of Movement*. Durham and London: Duke University Press.

Phuong C (2005) The removal of failed asylum seekers. *Legal Studies* 25(1): 117–141.

Rosenberger S, Winkler J (2014) Com/passionate protests – fighting the deportation of asylum seekers. *Mobilization: An International Journal* 19(2): 489–509.

Ruben R, Van Houte M, and Davids T (2009) What determines the embeddedness of forced-return migrants? Rethinking the role of pre-and post-return assistance. *International Migration Review* 43(4): 908–937.

Schuster L (2005) A sledgehammer to crack a nut: Deportation, detention and dispersal in Europe. *Social Policy and Administration* 39(6): 606–621.

Schuster L, Majidi N (2015) Deportation stigma and re-migration. *Journal of Ethnic and Migration Studies* 41(1): 635–652.

Schuster L, Majidi M (2013) What happens post-deportation? The experience of deported Afghans. *Migration Studies* 1(2): 221–240.

Tunaboylu S, Alpes J (2017) The EU-Turkey deal: What happens to people who return to Turkey? *Forced Migration Review* 54: 84–87.

Turton D, Marsden P (2002) *Taking Refugees for a Ride: The Politics of Refugee Return to Afghanistan*. Issue Paper Series. Kabul: Afghanistan Research and Evaluation Unit.

Tyler P (2017) *Discourse, Agency and Relationships Between the Deporting State, Deportees and Their UK Contacts*. Unpublished thesis. Sheffield: University of Sheffield.

UNAMA (2017) *Afghanistan Protection of Civilians in Armed Conflict: Annual Report 2016* Kabul: United Nations Assistance Mission in Afghanistan.

Walters W (2002) Deportation, expulsion and the international police of Aliens. In: De Genova N, Peutz N (eds) *The Deportation Regime: Sovereignty, Space and the Freedom of Movement*. Durham, NC: Duke University Press, 69–100.

Walters W (2016) Flight of the deported: Aircraft, deportation and politics. *Geopolitics* 21(2): 435–458.

Chapter 7

Displacement and the pursuit of urban protection

Forced migration, fluidity and global cities

Loren B. Landau

Introduction

This is an urban age. The post-industrial cities of Europe and North America have shaped the foundations of urban theory, but the urban future will be forged in the rapidly growing and consistently churning cities of the 'global south' (see UNDESA, 2014). Even if the contemporary global cities literature is slowly shifting its attention away from the imperial metropolises – London, Paris, Tokyo, New York – to their nouveau riche cousins – Dubai, Shanghai, Jakarta – the world's newest global cities are elsewhere (see Segbers, 2007). Lagos, Johannesburg and Chennai are already becoming well known, but those concerned with alternative global urbanism best turn their gaze to cities like Peshawar, Dadaab and Gaziantep. In places like Kabul and Khartoum, Beirut and Amman, refugees and the internally displaced significantly contribute to cities' rapid population growth (Beal and Esser, 2005: 6; Sanyal, 2014). Even where the displaced are proportionately less, their presence can rapidly reconfigure social and economic life. Elsewhere, the displaced move almost invisibly into cities, disappearing among longer-term residents who may share class, language, religious or other commonalities.

People displaced into urban areas due to war, persecution or climatic crisis have claimed an increasingly prominent position in humanitarian operations and scholarship (Zetter and Deikun, 2010). While for many years the United Nations High Commissioner for Refugees (UNHCR) resisted calls to work in urban spaces (often citing expense and an implicit belief in encampment), the organization and its partners have embraced the need for urban-oriented action (See UNHCR, 2009; Women's Refugee Commission, 2011a, 2011b; Zetter and Deikun, 2010; Lyytinen and Kullenberg, 2013). As UNHCR notes, 'only one-third of the world's 10.5 million refugees now live in camps' (www.unhcr.org/pages/4b0e4cba6.html). While any figure will soon be dated and inaccurate, as of January 2018, there were approximately 3.4 million Syrian refugees in Turkey. Of them, just over 10% were being housed in purpose-built camps or settlements. Similar proportions almost certainly hold for countries throughout the region. Across Africa, there is a growing awareness that the majority of refugees and other displaced people – in some places the vast majority of them – live and seek protection in what are often deeply impoverished, unequal and under-capacitated but increasingly global urban centres (see UN-Habitat, 2014).

'Urban refugees' is often used as a generic label referring to legally recognized refugees, asylum seekers, internally displaced persons and others living in 'refugee like' conditions. The urbanization of displacement and humanitarian action within broader global processes is logical given that more than half the world's population is urbanized. Given that the alternatives to urban settlement include decades in camps, administrative detention, or another 'protracted refugee situation', it is hardly surprising that the displaced increasingly find their ways to population centres (see Kamal, 2016). Although the urban displaced may not find golden paved streets, cities nonetheless offer at least the potential for upward economic mobility and physical freedom.

Knowledge about urban refugees has expanded dramatically over the past decade but there are still significant gaps. Part of this is technical and logistical – characterizing social realities in rapidly transforming urban centres is difficult without the added challenge of tracking new arrivals who may prefer to remain invisible (Jacobsen and Furst, 2011). Gaps are also due to researchers' understandings of displacement. We know, for example, that small towns and peri-urban areas are the most rapidly growing in the developing world (UNDESA, 2014) but most studies focus on countries' primary cities. Consequently, little is known about those living outside of the largest urban centres. This chapter replicates this bias in its focus on the presence of displaced people in capital cities across southern and eastern Africa and explores what the presence of displaced people means for understanding displacement and, particularly, durable solutions. There is much work to be done to understand whether these insights travel across specific sites and into small towns or cities.

The structures of global capitalism and urbanization means that displacement to or within Southern cities opens possibilities of desirable durable solutions – desirable for the displaced – premised on shunning solidarity. In an era in which finding economic security increasingly means spreading family and individual risk across multiple spaces (Halliday, 2006), displacement may create new opportunities within existing and emerging translocal relationships and diasporas. Moreover, given the challenges of rebuilding 'sending' communities, access to external resources and remittances may become central to families' sustainable economic security. Under such conditions, the most durable solution may well be the opportunity to continue moving within or across borders; what first appears as the (self) reservation of social marginalization and vulnerability in the form of alienation from family, kin and community represents a quest for freedom (of a certain kind). However, the nature of the South's conflicts and global cities – precarity crossed with potential fluidity and resistance – creates forms of almost perpetual displacement and mobility. In the global cities of the South, displaced people live alongside equally vulnerable 'hosts' – many of who may themselves be recent migrants. A key question, therefore, is how do migrants, IDPs, refugees and even long-term residents capitalize on cities' opportunities while avoiding the pitfalls of economic and physical precarity, and what, potentially, can be done to increase their chances of substantive protection?

Methods and site profiles

This chapter has as its focus displacement in African cities, and more specifically it draws on two research projects spanning almost 15 years. The first was carried out between 2006 and 2009 in Johannesburg (South Africa), Maputo (Mozambique), Nairobi (Kenya) and Lubumbashi (DRC), as part of a multi-sited collaborative research project (see Landau and Duponchel, 2011). The cities were selected due to their proximity to conflict and their importance for people seeking not only protection but also profit and passage. They also present a variety of legal regimes. In Johannesburg refugees and asylum seekers are formally encouraged to locally integrate and receive little direct humanitarian assistance. In Lubumbashi, almost all of the displaced populations are citizens from elsewhere in the country. While they may have legal rights to reside anywhere within the Democratic Republic of Congo, they are often treated with considerable hostility by local authorities the central government no longer recognizes people in Lubumbashi as internally displaced. In Mozambique, refugees are mandated to stay in camps, largely located in the country's northern provinces. Similarly in Kenya, refugees need (and are rarely granted) special permission if they wish to live outside of the country's sprawling refugee cities near Dadaab and Kakuma. With the exception of Mozambicans included in the Johannesburg survey, we selected groups—Somalis, Rwandans, Sudanese and Congolese—that straddle the line between purely economic migrants and those who might be considered – in substance, if not in law – forced migrants or displaced persons.

The second study draws on data from research in Nairobi, Johannesburg and Kampala (see Kihato and Landau, 2017). Each is a trade and political centre which has become a destination and transit point for a broad range of people generally falling under the 'urban refugee' label. While the specific needs of refugees vary among and within the cities, all face the generalized challenges confronting displaced persons, and many others, living in urban centres such as accessing secure housing, income, physical security and social services. In both Kenya and Uganda, the primary focus of humanitarian attention is on purpose-built camps and settlements. However, there is a growing awareness of urban refugees. In Nairobi these include refugees and asylum seekers from Africa's Great Lakes Region as well as from conflict and persecution across the Horn: the Sudans, Ethiopia, Eritrea, Uganda and Somalia. As the government of Kenya has repeatedly threatened to close Dadaab refugee camps, the urban 'case load' will only grow. Nairobi also hosts people internally displaced by ethnic conflicts, particularly those stemming from the 2007–2008 post-election violence. Kampala's urban refugee population is less well recognized although some have recently celebrated Uganda for its urban refugee programme (see Kigozi, 2017). It also includes people from across the Great Lakes Region and Horn of Africa as well as considerable numbers of people displaced by long-standing conflict in Northern Uganda. South Africa is somewhat exceptional in maintaining no purpose-built refugee camps, instead relying exclusively on a protection programme premised on temporary, local integration. New policy proposals may limit employment rights and free movement (Government of South Africa, 2017). For many years the world's leader in individual asylum claims, South Africa hosts asylum seekers and refugees from across Africa and from parts of South and Southeast Asia and central Europe.

The situation of urban refugees in Africa's cities is important to consider because estimates point to significant populations of displaced people in cities. In Kampala, the UNHCR conducted an urban refugee registration exercise and indicated that as of December 2014, there were 72,019 refugees in the city, contributing to the 1.72 million people living in the city (in 2012 according to the Ugandan Bureau of Statistics). No data were available on the number of internally displaced people (IDPs). In Kenya, a 2015 UNHCR report puts the number of registered refugees and asylum seekers in the country at 584,989. Of these, 51,757 were estimated to live in Nairobi, making up a significant portion of the city's 3.36 million residents (Central Intelligence Agency, 2015). Again, no data were available on the number of IDPs.[1] The UNHCR indicates that in December 2014, South Africa hosted 576,133 persons of concern including 112,192 refugees and 463,940 asylum seekers although there is no information on spatial distributions that could indicate how many live in the city. However, the 2011 census indicates that 12.7% (562,952) of the city's population (4,434,827) were born outside South Africa though their legal status is unknown it is likely that this constitutes a sizeable proportion of forced migrants. In addition there are sizeable, though unquantifiable, numbers of undocumented migrants living in cities where the most effective forms of protection are legal and social 'invisibility', even in situations where they might be eligible legal protection because of the risks associated with visibility (see Kihato, 2013).

The remainder of this chapter draws particular attention to the precarious nature of African urban life and how stability and fixity can work against displaced persons' ability to accumulate the social and material capital necessary to thrive or survive. The second part draws on survey data to explore the lives of displaced people in cities in Africa and shows the centrality of gender and social networks in making sense of the diversity of experiences. Thirdly it explores durable solutions and policy considerations. Lastly the chapter considers some ethical and epistemological concerns. Apart from problematizing teleologies of solidarity embedded in international refugee law, it speaks to how knowledge is constructed within 'refugee studies' and how that can exclude any real engagement with and understanding of the global south with all its diversity.

Urban lives: opportunities, obligations and uncertainty?

The challenges facing urban refugees have been documented in previous scholarly and applied research (See Sanyal, 2014; Simpson, 2013; Women's Refugee

Commission, 2011a, 2011b, 2011c; Campbell, 2006). These include economic and social marginalization, harassment from neighbours and the police, and challenges in accessing basic services and housing markets. Women are often singled out for facing high levels of gender-based violence. Yet in many ways, these are challenges facing millions of urban residents, regardless of their displacement histories. Indeed, the precarity of Southern city life is a familiar narrative underlying much academic and policy work. Many of these accounts note the tremendous growth rates (UNDESA, 2014; UN-Habitat, 2014) and that as cities swell, new arrivals (and long-term residents) find few new jobs. They also note that rather than embracing a swollen population, urban governance systems ostensibly designed to support the needy are instead captured by economic and political elites or crumbling from lack of resources and technical capacity. With a forthcoming 'youth bulge', cities are likely to swell further with little concomitant growth in formal economic opportunities (UN-Habitat, 2014). Apart from those profiting from the poor, the elite – political and economic – are largely disengaged from the cities' majority, often physically separating themselves in gated communities or new cities (Kermeliotis, 2013).

Yet for all of their evident shortcomings and risks, Africa's globalizing cities and their counterparts elsewhere nonetheless allure with their often elusive potential for profit, protection or passage elsewhere. Ideal by almost no imaginable metric, these sites nonetheless offer relative access to varied opportunities and possibilities, and urbanization is correlated with increased human development indices, a better quality of life and access to services and the possibility to earn (UNDESA, 2014). Even slum dwellers often live longer and healthier lives than those living beyond the city.

For present purposes, the question is what people – migrants, IDPs, refugees and even long-term residents – do to capitalize on cities' opportunities while avoiding the pitfalls of economic and physical precarity. With few possibilities for return to communities of origin or organized resettlement to a wealthy western country, *de facto* durable solutions for millions of displaced persons will be forged in these urban sites. In the absence of elaborate states or humanitarian interventions, these solutions, whatever their form, will be designed and realized by urban residents working alone, together, or with connections living beyond the urban edge. Simone (2006: 358) suggests, 'Cities everywhere exert pulls on each other in a force field in which the maintenance of localized coherence becomes increasingly problematic.' Part of this desire for constant restructuring and ongoing motion is rooted in the need to maintain an ever expanding or diversifying set of 'weak ties' (Granovetter, 1973). This may be accomplished from a fixed point or it may demand movement within cities or between them.

Reciprocal obligations along with the economic precarity of the post-industrial (or perhaps more accurately, the neo-liberal, non-industrial) era further encourage an impulse to decouple from local and distant social relations and the corollary connections to space. Take, for example, Worby's (2010) account of Zimbabwean refugees/migrants living in Johannesburg, Africa's best pretender to global city status. For him the desire for disconnection is rooted less in the nature of the city, *per se*, even though he recognizes the risks from police, employers and others. Rather, the need for consistent connection and reconnection stems from the elaborate and occasionally oppressive social networks extending among vulnerable populations migrant and otherwise. These take the form of demands from family and sending communities to send money, food, durable goods and clothing to their places of origin (see also Dzingirai, Mutopo and Landau, 2014; Kihato, 2013; Madsen, 2004). Perhaps more immediately, these demands may also manifest in requests to physically host and support relatives and friends – a flexible, often expansive category of people – in continual succession or even simultaneously. The result being a kind of dependency pyramid in which a refugee pioneer ends up hosting close relatives followed by ever more distant connections, often under cramped conditions: self-built houses, storage rooms, sub-let and sub-divided apartments, or even occupied offices.

Rather than offering comfort or social security, such relationships introduce not only material obligations and inconvenience but an additional source of uncertainty (Worby, 2010). For people living in the fluid, economically marginal neighbourhoods of Southern cities, denying others support when even marginally more resource endowed is almost unimaginable. For migrants, betraying expectations not only means exiting from potential reciprocal support at some indeterminate date, but may elicit explicit countermeasures ranging from reputational costs to curses, theft, or physical threats. In these cases, the strong social networks and sets of overlapping reciprocal obligations – social formations scholars and practitioners often celebrate for providing protection and resilience (see Madhavan and Landau, 2011; Deshingkar and Farrington, 2009, Aguilera and Massey, 2003; Kanaiapuni et al., 2005) – become burdensome and counterproductive (see also Landau et al., 2017). The failure to maintain them during periods of crisis can lead to what Kankonde (2010) terms, 'social death': one's indefinite social exclusion and stigmatization.

Confronted with the likely failure to meet social obligations or the sometimes onerous costs of doing so – not only short-term material costs, but comfort and capital accumulation possibilities – refugees hoping to make their lives in fluid, global cities often seek forms of social invisibility. For many, desiring disconnection and invisibility stems from the seemingly shameful activities one undertakes to make it in a new place (see Kankonde, 2010; Kihato, 2013; Malauene, 2004; for example). For those involved in sex work or other criminalized behaviours, the source of stigma is perhaps obvious even if many are proud for being able to support their families (Oliveira and Vearey, 2015). For others it may simply be the downgrading of skills – from accountant to taxi driver; from teacher to day labourer – they wish to shield from view. While many migrants send home glittering images of urban success which is critical to meeting family expectations and bolstering social status, stability and solidarity within a churning city brings with it observational disciplines and networks that risk revealing less laudable truths and spreading rumours.

Even if desires for disconnection are not universal, they nonetheless capture an important aspect of contemporary life in global cities of the South. Economic precarity, predatory policy and states and reciprocal obligations are giving rise to a desire for fluidity and ethics of disconnection that furthers what is perhaps a generic condition of city life. As Tonkiss notes,

> While a language of community has been important for articulating various politics of difference, I suggest that forms of *indifference* also afford certain rights to and freedoms in the city.
>
> (2003: 298)

Thus life in the city offers a constellation of reciprocity, translocal and transnational connections and obligations, economic opportunities alongside precarity and ontological insecurity.

Urban refugees: vulnerability and protection?

Quantitative analysis of refugees' lives in Nairobi, Johannesburg, Lubumbashi and Maputo set out to answer two primary questions. First, is there a set of characteristics distinctly associated with refugees? Second, recognizing that refugees – like all other population groups – are highly diverse, what accounts for higher levels of vulnerability and, conversely, the relative protection some are able to achieve? These questions stem from a challenge to the general presumptions of refugee vulnerability and a curiosity into if refugees were in fact categorically different from the often highly mobile and impoverished hosts that surround them. To these ends, we measured 'protection' in terms of access to housing, income and physical security. There are, of course, considerable variations across the cities discussed here. The experience of refugees is highly spatialized – not only by city, but by neighbourhood or even by block (Misago et al., 2010).

At first glance, the data in our research confirms what many refugee specialists presume and form their policies around: that displaced people face considerable disadvantages in urban settings. There are variations in experiences and one of the main intersections is gender. Women are considerably less likely to earn any income and where they do, they experience lower pay than their male counterparts. Women face a 12% lower probability of having a job and an 11% lower chance of earning more than about US$50 per week than men. What seems to matter most for both men and women is geographic background; having lived previously in an urban setting significantly increases earnings. Given that many people displaced into urban areas are from other cities, they often have a distinct advantage in terms of income generation over other migrants who may be newly urbanized. Indeed, across the four cities, foreigners were 10% more likely to earn a decent income than 'locals'. By contrast, they are less likely to be formally employed all things being equal. Rather, they tend to start small business or work in the informal sector.

There is also a gender difference in terms of accessing credit which would impact on the capacity to set up small businesses; men are better able to access this resource. The time since arrival positively and significantly increases financial security and so does the presence of relatives or friends in the city upon arrival. Both of these variables are likely to proxy the size of the migrant's network in the city where a larger network translates into a greater number of potential lenders. Thus having friends or relatives in the city on arrival provides a critical boost and while, as noted earlier this can drain the resources of those already in the city, for new arrivals these existing social networks are central to their experiences.

Having networks, especially on arrival to a city, also links to food security Refugee vulnerability to food insecurity ultimately appears to have as much to do with being new arrivals in the city as it does with being a refugee. Having people close by who you know – regardless of whether you are a refugee or just new to the city – who can provide you information even in the absence of direct material support is one of the best predictors of improved food security. If you move to a city with family and friends nearby, you are far more likely to do better in the initial phases than those coming alone. That said, over the long term, close family and acquaintances can be a burden on individual economic success, as noted above.

Having documents helps gain access to formal employment – an economic status which is almost exclusively available to the highly educated. However, education is not a commodity with much value in the highly informal economies where those without documents or formal legal status find work. Instead practical experience and hustle along with people's personal characteristics matter more than education. The informal economy is associated with low pay and a lack access to employment rights. Where remittances are an obligation this can put huge amounts of pressure on displaced people.

When it comes to physical security men appear to fare much worse than women. For instance, women are 9% less likely to be attacked *outside* their homes than men regardless of nationality and 21% less likely to be arrested by the police. (The survey excluded the forms of domestic violence which are almost uniquely aimed at women.) Unsurprisingly given its reputation, Johannesburg is the most dangerous place to live in. Indeed, the probability of being attacked is 24% lower in Maputo, 34% lower in Nairobi and 38% lower in Lubumbashi. In this regard, refugees are distinctly more vulnerable than domestic migrants: they are arrested more often and trust the police less all things being equal. Along with being the most dangerous, Johannesburg is also the place with the most hyperactive police and restrictive immigration controls (see Vigneswaran, 2014). As such, the probability of being arrested by the police is 25% lower in Nairobi and 38% lower in Lubumbashi than in Johannesburg. It is also important that even where foreigners do not face a higher chance of being attacked, they confront a significantly greater possibility of being arrested by the police. When it comes to crime or arrest, having documentation helps, but nationality matters more. Where nationalities are phenotypically 'foreign' (e.g., Somalis in South Africa;

Ethiopians in Mozambique), they are particularly likely to be targeted by police and citizens regardless of their legal status.

Interestingly, people claiming to have moved for economic reasons are statistically almost indistinguishable from those having fled war or persecution. This is at least partially explained by the costs of mobility and the archipelago of 'safe spaces' across the continent. The poor and highly vulnerable are, after all, less equipped to travel long distances or cover the costs associated with moving to cities. Instead, they typically move shorter distances and settle or find camp-based protection. Without denying the vulnerability of many refugees coming to cities, they are often less vulnerable than domestic migrants and far less vulnerable than those who remain closer to conflicts. There are some key points that are crucial when thinking about urban refuges.

First, the legal status as a refugee or asylum seeker is not a key determinant of welfare. It does, however, provide improved access to the labour market and, using the desire to stay put as an indicator, a gateway to a durable solution (i.e., local integration). Secondly, it makes little sense to presume that the conditions under which people left 'home' determine the levels of protection. Ignoring legal mandates, this suggests there may be little empirical or practical grounds for policy distinctions between those forced out by violence and those who have moved purely for economic or material circumstances. Thirdly there are clear gender differences in relation to economic resources, work and access to protection. Men are more likely to be the victims of physical attack, robbery and arrest. Women may generally be safer in public spaces due to the nature of their work, police profiling or other factors. However, they face greater challenges in accessing work, housing and services. Fourthly, people coming from rural settings are far more vulnerable in cities than people from urban backgrounds regardless of whether they have crossed an international border. In many instances, refugees from conflict-affected cities are better equipped to manage urban resettlement than domestic migrants driven by economic rationales.

The most significant factor in explaining urban 'success' (i.e., accessing food, jobs, housing and physical security) are social networks. In all cases, those who were joining friends or relatives already in a city were considerably more successful than those who migrated without such support. In most cases, urban 'anchors' were able to provide information and guidance before departure and, in some instances, accommodation or material support on arrival. Although additional work is needed to understand the full role these networks play, this point suggests that social networks and group membership, not legal status or welfarist interventions, are the lynchpin of protection and this raises questions about durable solutions for urban refugees.

Durable solutions and engaging cities of the South

In global cities where rooting is either undesirable or effectively impossible, Southern city residents – including the displaced – often see them as sites in which to gather the resources needed to further onward movement or build status and security beyond the city's boundaries (Geschiere, 2009). Doing so often means directly countering community and the forms of place-based solidarity – organic or mechanical – evoked by talk of 'durable solutions'. Proximate and translocal rooting may be important, but so too are regular shifts between rural (or peri-urban) and urban areas, within urban areas, or between cities. As such, migrants – including refugees and other displaced persons are turning parts of into stations, rather than destinations, as part of ongoing journeys. This helps generate a kind of permanent temporariness in which agency is visible by actively resisting incorporation (Kihato, 2013; Landau, 2014; Malauene, 2004). For many, urban sites are 'places of flows' (Castells, 1996) or 'nowherevilles' (Bauman, 2000) where rooting and local representation is not the goal and the burdens of connections and political participation are often something to be avoided (Kankonde, 2010; Madsen, 2004). Given the insecurity of land tenure, the possibility of violence, and ongoing economic deprivation, a durable solution means actively maintaining feet in multiple sites without firmly rooting themselves in any (Freemantle, 2010).

In such environments, formal citizenship and stability may have value for some, but with only limited enforcement capacity and a minimal reliance on state provided services – schools, clinics, jobs – it is safe to say that documentation and legal status often do little. At the most practical level they are poor predictors of people's welfare (Landau and Duponchel, 2011). Even in South Africa, arguably the continent's 'strongest' state, these processes are negotiated on the ground through a panoply of rationalities and calculations, sometimes involving laws and state actors but not always in predictable ways (Hansen and Stepputat, 2010). In such environments, finding space and resources within a city involves an ongoing process of forming and abandoning horizontal and vertical connections and constant, often constrained, calculations.

The forms of belonging and solidarity that matter for people increasingly are themselves fluid, syncretic and translocal. Even churches – often seen as instruments of local integration, community formation or stable transnational mobilization (see Cadge and Ecklund, 2007) – are now sites for 'tactical cosmopolitanism' and other forms of fluidity and liminality (see Landau and Freemantle, 2010; Garbin, 2012; Schiller, Caglar and Guldbrandsen, 2006). Within them and similar bodies, people find ways of maintaining the levels of social engagement and recognition necessary to negotiate everyday life, but without the kind of place-based fixity often associated with durable solutions. The forms of solidarity forged through these bodies are often inherently transient, translocal and even post-terrestrial. Not only do people frequently shift liturgical allegiances, but the churches themselves foster a kind of disconnection from those beyond the ever more fragmented congregations.

What does this mean for promoting refugee protection in Africa's cities or, more broadly, in the poorly legalized, often economically precarious cities of the South? A rethinking of the humanitarian enterprise as the policy changes most likely to result in improved protection for displaced people in urban areas may have little to do with migration, immigration or asylum *per se*. People moving into cities due to war or persecution are, by definition, 'displaced', but this status does not define them. Rather, they are also parents, traders, students, clients, service providers, consumers and potential investors. As such, their lives and economic impacts are shaped by policies and practices that intersect with but are not framed by protection or migration concerns.

Although there is no best approach or standard for engaging local authorities, humanitarians can benefit from using a systematic approach to assess and understand municipalities. Within a single country, municipalities are distinguished by the nature of their institutions, political priorities, resource bases, population and geography. Working across a region or on multiple continents further highlights the need to understand the varied institutions, interests and abilities likely to shape responses to people of concern. Providing incentives in the form of resources, prestige or opportunities for professional advancement are likely to be central to achieving any objectives. However, the specific language of one's approach or appeals needs to be tailored: what works well to mobilize sympathy and support in one setting may prove ineffective or potentially harmful in another. Similarly, appeals to principles – rights, inclusivity, justice, efficiency, obligations – will generate divergent results amongst planners and politicians steeped in different traditions, priorities and institutional or political incentives (see Donnely, 2003; Elias, 2008).

Humanitarians working in urban settings characterized by generalized poverty and fluidity must begin their work from the position that refugees are almost universally a low political priority for local authorities. While displaced people continue to be used as political tools across a range of settings, their protection is rarely at the forefront of local political agendas. This may seem obvious, but it nonetheless bears emphasis to temper humanitarians' expectations and approach. This is especially important in instances of widespread scarcity – a condition that describes the majority of refugee-hosting municipalities across the world – where simply highlighting humanitarian needs is unlikely to elicit a strong response. Ironically, the more democratic and participatory local governments become, the less likely they may be to dedicate scarce resources to persons of concern. Unless there is a strong local constituency concerned with refugees' rights and welfare, politicians will do as little as possible to promote refugee rights especially when they need to win popular support. Where local populations are hostile to refugees and displaced people – as they are in Nairobi and Johannesburg – local authorities may win points through policies that explicitly exclude or deny them access to rights and access to services (see Kihato and Landau, 2017; Hopkins, 2010). Under such circumstances, overt or public demands for refugee rights to services and opportunities may only provide fodder for populist politicians.

Local institutional literacy

The first principle of effective engagement is to develop a high degree of 'local institutional literacy'. Building on the recognition of refugees' limited political caché means moving beyond appeals to blunt principles or international protocols. Rather it requires deep engagement in the kind of local politics that often unsettles 'neutral' accountable humanitarian actors. Such anxieties are in part due to the need to stray from humanitarians' legalistic and technocratic expertise. Indeed, engaging effectively requires strong understandings of varied institutional configurations, the language of urban development, and the politics surrounding diversity, poverty reduction and immigration. Recognizing that 'human/refugee rights' and 'protection' are only powerful terms for mobilizing authorities and populations under particular circumstances; humanitarians must develop nuanced understandings of the political language, institutional capacities, and interests informing local government policy and practice. Moreover, there is a need to recognize that protection occurs when humanitarian and political/institutional interests align.

In illustrating local literacy's value, we can take differences in political priorities between Johannesburg and Nairobi. For South African municipalities, authorities typically measure success by their performance in countering economic and social exclusion. While authorities may not universally consider refugees among the marginalized groups deserving assistance, advocates have found ways of using the language of inclusion to help refugees be inserted into policy. Rather than making appeals to their rights as refugees, municipal authorities have responded to arguments about persons of concerns' general economic and physical vulnerability. The substance of the appeals may differ little, but the rhetorical shift matters greatly.

Counter this with Nairobi. In the Kenyan capital – and to some degree in Kampala – officials have little direct responsibility and express little moral commitment to providing the kind of inclusive, transformative services available to some Johannesburg residents. As such, demands for inclusion or access to state services are unlikely to garner support or an effective response. This is so even where residents may be legally entitled to such services. Where refugees are a low political priority and states provide little to their own citizens, few gains will come from demonstrating that persons of concern have unmet protection needs. Similarly, remonstrating officials for falling short of their legal obligations to persons of concern will accomplish little where officials and citizens expect little in this regard. Rather, Kenyan officials see their role as fostering opportunities for business formation and self-reliance. Under such conditions, appeals to improve conditions for entrepreneurialism (i.e., improved physical security, licencing and market access) may be the most effective way to expand the protection space. This need not mean abandoning quests for improved health care, housing or other services, but rather it means bringing one's strategies in line with Kenya's market-based ethos.

Smaller, smarter, stealthier

The illustrations above lead us to a series of ancillary principles humanitarians should consider in developing strategies for municipal engagements. Most critical here is that *de facto protection will be negotiated outside refugee law*. Even where refugee law explicitly entitles refugees to a range of services – under South Africa's Refugees Act (1998) they are entitled to public health care, work opportunities and potentially public housing – claiming those rights may well require incentivizing local authorities or modifying sectoral regulations and practices. In Johannesburg, refugees may already be formally eligible for varied forms of subsidized housing but are excluded due to rationing or ignorance on the part of officials and advocates. By providing limited support to the city's department of housing or even to specific housing schemes, it may prove possible to negotiate access to secure accommodation. In Nairobi, the assessment tool identified a pool of resources dedicated to disaster management while there were no funds set aside for assistance. Under such circumstances, working with officials responsible for disaster management can unlock funding for refugee-related initiatives that would otherwise remain untouched. The more decentralized the institutional configurations, the greater the need to engage across a range of levels and sector.

Where rights to services and/or markets are not clearly delimited in refugee legislation, authorities may be similarly persuaded to create environments in which persons of concern are empowered as citizens and long-term residents to access opportunities. This can be done through small-scale engagement to amend by-laws, trade licences and other regulations. Indeed, the most rapid change in protection outcomes can be achieved through highly localized, sectorally specific advocacy. In politically hostile or contentious environments, a stealthy approach may be the way to go. Although working against the grain of those striving for legal recognition and protection, positive change in local regulations or by-laws can be achieved without making explicit reference to the inclusion of refugees or others of concern. Removing provisions that provide free access to public services only to host populations (as is the case with Nairobi's public 'Iko' toilets) at least formally enables refugees access. More significantly, rights to services flow from being urban residents, not refugees.

In all three cases, the most effective forms of protection are also those relying on legal and social 'invisibility'. Secondary research in Johannesburg, for example, highlights the degree to which some people eligible for legal protection may instead prefer invisibility as noted earlier (see Kihato, 2013). Understanding how persons of concern integrate into markets and services may ultimately lead humanitarians to pragmatically adopt strategies of 'benign neglect': allowing people to negotiate their own ways of accessing urban services and economic opportunities. This falls short of guaranteeing universal access, but it may be quicker, cheaper and more politically and economically sustainable than making such universal demands. This may be done while working to open legal spaces for protection for those needing such avenues, but organizations must not presume that legal status is a gateway to other substantive needs (see Landau and Duponchel, 2011).

Direct service provision in urban areas is expensive and typically unsustainable. However, unlike camps or other purpose-built settlements, municipalities often come equipped with existing networks of service providers, security mechanisms, and markets. These may be imperfect, even for long-term residents, but are likely to be more cost effective for humanitarian organizations to reform, expand or supplement than building parallel systems. RefugePoint's clever actions in Nairobi illustrates how this may work: rather than paying for health services or supporting refugee health clinics, RefugePoint worked to incorporate legally recognized refugees in the National Health Insurance Fund (NHIF). Instead of making this a national issue which may have resulted in a parliamentary backlash resulting in refugees' ineligibility for coverage – the organization worked with a mid-level bureaucrat to quietly enrol refugees into the system. By completing the paper work themselves, they secured care for hundreds of people at almost no cost, with little publicity, and with no political backlash. In aligning their incentives (health care for refugees) with the bureaucrat's (achieving performance targets), they achieved a double win. Without a sophisticated understanding of local policies and a sound reading of performance incentives, such success would have likely remained elusive.

Support for existing mechanisms can also win popular political favour for populations that would otherwise be stigmatized or scapegoated. This can come by providing additional resources to health providers to expand services; vouchers or supplements to housing programmes already established for the poor; or technical assistance to city planners so that their initiatives better serve long-term residents and persons of concern. Such technocratic engagements also open multiple spaces for engagement. Rather than relying on rights to 'trickle down' from national policy pronouncements – although this may be required in highly centralized systems like Kampala – a sectorally specific approach opens multiple spaces for engagement. Engaging with municipal or sub-municipal bureaucrats may do little to change national policy, but appeals to professional values can often do more and do it more quickly than high level policy reform. Wherever possible, humanitarians should build on the possibilities for 'bureaucratic incorporation'.

This does not mean abandoning humanitarians' traditional focus on documentation, legal status or reform to refugee and immigration laws. Such campaigns remain important symbolically even if – as discussed above – documentation and formal rights translate into practical protection far less directly than advocates often presume (Landau and Duponchel, 2011). Instead the approach presented here suggests that in engaging with local authorities, humanitarians look for opportunities to build local solidarity with citizens and officials by appealing to interest beyond immediate humanitarian needs. Doing this requires a perspective recognizing the decentralization and privatization of political authority (Soysal, 1995). Marrow's (2009: 758) work on bureaucratic incorporation of immigrants into the United States can provide one route. She speaks about how 'bureaucrats' responses to immigrants' interests precede those of elected officials and are driven by strong professional norms'. Elsewhere appealing to more generalized interests, around housing, crime or other concerns (i.e., not rights), can help appeal to local political incentives in ways that do not draw lines or make references to discourses which are seen as foreign, threatening or unwelcome. In all cases, the language must resonate locally, the interventions must be locally legitimate and the approach must be gradual and cautious.

Conclusions: practical, ethical and epistemological reflections

For all of their evident shortcomings and risks, Africa's globalizing cities and their counterparts elsewhere nonetheless allure with their often elusive potential for profit, protection or passage elsewhere. While far from ideal, these sites nonetheless offer relative access to varied opportunities and possibilities, and urbanization is correlated with increased human development indices, a better quality of life and access to services and the possibility to earn (UNDESA, 2014). The potential for investment and work in rapidly expanding urban markets offer comparative advantage in terms of trade and economies of scale when compared to Africa's relatively sparsely populated rural hinterlands. Consequently, understanding the meaning of solutions forged within urban spaces demands moving beyond immediate efforts to improve service delivery and protection. We must instead delve more deeply – empirically and philosophically – into the nature of contemporary urban life. Doing so reveals extraordinarily high levels of economic and physical precarity associated with living in Africa's urban centres and residents' tactical and strategic responses to these conditions. While, for the most part, such risks face all poor urban residents, they can be potentially exacerbated by a history of displacement.

In engaging with such spaces, humanitarians may need to all but abandon the language of rights and protection embedded in humanitarian law and guiding principles. Such instruments may continue to inform and guide humanitarians' work, but through locally appropriate language informed by a close reading of politics, interests and opportunities. This will not be easy for agencies and individuals steeped in the humanitarian *status quo*. As Fassin (2011) notes in discussing reforms to the humanitarian systems, there are great institutional and personal interests invested in preserving both the universal language and mechanisms long used in mobilizing for rights. People have almost religious faith in past approaches and principles and may be deeply unsettled by needing to think in new, more pragmatic shades of grey. Organizations built around a rights discourse may fear for their relevance and funding. Indeed, the kind of political approach called for here may be used against organizations like the UNHCR or its partners who are expected to remain politically neutral. But there is a place for all these strategies; the diversity of spaces in which we push for social justice demands as many strategies and appeals.

Apart from fundamental questions of policy intervention, the trends outlined above raise epistemological questions for scholars seeking to understand displaced persons' agency under constrained circumstances. Arguing that striving for ongoing flux and mobility is part of a durable solution and a demonstration of agency raises significant methodological challenges to the observer. It is, after all, difficult to know if someone is in constant movement because they are unable to settle or because they have read the environment in which they operate and are actively choosing to remain unrooted and potentially in motion. However, churning is part of what contemporary urban life requires and that suggests a degree of vulnerability and structural constraints that all residents – particularly those who are relatively poor – experience. But this is no more apparent than for than those who remain trapped in place, limiting their ability to capitalize on the potential benefits of migration which, after all, may include basic physical security, basic needs, and the possibilities for more (cf. Lubkemann, 2008). In a world in which economic precarity can be thrust on individuals by local policies, global structures, and even one's family and kin, the desire to move and the ability to do so is of enormous tactical importance. In this regard we must take the lead from critiques of the human trafficking and sex work literature which ask us to problematize questions of victimization. Yet, as Sen (1997) and others note, choice under highly constrained situations is itself a problematic concept, and people's desires are often shaped as much by perceived possibilities and objective or consistent moral principles and commitments.

Finally, there is much to gain from embedding our approaches to displacement within a broader scholarship on the places and processes in which refugees participate. In this case, urban studies and the study of African urbanism helps to reframe the meaning of durability and its potential desirability in the ways it has typically been understood. It also helps us recode actions that may in part appear to represent signs of constraint to ones of empowerment or, more mildly, agency. There are further gains from following the Comaroffs' (2012) suggestion to begin more substantially theorizing from the South. We tend to look towards the South as a source of data to flesh out models formed in the backyards of the more powerful knowledge producers. A number of urbanists have begun this process (see Parnell and Robinson, 2012; Watson, 2009; Mbembe and Nuttall, 2004), and there is much to learn from them. However, given that the humanitarian enterprise and the headquarters of most global humanitarian agencies are rooted primarily in 'the North' and operate through knowledge forged there (see Fassin, 2011; Chimini, 2009; Malkki, 1995, 1996), it is often difficult for 'refugee studies' to shift fundamental frames. Indeed, if we take seriously the question of agency, we must then also take seriously the question of how we theorize about the agency of refugees. Beginning from a position that 'solutions' are compatible with state objectives and looking at how refugees and displaced people might ultimately be accommodated within them, still grants an unnecessarily privileged position to global and national regulatory frameworks. If instead we start from the perspective of what is required – or what is perceived to be so – among refugees, our understanding of 'solutions' – durable or otherwise – begin to look substantially different. As scholars we must not allow our desire for relevance and policy influence to foreclose the possibilities and critiques emerging from authors generating insights from a wide range of geographic and intellectual sites and traditions.

Note

1 Interview with Humanitarian Reporting Officer, OCHA, by C.W. Kihato (February 2015, Nairobi).

Bibliography

Aguilera MB, Massey D (2003) Social capital and the wages of Mexican migrants: New hypotheses and tests. *Social Forces* 82(2): 671–701.
Bauman Z (2000) *Globalization: The Human Consequences*. New York: Columbia University Press.
Beal J, Esser D (2005) *Shaping Urban Futures: Challenges to Governing and Managing Afghan Cities*. Kabul: Afghanistan Research and Evaluation Unit.
Cadge W, Ecklund EH (2007) Immigration and religion. *Annual Review of Sociology* 33: 359–379.
Campbell HE (2006) Urban refugees in Nairobi: Problems of protection, mechanisms of survival, and possibilities for integration. *Journal of Refugee Studies* 19(3): 396–413.
Castells M (1996) The space of flows. In: Susser I (ed) *The Castells Reader on Cities and Social Theory*. Oxford: Wiley Blackwell, 314–365.
Central Intelligence Agency (2015) *The World Factbook*. Washington, DC: Central Intelligence Agency. Available at: www.cia.gov/library/publications/the-world-factbook/geos/ke.html [Accessed 1.2015].
Chimini BS (2009) The birth of a 'discipline': From refugee to forced migration studies. *Journal of Refugee Studies* 22(1): 11–29.
Comaroff J, Comaroff J (2012) *Theory from the South, or, How Euro-America Is Evolving Toward Africa*. New York: Paradigm.
Deshingkar P, Farrington F (eds) (2009) *Circular Migration and Multilocational Livelihood Strategies in Rural India*. Oxford: Oxford University Press.
Donnely J (2003) *Universal Human Rights: In Theory & Practice*. Ithaca: Cornell University Press, 2nd Edition.
Dzingirai V, Mutopo P, and Landau LB (2014) *Confirmations, Coffins and Corn: Kinship, Social Networks and Remittances from South Africa to Zimbabwe*. Migrating out of Poverty Research Consortium Working Paper 18, Sussex: University of Sussex.
Elias J (2008) Struggles over the rights of foreign domestic workers in Malaysia: The possibility and limitations of "Rights Talk". *Economy and Society* 37(2): 282–303.
Fassin D (2011) *Humanitarian Reason: A Moral History of the Present*. Berkeley: University of California Press.
Freemantle I (2010) *You Can Only Claim Your Yard and Not a Country: Exploring Contexts, Discourse and Practices of Quotidian Cosmopolitanism Amongst African Migrants in Johannesburg*. Unpublished doctoral thesis. Johannesburg: University of Witwatersrand.
Garbin D (2012) Marching for god in the global city: Public space, religion and diasporic identities in a transnational african church. *Culture and Religion* 13(4): 425–447.
Geschiere P (2009) *The Perils of Belonging: Autochthony, Citizenship, and Exclusion in Africa and Europe*. Chicago, IL: University of Chicago Press.
Government of South Africa (2017) *Draft White Paper on International Migration in South Africa*. Pretoria: Department of Home Affairs.
Gow G (2005) Rubbing shoulders in the global city: Refugees, citizenship and multicultural alliances in Fairfield, Sydney. *Ethnicities* 5(3): 386–405.

Granovetter M (1973) The strength of weak ties. *American Journal of Sociology* 78: 1360–1380.

Halliday T (2006) Migration, risk, and liquidity constraints in El Salvador. *Economic Development and Cultural Change* 54(4): 893–925.

Hansen TB, Stepputat F (eds) (2010) *States of Imagination: Ethnographic Explorations of the Postcolonial State.* Durham, NC: Duke University Press.

Hopkins D (2010) Politicized places: Explaining where and when immigrants provoke local opposition. *American Political Science Review* 104(1): 40–60.

Jacobsen K, Furst R (2011) *Developing a Profiling Methodology for Displaced People in Urban Areas.* Medford: Feinstein International Center.

Kamal, B. (2016) Now 1 in 2 world's refugees live in urban areas. *Inter Press News Service*, 19 May 2016. Available at: www.ipsnews.net/2016/05/now-1-in-2-worlds-refugees-live-in-urban-area/.

Kanaiapuni S, Donato K, Thompson-Colon, T, and Stainback M (2005) Counting on lin: Social networks, social support, and child health status. *Social Forces* 83(3): 1137–1164.

Kankonde P (2010) Transnational family ties, remittance motives, and social death among congolese migrants: A socio-anthropological analysis. *Journal of Comparative Family Studies* 41: 225–244.

Kermeliotis T (2013) Africa's "new cities": Urban future or utopian fantasies. *CNN Online*, 30 May 2013. Available at: http://edition.cnn.com/2013/05/30/business/africa-new-cities-konza-eko/.

Kigozi D (2017) The reality behind Uganda's refugee model. *Refugees Deeply*, 30 May 2017. Available at: www.newsdeeply.com/refugees/community/2017/05/30/the-reality-behind-ugandas-glowing-reputation.

Kihato CW (2013) *Migrant Women of Johannesburg: Everyday Life in an in-Between City.* London: Palgrave Macmillan.

Kihato CW, Landau LB (2017) Stealth humanitarianism: Negotiating politics, precarity, and performance management in protecting the urban displaced. *Journal of Refugee Studies* 30(3): 407–425.

Landau LB (2014) Conviviality, rights and conflict in Africa's urban estuaries. *Politics & Society* 14(3): 359–380.

Landau LB, Bule B, Malik AA, Kihato CW, Irvin-Erickson Y, Edwards B, and Mohr E (2017) *Displacement and Disconnection? Exploring the Role of Social Networks in the Livelihoods of Refugees in Gaziantep, Nairobi, and Peshawar.* Washington, DC: Urban Institute.

Landau LB, Duponchel M (2011) Laws, policies, or social position? capabilities and the determinants of effective protection in four African cities. *Journal of Refugee Studies* 24(1): 1–22.

Landau LB, Freemantle I (2010) Tactical cosmopolitanism and idioms of belonging: Insertion and self-exclusion in Johannesburg. *Journal of Ethnic and Migration Studies* 36(3): 375–390.

Lubkemann S (2008) Involuntary immobility: On a theoretical invisibility in forced migration studies. *Journal of Refugee Studies* 21(4): 454–475.

Lyytinen E, Kullenberg J (2013) *Urban Refugee Research and Social Capital: A Roundtable Report and Literature Review.* New York: International Rescue Committee.

Madhavan S, Landau LB (2011) Bridges to nowhere: Hosts, migrants and the chimera of social capital in three African cities. *Population and Development Review* 37(3): 473–497.

Madsen ML (2004) Living for home: Policing immorality among undocumented migrants in Johannesburg. *African Studies* 63: 173–192.

Malauene D (2004) *The Impact of the Congolese Forced Migrants' "permanent transit" Condition on Their Relations with Mozambique and Its People*. Unpublished MA thesis. Johannesburg: University of the Witwatersrand.

Malkki LH (1995) Refugees and exile: From "refugee studies" to the national order of things. *Annual Review of Anthropology* 24: 495–523.

Malkki LH (1996) Speechless emissaries: Refugees, humanitarianism, and dehistoricization. *Cultural Anthropology* 11(3): 377–404.

Marrow HB (2009) Immigrant bureaucratic incorporation: The dual roles of professional missions and government policies. *American Sociological Review* 74(5): 756–777.

Mbembe A, Nuttall S (2004) Writing the world from an African metropolis. *Public Culture* 16(3): 347–372.

Meyers G (2011) *African Cities: Alternative Visions of Urban Theory and Practice*. Chicago, IL: University of Chicago Press.

Misago JP, Gindrey V, Duponchel M, Landau L, and Polzer T (2010) *Vulnerability, Mobility and Place: Alexandra and Central Johannesburg Pilot Study*. Johannesburg: Forced Migration Studies Programme and the South African Red Cross Society.

Oliveira E, Vearey J (2015) Images of place: Visuals from migrant women sex workers in South Africa. *Medical Anthropology: Cross-Cultural Studies in Health and Illness* 34(4): 305–318.

Parnell S, Robinson J (2012) (Re)theorizing cities from the global south: Looking beyond neoliberalism. *Urban Geography* 33(4): 593–617.

Potts D (2010) *Circular Migration in Zimbabwe and Contemporary Sub-Saharan Africa*. Oxford: James Currey.

Sanyal R (2014) Urbanizing refuge: Interrogating spaces of displacement. *International Journal of Urban and Regional Research* 38(2): 558–572.

Schiller NG, Caglar A, and Guldbrandsen TC (2006) Beyond the ethnic lens: Locality, globality, and born-again incorporation. *American Ethnologist* 33(4): 612–633.

Simpson G 2013. *'You Are All Terrorists': Kenyan Police Abuse of Refugees in Nairobi*. New York: Human Rights Watch.

Segbers K (ed) (2007) *The Making of Global City Regions: Johannesburg, Mumbai/Bombay, São Paulo, and Shanghai*. Baltimore: Johns Hopkins University Press.

Sen A (1997) Capability as well-being. In: Nussbaum M, Sen A (eds) *The Quality of Life*. Oxford: Oxford University Press.

Simone AM (2006) Pirate towns: Reworking social and symbolic infrastructure in Johannesburg and Doula. *Urban Studies* 43(2): 357–370.

Soysal, YN., (1995). *Limits of Citizenship: Migrants and Postnational Membership in Europe*. University of Chicago Press.

Tonkiss F (2003) The ethics of indifference: Community and solitude in the city. *International Journal of Cultural Studies* 6(3): 297–311.

UN-HABITAT (2014) *African Cities 2014: Re-Imagining Sustainable Urban Transitions*. Nairobi: UN-HABITAT. Available at: http://unhabitat.org/the-state-of-african-cities-2014.

United Nations Department of Economic and Social Affairs Population Division (UNDESA) (2014) *World Urbanisation Prospects: The 2014 Revision : Highlights*. New York: UNDESA.

United Nations High Commissioner for Refugees (UNHCR) (2009) *UNHCR Policy on Refugee Protection and Solutions in Urban Areas*. Geneva: UNHCR.Vigneswaran D

(2014) The contours of disorder: Crime maps and territorial policing in South Africa. *Environment and Planning D: Society and Space* 32(1): 91–107.
Watson V (2009) Seeing from the South: Refocusing urban planning on the globe's central urban issues. *Urban Studies* 46: 2259–2275.
Women's Refugee Commission (2011a) *Bright Lights, Big City: Urban Refugees Struggles to Make a Living in New Delhi*. New York: Women's Refugee Commission.
Women's Refugee Commission (2011b) *No Place to Go but Up: Urban Refugees in Johannesburg: South Africa*. New York: Women's Refugee Commission.
Women's Refugee Commission (2011c) *The Living Ain't Easy, Urban Refugees in Kampala*. New York: Women's Refugee Commission.
Worby E (2010) Address Unknown: The temporality of displacement and the ethics of disconnection among Zimbabwean migrants in Johannesburg. *Journal of Southern African Studies* 36(2): 417–431.
Zetter R, Deikum, G (2010) Meeting humanitarian challenges in urban areas. *Forced Migration Review* 34: 5–7.

Chapter 8

Mobile technologies and forced migration

Giorgia Donà and Marie Godin

Introduction

Information and communication technologies (ICTs) increasingly influence our social relations, political imaginations, economic transactions, cultural productions and affective lives. We live in networked societies (Castells, 2011) where smartphones, instant messaging, navigation devices and social media applications create new kinds of daily experiences and social interactions (Elliott and Urry, 2010). Mobile technologies refer to those systems, applications and material objects which can be easily transported and transferred.

These 'digital infrastructures' are composed of devices such as mobile apps, websites, messaging and calling platforms, social media and translation services (Gillespie et al., 2016). In recent years, there has been a growing interest in the use of mobile technologies, not only among the general population, but also among relatively settled forced migrants and diasporas who increasingly lead transnational lives (see, for example, Diminescu, 2012; Everett, 2009; Oiarzabal and Ulf-Dietrich, 2012; Schapendonk, 2012), while the so-called European refugee 'crisis' has generated new questions about the intersection between forced migration and mobile technologies in the context of refugees' increasingly long, complex and fragmented journeys.

In novel ways, states themselves have increased their use of technological devices to manage cross-border migration, securitise borders and monitor the movement of people within nation-state borders (Andersson, 2015). Migrants and activists have responded to these technologically secured 'borderscapes' (Rajaram and Grundy-Warr, 2007) by engaging in counter-bordering technological strategies of resistance. Humanitarian workers have embraced technological innovations to respond to the changing humanitarian and technological needs of forced migrants in transit.

Understanding the role of mobile technologies in forced migrants' lives and journeys in rapidly changing contexts is a key issue in forced migration studies for two main reasons. First, given the increasing relevance and multi-functional purposes that mobile technologies have in the everyday lives of migrants, it is important to understand the ways in which they are used, the functions they fulfil, the roles they play and the challenges they create. Such analysis contributes to the understanding of an under-researched dimension of the experience of forced migrants, and the role of mobile technologies in enabling, constraining and transforming human mobility. Second, the use of mobile technologies influences research methodologies and concepts in the field of forced migration. Scholars need to revisit concepts like transnationalism, belonging, security, activism and humanitarianism through the digital lens, and examine whether the use of ICTs alters in cosmetic or substantial ways the conceptualisation of the world in which migrants live.

In this chapter, we adopt a comprehensive approach to examine the role of mobile technologies among forced migrants in transit. The chapter is divided into three parts. In the first, we present a literature review of the ways in which established diasporas, migrants and refugees use mobile technologies to form online transnational connections, experience new modes of belonging and engage in transnational political activism. Second, we examine the ways in which forced migrants in transit use mobile technologies to negotiate their movements in increasingly securitised 'techno-borderscapes', a term that we develop from Appadurai (1996)'s notion of technospaces. Lastly, we examine the use of mobile technologies among forced migrants in transit in Calais, at the border between France and the United Kingdom (UK). Until very recently, it was unusual for refugees who entered Europe to find themselves living in informal camps outside conventional forms of protection and assistance in what Agier (2016) calls borderlands. We argue that in these new settings, mobile technologies become multi-functional devices that organise various aspects of forced migrants' lives and life-saving tools which influence practical, affective, economic, social and political dimensions of forced migrants' lives.

Taking a different approach from that of existing literature, we examine the real and virtual connections that unfold among different social actors (migrants, humanitarians, border guards and activists) who are simultaneously embedded in 'techno-borderscapes'. With a focus on forced migrants, we show how their use of mobile technologies shapes and is shaped by their relations with others and their surrounding environment.

In this chapter, we use the terms 'forced migrants', 'refugees' and 'asylum seekers' to describe the nature of human mobility across borders. The journeys of forced and voluntary migrants are often similar: individuals have mixed motivations to move, and in transit places people whose immigration status is still undetermined reside together. It is for these reasons that we also use the more general terms 'migrant' and 'transit migrant' to refer to people on the move in general, which includes both forced and voluntary movement.

Mobile technologies for belonging among relatively settled forced migrants and diasporas

Movement and spaces feature prominently in the experiences of forced migrants, as individuals cross international borders, enter into longer and more fragmented journeys, spend time in transit and, even after arrival at places of destination, may move onwards, return, or move back and forth between places. Conversely, the virtual occupies no physical territory, as time and place shrink on computer and smartphone screens. Despite its placeless features, the virtual medium allows for the (re-)creation of place, making it simultaneously place-dissolving and place-generating (Diamandaki, 2003).

The use of new ICTs, especially mobile telephony, fulfils two distinct functions among forced migrants and diasporas. First, it contributes to the formation of new online places of transnational belonging that collapse conventional distinctions between homeland and hostland, the national and the transnational. Second, ICTs facilitate the online articulation, dissemination and promotion of social issues that unfold in the offline world. For relatively settled forced migrants and diasporas, smartphones and the internet become 'mobile technologies for belonging'.

In a time of 'personalised diasporas' (Mitra, 1997), migrant, refugee and diasporic communities use virtual sites to build a 'home away from home' which collapses conventional distinctions between the national and transnational and to create transnational communities among migrants who live in different countries and are unable to meet in person (Donà, 2014). Because of its widespread accessibility, the internet has become 'the social glue of migrant transnationalism' (Vertovec, 2009: 54). Mobile technologies also play an important role in the creation of de-territorialised spaces of belonging for immobile populations. Somali refugees transcend their immobility by interacting with family members and friends in transnational spaces (Horst, 2006a), while Palestinians living in camps use the internet as a mediating space through which they imagine a transnational Palestinian community (Aouragh, 2011). Similarly, asylum seekers confined in detention centres rely on mobile phones to keep in touch with the 'outside world' (Leung, 2011). The often repressive material conditions of encampment, detention and surveillance are among the reasons why 'home' is found elsewhere, in de-territorialised spaces (Donà, 2015). Mobile technologies also shape the process of identity formation, by offering the symbolic 'proto-material' – images, representations, discourses and interactions – from which transnational online identities are made (Diamandaki, 2003).

If mobile technologies contribute to the formation of new online spaces of transnational belonging, they also mirror real-life interactions and preoccupations. Chatrooms, newsgroups and blogs foster direct interaction and can, over time, create a sense of familiarity and intimacy among their regular users (Eriksen, 2006). These interconnected networks become transnational spaces for the expression of nostalgic ideas of the lost home, where uprootedness, dislocation, suffering, pain and remembrance are shared among digital diasporas. In a different manner, for refugees who are members of nations or groups without a state, the focal online discourse is projected towards the future homeland and the 'right to return'. In addition to being a forum for the articulation of real-life preoccupations, mobile technologies also facilitate the actualisation of offline interactions and engagements. Migrants use social media to communicate, interact, exchange information and promote cultural and religious practices that take place in the real world (Oiarzabal and Ulf-Dietrich, 2013). Migrants also advocate for real-life political changes that transcend homeland and host societies while also remaining connected to them (Godin and Donà, 2016).

The political nature of refugee movements means that politics are relevant for forced migrants in exile. The internet has transformed the ways in which refugees engage in political mobilisation across borders (Bernal, 2006; Oiarzabal and Ulf-Dietrich, 2012) through long-distance nationalism (Conversi, 2012; Mazzucchelli, 2012). But if transnational political engagements on the web are focused on the home country, they also reconfigure modes of citizenship (Kissau, 2012; Siapera, 2011) and engage with a range of transnational and trans-ethnic social actors (Anat, 2012; Graziano, 2012). Thus, the phrase 'mobile technologies for belonging' captures the formation and transformation of online as well as offline transnational social processes, relations and activities among relatively settled migrants, refugees and diasporic individuals.

The so-called European refugee 'crisis' that has unfolded since 2015 has generated new research on the intersection between mobile technologies and forced migration, especially for people who are on the move. Differing from research conducted with relatively settled forced migrants and diasporas, this emerging scholarship examines emergencies which occur during migration and the ways in which people on the move use smartphones and applications to navigate increasingly complex techno-borderscapes. We refer to this phenomenon with the term 'mobile technologies for survival'. Technologies for belonging and survival are interrelated and coexist, but they also have distinctive functions and roles. The following section gives an overview of the emerging research on 'mobile technologies for survival'.

Mobile technologies for survival during journeys and in transit

Similarly to relatively settled populations, people on the move use mobile phones to connect, stay in touch and reconnect. Smartphones have become the 'network capital' that enables transit migrants to communicate with families and friends as well as other migrants on the move (Gillespie et al., 2016), and function as archival technologies in which memories are stored through live photo albums and other digital media (Gillespie et al., 2016). In this regard, they function as technologies for belonging.

However, people on the move increasingly use mobile technologies to navigate securitised borderscapes. We refer to this emerging strategy as 'mobile technologies for survival'. Gillespie et al. (2016)'s study on the current refugee 'crisis' shows that refugees rely on smartphones, Global Positioning System (GPS) and Google Maps to navigate their journeys. These applications become digital guides and travel companions, which can complement or replace the role of smugglers and agents, the latter of whom use smartphones and social media applications to 'recruit' refugees and to alert authorities to 'rescue' refugees whom they had in fact smuggled across borders. On the other hand, refugees lost at sea use smartphones to contact rescuers, while forced migrants on the move use new technologies to seek information from people who left before them in order to follow in their path. Smartphones and social media platforms (Facebook, WhatsApp and Twitter) are thus used by migrants and refugees to crowd-source information.

However, social media sources are not always reliable. Refugees may have to depend on inaccurate information spread by smugglers that exposes them to danger (Gillespie et al., 2016). Mobile technologies can also pose a threat to migrants because they leave digital traces which can make transit migrants vulnerable to surveillance by both state and non-state actors (Gillespie et al., 2016). Additionally, not all migrants on the move have access to mobile technologies. In the same way in which class affects routes taken, means of migration and destinations (Van Hear, 2006), differential access and use of mobile technologies reproduce social inequalities among migrants. Mobile technologies can in fact reinforce power inequalities between the 'haves' and the 'have-nots' among forced migrants, facilitating the journeys of some while making journeys more difficult for others.

Ownership of mobile phones by migrants can also be a double-edged sword. Schapendonk (2012)'s research on African migration to Europe describes how networked connections used by migrants can be traced back to the SIM cards in their mobile telephones. For this reason, mobile phones are the first assets confiscated by border guards when arresting transit migrants, with the goal of 'taking them out of the network' (p. 134). In another context, Newell et al.'s (2016) study on information seeking and technology use among migrants at the United States-Mexico border shows how the disclosure of phone numbers of a migrant's contacts or family members can lead to extortion and abuse. The mobile phone, often a lifeline until migrants reach the border, thus becomes a liability which places migrants, and their families back home, at risk. These limitations show that mobile technologies can empower migrants, but can also jeopardise their itineraries, resilience and survival.

Mobile technologies, albeit with negative as well as positive effects, have nonetheless become essential multi-functional tools which can determine forced migrants' access to vital services and support networks. During their journeys, migrants and refugees interact with other social actors, namely state agents, activists and humanitarians, all of whom also use mobile technologies. Taking a different approach to that of the existing literature, which tends to examine digital securitisation, activism and humanitarianism separately, we integrate these factors to show their interconnections within techno-borderscapes.

Digital surveillance, activism and humanitarianism

States use ICTs, including mobile technologies, to monitor and control the movement of people across and within borders. Monitoring devices such as motion sensors, infra-red equipment and surveillance cameras are widely used by state agents to manage cross-border movements and enact the surveillance of those who have crossed borders. These digital practices are especially concentrated at the edges of state territories – in their borderzones. For example, in Europe the border agency Frontex has established multiple surveillance mechanisms to monitor, intercept, apprehend and push back or halt the passage of migrants between Greece and Turkey (Topak, 2014). The use of drone technology in border surveillance has increased over the last few years, challenging migrant and refugees' human rights (Marin and Krajíková, 2016).

The use of these technologies creates new 'digital borders' which are distinct from physical and geographical borders (Bigo, 2014; Broeders, 2007). State controls extend over bounded territories and populations (Kuster and Tsianos, 2016). Transnational surveillance practices, which rely on ICTs, are increasingly addressing a public that is no longer defined exclusively as the citizenry of the nation-state. Through the notions of bona fide global citizens and 'crimmigrant' others, Aas (2011) details how the seeming universality of citizenship is punctuated by novel categories of globally included and excluded populations. Because digital bordering practices alone cannot stop irregular migration, states also turn to internal control measures. Eurodac, an information, communication and technological tool of control, stores the fingerprints of asylum seekers and irregular migrants, regulating the mobility of non-EU citizens within the EU (Kuster and Tsianos, 2016). The identification and registration of people at the border is crucial for sorting legal and undocumented migrants, and subsequently excluding irregular migrants from societal institutions, discouraging their stay or deporting those who are apprehended (Broeders, 2009). Risk profiling thus becomes a tool of digital governance, through which 'legitimate' and 'illegitimate' mobilities are kept separate (Amoore, 2006).

It is worth mentioning the 'failed' attempt by Frontex to commission tech firms to design smartphone apps and databases to track and manage the arrival of refugees to Europe (Taylor and Graham-Harrison, 2016). Refugee support groups and privacy organisations have argued that it would be difficult to convince refugees to download an app for their 'safety' (weather and routes) which could then be used to apprehend them. In spite of the existence of digital bordering practices, migrants appear to be able to negotiate such constraints (Warren and Mavroudi, 2011) and continue to cross borders (Topak, 2014).

In response to state digital securitisation, activists use mobile technologies to challenge and undermine current border regimes. For example, activist groups at the Mexico–US border use digital photography and video recording equipment to monitor state agents, while vigilante organisations use technologies to coordinate citizen-organised foot patrols that locate and assist migrants in danger. Such groups use Geographic Information Systems (GIS) to organise the provision of water and give high-resolution border maps to migrants to assist their journeys (Walsh, 2010). Asylum seekers have begun to record the testimonies of their journeys while crossing on boats, trucks and planes, and disseminate their stories via social media. In this way, asylum seekers become producers of their own narratives. These accounts challenge stigmatising perceptions of asylum seekers as security threats, and advocate for their rights as global citizens who are forced to flee because of a lack of democracy in their homelands (Whitlock, 2015).

Increasingly, activists and migrants have responded to the escalating presence of technologically secured 'borderscapes' (Rajaram and Grundy-Warr, 2007) by engaging in counter-bordering technological strategies of resistance. The smartphone revolution shapes not only the ways in which migrants, states and activists operate, but also how relief workers deliver aid to forced migrants in transit and the kind of aid they deliver. The European refugee 'crisis' has generated a dynamic response from a novel and diverse constellation of actors: humanitarian organisations, state institutions, development cooperatives, non-governmental organisations and grassroots activists (Mason, 2016). Their responses are increasingly reliant on ICTs. 'Digital humanitarianism' extends the conventional delivery of aid to include the provision of technology-related services. WatchTheMed Alarm Phone, for example, is an organisation that offers an emergency phone service through which the nearest coastguards can be alerted in response to SOS calls from migrants whose boats experience crises in various stretches of sea around Europe. The organisation has received around 1,400 distress calls in the 15 months up to February 2017 (Taylor and Graham-Harrison, 2016).

Within digital humanitarianism, mobile technologies become a form of aid in themselves. The Central European University in Budapest, Hungary, developed battery-powered Wi-Fi hotspots that can be worn in a backpack, along with charging banks assembled from components bought from high-street stores, to help refugees charge their phone batteries as they move across Europe. In Jordan, UNHCR launched a new programme which gives Syrian refugees custom-designed mobile phone SIM cards through which they can receive mass information messages (IRIN, 2013). These examples indicate that digital humanitarianism is increasingly expanding to include the provision of emergency technological services, the use of technologies to deliver aid more effectively, and suggest that telephonic technology is becoming a form of aid provision.

Reliance on new technologies changes the needs of refugees, who need not only food, shelter and protection but also access to electricity and Wi-Fi, services that would have been an afterthought only a few years ago (UNHCR, 2016). As one refugee from Syria told AFP news agency, 'Our phones and power banks are more important for our journey than anything, even more important than food' (Worley, 2016: 1). However, the tendency to substitute old humanitarian tools with new ones, especially with digital innovations, has progressively led to what Scott-Smith (2016) labelled 'humanitarian neophilia', in which markets and technologies are presented as solutions to a failed aid system. Their supporters 'understate' the role of the state and 'overstate' the objects and vision of self-reliant subjects (Scott-Smith, 2016). It is therefore important to question how digital humanitarian innovations are genuinely benefiting their intended beneficiaries and remain autonomous in increasing complex environments.

To conclude, various social actors use mobile technologies in ways that intersect, reinforce and challenge one another. In the next section, we present the case study of the use of mobile technologies by migrants and refugees in the techno-borderscapes of Calais. We aim to offer a comprehensive analysis of the centrality of mobile technologies, with enabling and constraining consequences, for forced migrants and the actors with whom they engage.

Forced migrants in transit at the border in Calais

Since the late 1990s, migrants and refugees have been gathering in informal camps at Calais, near the securitised border between France and the UK. In 1999 the Red Cross set up a centre at Sangatte, which was closed down three years later. However, over the years informal settlements continued to form, only to be demolished, and then reconstituted. Prior to its official closure in October 2016 and the eviction of its residents, around 8,000 individuals lived in what was known as the Calais Jungle (Help Refugees, 2016). Even though the camp was dismantled, people continued to congregate at the border in Calais to attempt to cross the Channel. The formation of the Jungle and of the Sangatte Centre beforehand, together with other informal settlements for transit migrants that are situated outside conventional forms of protection, citizenship and belonging, and which continue to proliferate across Europe, comprises a new phenomenon in Europe, making it a key issue in contemporary forced migration studies. In a traditional country of permanent resettlement, the camp signals the existence of informal sites of migrants who are contained within the borders of nation-states but exist outside the nation-state imagination. They are 'in' but not 'of' (Baumann, 2002) the national space of belonging.

So, while the Calais Jungle was located in French territory, its residents did not benefit from mainstream services. In the camp there was no running water, latrines were temporary and portable, and electricity was only available in the few places which had generators. Migrants in transit have limited access to emergency health or welfare services. Informal solidarity networks of activists and volunteers, rather than government agencies or formal aid organisations, deliver assistance to the migrants. In the Calais informal settlement, transit migrants experience informality of responses and precarity of existence. In this new European context, securitisation and control of migration become tighter, undocumented border crossings are on the increase and official responses are limited. It follows that precarity of status prevails. In this informal borderscape, migrants and refugees rely heavily on mobile technologies for multiple purposes, one of which is to facilitate engagement with other social actors who also use mobile technologies. Mobile technologies thus comprise the means through which migrants and refugees and other social actors become embedded in techno-borderscapes.

Our study on the use of mobile telephony among forced migrants in the Calais Jungle stems from a civic engagement project run by the Centre for Narrative Research at the University of East London, which delivered accredited short university courses on 'Life Stories' to migrants in transit. Participant observation, life narratives and informal conversations about the use of technology with (now former) residents of the Calais camp, including those with whom we had developed contacts and relationships through the 'Life Stories' project,[1] took place between September 2015 and October 2016. We adopted the role of researcher/activist/volunteer at different points in time. The mobile phone, and in particular smartphones, became an important methodological tool for collecting information, maintaining contact with the residents and supporting them in their day-to-day survival. The field of forced migration has undergone a shift from research framed by methodological nationalism towards multi-sited research and, more recently, digital methodologies (Donà, 2014). Digital research with forced migrants can be divided into three broad categories: the analysis of online sites and web posts used by forced migrants and diasporic groups (Brinkerhoff, 2006; Diminescu, 2012; Doná, 2010; Donà, 2014); interviews and group discussions with forced migrants about their use of mobile technologies (Wall et al., 2015; Aouragh, 2011); and the mixed-method integration of online and onsite methods (Aouragh, 2011; Brinkerhoff, 2006; Godin and Donà, 2016; Halilovich, 2013). Our research project relies on the use of mixed-methods both online and onsite.

The mobile phone as lifeline

In the context of precarity during transit migration, mobile phones become multi-functional devices around which various spheres of forced migrants' lives revolve. They are not accessories but essential lifeline tools, used to promote local and transnational belonging and survival in ways that are context dependent. Mobile technologies allow people in transit to keep in touch with family and friends. Communicating with family back home or across locations reassures loved ones that the journey is almost ending and to lessen their worry. This means that sometimes, forced migrants send back selfies in front of houses, cars or at the beach in Calais instead of images of the refugee camp as ways of concealing the reality of their circumstances.

Mobile phones also enable forced migrants to connect with other residents of the camp, be they others on the move or smugglers. Everyday survival in the camp depends on relationships between residents as well as between resident and non-resident volunteers. Social interactions among residents and volunteers in such a volatile environment are built around trust and personal relationships that are fostered through social networking. These interactions are conducted in person but also via text or phone. During one of our visits, one refugee from Afghanistan was called innumerable times by phone to interpret for a co-national who did not speak English and needed to be registered with French authorities. Refugees therefore become providers of social services in the camp, a role enabled through their use of mobile technologies. Late at night, one woman residing in the fenced compound inside the Jungle used her text messaging service to ask a volunteer to bring some water rather than taking the risk of going out alone. The registration of migrants in the camp, the organising of translation sessions, and the filling out of forms are just a few examples of the micro-coordination that mobile phones enable in techno-borderscapes. Smartphones are also used to keep up-to-date with news, culture and sport in countries of origin and the diaspora. They are recreational devices for listening to music, watching videos and playing games in native languages and scripts, and for sharing practical information about Calais, routes into the UK, or the European asylum system.

Transit migrants living in the Jungle camp also used mobile phones to engage in transnational politics but also used mobile phones to address local and context specific issues. First, they documented directly the violence that police and fascist groups used against them. They used the internet as a form of digital activism with which they could bear witness to the violence. Second, some of the inhabitants of Calais used social media to criticise European refugee and asylum policies generally, as well as at the border between France and the United Kingdom, denouncing their inadequacies in addressing their reality of movement. Third, Calais residents shared information about the political situation back home, not only with the aim of changing the situation in their countries of origin, but also to raise awareness about the legitimacy of their presence in Europe as refugees. They shared online images of widespread and protracted violence in their countries of origin (e.g., Pakistan, Afghanistan and Iran) to explain their presence in Europe and to provide visual documentation of the dangers awaiting them in the event of their being repatriated. Lastly, the Calais residents raised awareness of the experience of being a refugee in the Jungle by using social media to articulate a politics of the representation of refugee voices, through which they could become technologically visible figures of identification and empathy. Through these uses of mobile technologies, online political engagements intersected with offline political activism, such as participating in demonstrations, undertaking hunger strikes and talking to the media.

Securitisation and safety

The Calais case shows that mobile phones are used not only for belonging but also for survival in the new techno-borderscape of securitisation and insecurity. The Calais Jungle was located beside the highly securitised border of the Channel Tunnel, surrounded by high white walls, barbed wires, cameras and surveillance mechanisms. Inside the Jungle, technology was used to control and to enable securitisation, but also to give protection to vulnerable residents, most notably single women, girls, mothers and children, on the grounds of health and safety concerns. Migrants in Calais used their phones to find safety in the knowledge that friends and agents could monitor their journey and that they in turn could monitor the crossing of the Channel made by family and friends. One Afghan resident who had opted to apply for asylum in France but whose sister, her two children and husband, were trying to cross the France–UK border at Calais, explained how he was going to follow their journey step-by-step, and that this made him feel like a smuggler, checking for safety but also controlling their movement. Similarly to African refugees in Italy who used their phones to share with other migrants news of imminent threats of police roundups (Harney, 2013), activists and residents in Calais used mobiles to alert residents of imminent police raids. On 14 October 2016, we saw activists going around the camp alerting residents of a forthcoming raid on 'commercial' sites. This was often done via WhatsApp, a cross-platform instant messaging application for smartphones users that is less subject to monitoring and surveillance than other social media platforms, such as Facebook or Twitter (Gillespie et al., 2016: 24). An activist read aloud text messages to small groups of migrants alerting them that security forces were about to arrive. In response, shops' curtains were drawn, a television standing in the corner of a restaurant was removed and customers left the premises, returning only after activists had informed them that the anticipated raid was not going to take place on that day.

Access to mobile technologies can also have negative impacts for security. While mobile technologies enable the exercise of belonging and the reconfiguration of political subjectivities and modes of citizenship, they also generate new forms of insecurity, surveillance and control of everyday life (Siapera, 2011). In addition to economic, social and political precarity, forced migrants experience a more specific category of information precarity, in which their access to news as well as personal information is insecure, unstable and unreliable, leading to potential threats to their well-being (Wall, Campbell and Janbek, 2015). As phone cameras are more and more used for 'citizen witnessing', they become dangerous objects that need to be placed under surveillance. In Calais, a notice posted on the door of a shop had a recognisable blue rectangle with the word 'Facebook' printed on it and underneath a warning sign:

> BEWARE: Refugees and Volunteers – The UK Home Office will look at your Facebook account and they will use photos of you in Calais or other European countries to try and deport you. Be VERY careful about who you add, your profile pictures, what pictures you are tagged in/who you tag and your privacy settings!

It also warns volunteers to

> Be careful about what you put on Facebook! Consent is not only someone being happy to have their photo taken/face shown. It is also about knowing what is going to be done with the photo and what risks this involves both in the UK and in people's home countries.

Digital humanitarianism and activism

If mobile technologies shape the ways in which refugees and activists operate, they also alter the ways in which aid is given, and shape interactions among volunteers and residents in the Jungle. These new types of digital 'volunteer humanitarianism' (Sandri, 2017) are heavily reliant on online social networking sites, which are instrumental in galvinising support and mobilising volunteers and activists. They form networks and online communities of solidarity that are highly flexible, spontaneous and mobile.

Technology, in particular the social networking site Facebook, facilitates information sharing about needs, creation of projects and coordination of operations among these informal, mixed networks of volunteers, activists and camp residents. An online analysis of digital volunteer humanitarian sites (in October 2016, before the camp was dismantled) showed that there were more than 85 English language Facebook pages of groups containing the word 'Calais' or 'Jungle'.

These virtual platforms of solidarity, action, compassion, volunteering, care and aid are both national sites and locally based solidarity groups. Given the lack of infrastructure and facilities in the Jungle, coordination of aid took place online as well as offline in the provision of medical equipment and medicines, the delivery and preparation of food in the 'Calais Kitchen', or the provision of suitable shelter via the Caravans for Calais mobile crisis support units. Volunteers and residents used Facebook pages to coordinate specific activities such as 'Clean the Calais Jungle', or 'Calais Jungle waste and sanitation group'. Facebook pages also give us a glimpse of the targeted projects for women or children in 'The "unofficial" women and children's centre', which was located in a blue double-decker bus near the family area of the camp, or the 'Hummingbird Project' for children. Activists used Facebook to call for demonstrations such as 'Calais – No Eviction Without Solution', 'Calais Calling' or 'Hunger Strike Calais'. Finally, in spite of the dangers of making one's presence in Calais known, residents set up their own sites, like 'Riaz 4 Calais' and 'Calais Voices of Refugees', where they gave updates on the conditions in the camp. Since the Jungle was demolished, transit migrants are still congregating at the Calais border and therefore some groups of volunteers that were active in the camp continue to be active at the border. Refugees who have moved to some localities in France and those who have made it to the UK also continue to keep their Facebook pages active.

Digital humanitarianism is also visible in the ways in which mobile technologies (phones, phone credits) become technologies of aid. The most exemplary case is that of the Facebook group 'Phone credit for refugees and displaced people',[2] which was set up in February 2016 by a British volunteer who had been in Calais. This was at first an online-only network gathering for the refugees, friends and volunteers who the group founder had met at the camp. The site quickly became an online platform allowing refugees, administrators and phone credit donors to interact with each other. The Facebook page reported that in October 2016 the group had 27,140 members and 27 administrators. By the end of January 2017, the service had recently completed 20,000 top-ups and raised almost £500,000. Since the dismantling of the Calais Jungle in October 2016, this platform has expanded its support to cover refugees across Europe and the

Middle East.[3] This digital fundraising platform, which is a shared space between refugees, donors and administrators, gives vital phone credit to refugees in crisis to help them to connect with their loved ones, gain access to vital services, news and information and to keep themselves safe.

The mobile phone as the most precious possession: the emergence of mobile-centred economies and infrastructures

We also observed the emergence, in response to the spontaneous and informal nature of the Calais Jungle, of economies and infrastructures that revolve around the needs of mobile phone users and consumers. This is an under-researched dimension of the relationship between mobile technologies and forced migration, where in addition to the impact of mobile technologies on the lives of forced migrants in transit and those around them, we also observed the creation of mobile-focused economies and temporary infrastructures that support the electric and Wi-Fi systems.

In the volatile camp environment, forced migrants cannot risk that their phone battery runs out or their phone breaks down. Spaces which are usually associated with recreation, learning and sociability, such as the Afghan Restaurant, the Kids' Café and the Jungle Library, were therefore transformed into communal charging spots, where it was possible to charge devices for free. Refugees could connect to a wireless network called 'Jangala', beamed into the camp from a hand-built antenna sitting atop a battered blue track, called the Refugee Info Bus.[4] This innovative mobile tech hub provided 150 individuals a day with a free Wi-Fi connection. A lack of access to electricity lines and a reliance on generators meant that electricity was a precious commodity whose scarcity posed the possibility of considerable tensions.

The need for technology generated a market in the Jungle for smartphone infrastructure support. On shop counters, Lycamobile prepaid phone cards, SIM cards, headphones, chargers and second-hand phone batteries were sold beside tomatoes, oil, bread and cigarettes. In the Jungle, residents could buy monthly connectivity, purchasing 12 GB of data for around £20. Interestingly, some of this memory data was transferred from abroad when relatives residing in the UK sent Calais residents digital remittances to be exchanged for cash to purchase food and clothes in the informal camp market. In the absence of banks or Western Union shops, mobile data complemented or replaced traditional money transfers. Horst (2006b) writes that the receipt of remittances via smartphones has changed in significant ways: the mobile phone has made it easier to receive money regularly but also for specific purposes; money can be received on an occasional basis as well as in emergencies.

In the context of Calais, we see a further transformation whereby technological connectivity becomes the remittance per se, replacing money that cannot be withdrawn in the absence of identity documents, access to banks and availability of money transfer shops. Our research shows that technological connectivity is also the means through which family members in the diaspora support refugees in the camp. The existence of a second-hand information technology (IT) market also suggests quite strongly that there is a need for maintenance services. We saw evidence of this in examples like a handwritten sign on the outside door of one of the shops selling IT items, which read 'phone repair' and underneath 'phone unlock' with French contact details (first name and mobile number). Smartphones have thus become a 'form of currency', which can be bought and sold, traded and upgraded, exchanged for goods, stolen, lost and found (Gillespie et al., 2016).

The digital intersectional divide

As mobile technologies become more diffused among migrants and refugees, they also create new kinds of inequalities and challenges. Differential access to mobile technologies creates new forms of digital and social stratification. Gender and generational differences in refugee experiences of smartphones are rarely touched upon but are of great significance (Gillespie et al., 2016).

In Calais, on one side of the spectrum were those like Mohammed, an Afghan translator, who owned two mobile handsets with two separate SIM cards, a French and a UK one. Like others, Mohammed was sufficiently digitally literate to know that (at that time) it was cheaper to access the internet with a UK SIM card than a French one, and that the use of two SIM cards and sometimes more than one phone was a cost-reducing strategy. Forced migrants thus became active agents in negotiating the complexities of the tele-communication techno-borderscape while also creating a transnational, cross-border market for UK SIM cards to be used in French territory.

On the other side of the fragmented digital world, a gender divide appears, with women in Calais tending to own basics phones, such as candy bar models, rather than the smartphones that men, especially young men, tended to own. For women, communication took place via text messages and calls made after having purchased €5 Lycamobile prepaid phone cards on sale in the Jungle shops. However, smartphones are also shared within family units with the person (often the youngest and the men) being the most digitally literate and the ones in charge of keeping the others informed. There is also a generational divide, such as is seen in the story of an older Kuwaiti migrant. He had been in Calais for a year when we met him and was unable to communicate with his family because his old mobile phone did not have enough memory to upload new applications such as Viber. National inequalities are also visible. As mentioned earlier, not all migrants have smartphones and virtual online lives. Research has found that on the Balkan route, Syrians tend to have the most money and the best technology while Afghans, Pakistanis, Bangladeshis, Eritreans and Somalis are among the poorest, and their journeys are usually the toughest, with little help from internet resources (McLaughlin, 2015).

We also observed that there were different types of phones among migrants from different countries, with Sudanese, Eritrean, Ethiopian and Somali migrants being less likely to have smartphones than migrants from the Middle East. This trend intersected with age and gender. Migrants and refugees also experienced a stratified 'mobility regime' (Shamir, 2005) in which access to mobile technology is unstable and characterised by frequent periods of disconnection, and thus creating or reinforcing digital inequalities. In fact, pre-existing digital inequalities in terms of access, usage, skills and self-perceptions can reinforce social inequalities between refugees while on the move and in the camp.

Conclusion

In this chapter, we adopted a comprehensive approach to examine the role of mobile technologies during forced migration, which we refer to as mobile technologies for belonging and survival. Our ethnographic research in Calais shows the pivotal role of mobile technologies in forced migrants' lives in rapidly changing techno-borderscapes and contributes to our understanding of an emerging, currently under-researched dimension of the migrant experience. In the informal Calais camp, mobile technologies were used as multi-functional devices that overlap with all aspects – survival, practical, affective, economic, social and political – of forced migrants' lives, combining both technologies for belonging and survival.

We looked at migrant's agencies through the complex use of mobile technologies not by migrant themselves in isolation, but within techno-borderscapes in which a range social actors, including transit migrants, are embedded. We explored the ways in which the environment alters the uses of mobile technologies among refugees, and how mobile technologies can facilitate migrant's journeys while simultaneously constraining them. We also examined the new interfaces created by mobile technologies that allow for new types of social interactions to take place among different social actors who do not necessarily share the same motives. The ongoing transformation of the use of mobile technologies by forced migrants embedded in techno-borderscapes needs to be studied contextually, across time and space.

By focusing on migrant's agencies at the Calais border, we were able to reveal a complex interplay between mobile technologies for survival and belonging and the formation of digital sociabilities and infrastructures. We attempted to avoid falling into the trap of technological determinism, which either offers a glowing picture of what technologies can bring to refugees or a dark vision of how technologies are being used to 'manage' and 'control' the flow of refugees in Europe. We showed that differentiated access to mobile technologies and their use among national and social groups differently shapes the experiences of migrants in the camp and can provide opportunities, but can also reinforce inequalities.

Future research needs to better understand complex emerging forms of digital divisions in migration, and we suggest that adopting an intersectional lens that looks simultaneously at racial, geographic, gender, class and age divides may represent a way forward.

Notes

1 For more details on the 'Life Stories' project: www.uel.ac.uk/schools/social-sciences/our-research-and-engagement/research/centre-for-narrative-research/collaborative-research-events/life-stories-at-the-jungle-refugee-camp-calais
2 www.facebook.com/groups/1709109339334305/
3 Since October 2016, new members have seen the Facebook group almost triple in size with almost 60,000 members at the end of September 2017.
4 http://refugeeinfobus.com/. The organisation became involved in Greece in early 2017, and it plans to get involved in the north of France as refugees are still there.

Bibliography

Aas KF (2011) 'Crimmigrant' bodies and bona fide travellers: Surveillance, citizenship and global governance. *Theoretical Criminology* 15(3): 331–346.

Agier M (2016) *Borderlands: Towards an Anthropology of the Cosmopolitan Condition*. Cambridge: Polity Press.

Amoore L (2006) Biometric borders: Governing mobilities in the war on terror. *Political Geography* 25(3): 336–351.

Anat B (2012) The Palestinian diaspora on the web: Between de-territorialisation and re-territorialisation. *Social Science Information* 51(4): 459–474.

Andersson R (2015) Hardwiring the frontier? The politics of security technology in Europe's 'fight against illegal migration'. *Security Dialogue* 47(1): 22–39.

Aouragh M (2011) *Palestine Online: Transnationalism, the Internet and the Construction of Identity*. London: IB Tauris.

Appadurai A (1996) *Modernity at Large: Cultural Dimensions of Globalization*. Minneapolis, MN: University of Minnesota Press.

Baumann Z (2002) Up the lowly nowherevilles of liquid modernity: Comments on and around Agier. *Ethnography* 3(3): 343–349.

Bernal V (2006) Diaspora, cyberspace and political imagination: The Eritrean diaspora online. *Global Networks* 6(2): 161–179.

Bigo D (2014) The (in)securitization practices of the three universes of EU border control. *Security Dialogue* 45(3): 209–225.

Brinkerhoff JM (2006) Digital diasporas and conflict prevention: The case of somalinet.com. *Review of International Studies* 32(1): 25–47.

Broeders D (2007) The new digital borders of Europe: EU databases and the surveillance of irregular migrants. *International Sociology* 22(1): 71–92.

Broeders D (2009) *Breaking Down Anonymity: Digital Surveillance of Irregular Migrants in Germany and the Netherlands*. Amsterdam: University Press.

Castells M (2011) *The Rise of the Network Society: The Information Age, Economy, Society and Culture*. Chichester: John Wiley & Sons.

Conversi D (2012) Irresponsible radicalisation: Diasporas, globalisation and long-distance nationalism in the digital age. *Journal of Ethnic and Migration Studies* 38(9): 1357–1379.

Diamandaki K (2003) Virtual ethnicity and digital diasporas: Identity construction in cyberspace. *Global Media Journal* 2(2): 26.

Diminescu D (2012) Introduction: Digital methods for the exploration, analysis and mapping of e-diasporas. *Social Science Information* 51(4): 451–458.

Donà G (2010) Collective suffering and cyber-memorialisation in post-genocide Rwanda. In: Broderick I, Traverso A (eds) *Trauma, Media, Art: New Perspectives*. Newcastle on Tyne: Cambridge Scholars Press, 16–35.

Donà G (2014) Forced migration, and material and virtual mobility among Rwandan children and young people. In: Veale A, Donà G (eds) *Child and Youth Migration: Mobility-in-Migration in an Era of Globalisation*. Basingstoke: Palgrave Macmillan, 113–139.

Donà, G (2015) Making homes in limbo: Embodied virtual "homes" in prolonged conditions of displacement. *Refuge* 31(1): 67–73.

Elliott A, Urry J (2010) *Mobile Lives*. London: Routledge.

Eriksen T (2006) Nations in cyberspace. *Short Version of the 2006 Ernest Gellner Lecture, Delivered to the ASEN Conference, London School of Economics*. Available at: http://tamilnation.co/selfdetermination/nation/erikson.htm [Accessed 12.2017].

Everett A (2009) *Digital Diaspora: A Race for Cyberspace*. New York: Suny Press.

Gillespie M, Ampofo L, Cheesman M, Faith B, Iliadou E, Issa A (2016) *Mapping Refugee Media Journeys: Smartphones and Social Media Networks*. Milton Keynes: The Open University/France Médias Monde.

Godin M, Donà G (2016) 'Refugee voices', new social media and the politics of representation: Young Congolese in the diaspora and beyond. *Refuge* 32(1): 60–71.

Graziano T (2012) The Tunisian diaspora: Between 'digital riots' and Web activism. *Social Science Information* 51(4): 534–550.

Halilovich H (2013) Bosnian Austrians: Accidental migrants in trans-local and cyber spaces. *Journal of Refugee Studies* 26(4): 524–540.

Harney N (2013) Precarity, affect and problem solving with mobile phones by asylum seekers, refugees and migrants in Naples, Italy. *Journal of Refugee Studies* 26(4): 541–557.

Help Refugees/L'Auberge des Migrants (2016) *Census Report*. October 2016. Available at: www.helprefugees.org.uk/news/new-calais-census-released-568-children-calais-74/ [Accessed 12.2017].

Horst C (2006a) In "virtual dialogue" with the Somali community: The value of electronic media for research amongst refugee diasporas. *Refuge: Canada's Journal on Refugees* 23(1): 51–57.

Horst H (2006b) The blessings and burdens of communication: Cell phones in Jamaican transnational social fields. *Global Networks* 6(2): 143–159.

IRIN (2013) *Syrian Aid in the Tech Age*. 14 November 2013. Available at: www.refworld.org/docid/5285f7964.html [Accessed 3.4.2017].

Kissau K (2012) Structuring migrants' political activities on the Internet: A two-dimensional approach. *Journal of Ethnic and Migration Studies* 38(9): 1381–1403.

Kuster B, Tsianos VS (2016) How to liquefy a body on the move: Eurodac and the making of the European digital border. In: Bossing R, Carrapiço H (eds) *EU Borders and Shifting Internal Security: Technology, Externalization and Accountability*. London: Springer International Publishing, 45–63.

Leung L (2011) *Taking Refuge in Technology: Communication Practices in Refugee Camps and Immigration Detention*. Geneva: UNHCR, Policy Development and Evaluation Service.

Marin L, Krajcíková K (2016) Deploying drones in policing European borders: Constraints and challenges for data protection and human rights. In: Zavrsnik A (ed) *Drones and Unmanned Aerial Systems: Legal and Social Implications for Security and Surveillance.* New York: Springer International Publishing, 101–127.

Mason B (2016) *ICT4Refugees: A Report on the Emerging Landscape of Digital Responses to the Refugee Crisis.* Bonn: GTZ. Available at: https://regasus.de/online/datastore?epk=74 D5roYc&file=image_8_en [Accessed 12.2017].

Mazzucchelli F (2012) What remains of Yugoslavia? From the geopolitical space of Yugoslavia to the virtual space of the Web Yugosphere. *Social Science Information* 51: 631–648.

McLaughlin D (2015) Mass movement guided by mobiles and social media: Wifi, texts and newsfeeds serve as torches to navigate the long road ahead. *The Irish Times*, 9 September 2015.

Mitra A (1997) Virtual commonality: Looking for India on the Internet. In: Jones S (ed) *Virtual Culture: Identity and Communication in Cybersociety.* Thousand Oaks: Sage Publications, 55–79.

Newell BC, Gomez R, and Guajardo VE (2016) Information seeking, technology use, and vulnerability among migrants at the United States – Mexico border. *The Information Society*. 32: 3, 176–191. Available at: https://doi.org/10.1080/01972243.2016.1153013 [Accessed 12.2017].

Oiarzabal PJ, Ulf-Dietrich R (2012) Migration and diaspora in the age of information and communication technologies. *Journal of Ethnic and Migration Studies* 38(9): 1333–1338.

Rajaram PK, Grundy-Warr C (eds) (2007) *Borderscapes: Hidden Geographies and Politics at Territory's Edge.* Minneapolis, MN: University of Minnesota Press.

Sandri S (2017) 'Volunteer humanitarianism': Volunteers and humanitarian aid in the Jungle refugee camp of Calais. *Journal of Ethnic and Migration Studies* 44(1): 65–80.

Schapendonk J (2012) Mobilities and sediments: Spatial dynamics in the context of contemporary Sub-Saharan African migration to Europe. *African Diasporas* (5): 117–142.

Scott-Smith T (2016) Humanitarian neophilia: The 'innovation turn' and its implications. *Third World Quarterly* 37(12): 2229–2251.

Shamir R (2005) Without borders? Notes on globalization as a mobility regime. *Sociological Theory* 23(2): 197–217.

Siapera E (2011) *Understanding New Media.* London: Sage Publications.

Taylor D, Graham-Harrison E (2016) EU asks tech firms to pitch refugee-tracking systems. *The Guardian*, 18 February 2016. Available at: www.theguardian.com/world/2016/feb/18/eu-asks-tech-firms-to-pitch-refugee-tracking-systems [Accessed 1.2018].

Topak ÖE (2014) The biopolitical border in practice: Surveillance and death at the Greece-Turkey borderzones. *Environment and Planning D: Society and Space* 32(5): 815–833.

United Nations High Commissioner for Refugees (UNHCR) and Accenture (2016) *Connecting Refugees: How Internet and Mobile Connectivity can Improve Refugee Well-being and Transform Humanitarian Action.* Available at: www.accenture.com/us-en/insight-refugee-connectivity-unhcr [Accessed 12.2017].

Van Hear N (2006) 'I went as far as my money would take me': Conflict, forced migration and class. In: Crepeau F, Nakache D, Collyer M, Goetz N, Hansen A, Modi R, Nadig A, Spoljar-Vrzina S and Willigen M (eds) *Forced Migration and Global Processes: A View from Forced Migration Studies.* Oxford: Lexington Books, 125–158.

Vertovec S (2009) *Transnationalism.* London: Routledge.

Wall M, Campbell M, Janbek D (2015) Syrian refugees and information precarity. *New Media & Society* 19(2): 240–254.

Walsh JP (2010) From border control to border care: The political and ethical potential of surveillance. *Surveillance & Society* 8(2): 113–130.

Warren A, Mavroudi E (2011) Managing surveillance? The impact of biometric residence permits on UK migrants. *Journal of Ethnic and Migration Studies* 37(9): 1495–1511.

Whitlock G (2015) The hospitality of cyberspace: Mobilizing asylum seeker testimony online. *Biography* 38(2): 245–266.

Worley W (2016) Syrian woman explains why refugees need smartphones: For refugees, smartphones are far more than just Snapchat and Instagram. *The Independent*, 12 May 2016. Available at: www.independent.co.uk/news/world/europe/why-do-refugees-have-smartphones-syrian-woman-explains-perfectly-refugee-crisis-a7025356.html [Accessed 12.2017].

Chapter 9

Second generation from refugee backgrounds

Affects and transnational ties and practices to the ancestral homeland

Milena Chimienti, Anne-Laure Counilh and Laurence Ossipow

Introduction

This chapter engages with and explores the intersections between two important current issues in forced migration: second generation from refugee backgrounds and transnationalism. There has been a growing body of research and scholarship on transnationalism since the 1990s, and it is increasingly central both in terms of modes of global engagement and in relation to integration. However, little is known about second generation from refugee backgrounds[1] and how their backgrounds impact on them as transnational actors and in turn how this impacts on their feelings about home and their identity and belonging. In bringing these areas together, this chapter integrates theoretical ideas with empirical data in order to highlight the importance of understanding the complex relationships that second generation from refugee backgrounds – an ever-growing cohort – have with the countries to which they are connected either physically through everyday life or visits or through virtual intra-diasporic engagement.

The literature on migrant second generation focused initially on their socio-economic, political and cultural integration in the host country (Alba and Nee, 1997; Bolzman, Fibbi and Vial, 2003; Crul and Vermeulen, 2003; Heckmann and Schnapper, 2003; Juhasz and Mey, 2003; Portes and Zhou, 1993). It was not until the early 2000s that the second generation's transnational relationships with the parents' home country became a focus of research (Levitt and Waters, 2002; Portes and Rumbaut, 2001). Literature specifically on the transnational ties and practices of second generation with refugee backgrounds is recent and still limited (Bloch, 2017a; Hammond, 2013; McMichael et al., 2017).

The second generation are considered less transnational than their parents who are often seen as the facilitators of transnational ties and activities for their children (Alba and Nee, 2003; Haikkola, 2011). Despite the inter-generational erosion of transnational ties and practices, it is assumed that members of the second generation still have shared behavioural characteristics on the grounds of common descent or of a common migratory background. These studies have as standpoint that the identity and sense of belonging of second generation are different to those of their peers with no migratory background and to those of their migrant parents (Levitt and Waters, 2002).

In this chapter, we add a third hypothesis exploring the specific case of children of refugees living in Switzerland. We assume that their transnational ties and practices might be different from those of other second-generation migrants because of the violence and/or trauma that their parents may have suffered and the limited rights that some will have been subjected to as asylum seekers when they arrived in the receiving country. This is a timely issue because refugees arriving in Europe have become more diverse and their number has increased significantly, since the 1960s and so their European-born children are now adults. In view of the growing number of refugee families who came, over the past decades, their precarious situation for years and the politicisation of their situation makes the analysis of the children of refugees' transnational ties and practices particularly significant. It is an important issue to study also because second generations from refugee backgrounds have the potential to contribute financially, politically, socially and culturally to development and humanitarian aid in 'countries of emigration' and push 'countries of immigration' to decrease their discriminatory 'regime of mobility' in terms of race, gender and class (see among others Glick Schiller and Salazar, 2013).

Most commonly, transnationalism is used to refer to migrants' durable ties across countries (Bauböck and Faist, 2010) implying generally their society of origin and the one of their everyday life (Glick Schiller et al., 1995) though these ties can be much wider and include a number of countries. This chapter looks at transnationalism from the specific angle of transnational ties and practices with the ancestral homeland. It examines how second generation from refugee backgrounds feel or do not feel attached to the homeland of their parents and how these perceptions and feeling affect their transnational ties and practices. We will focus on the specific case of the adult children of refugees from Vietnam, Turkey and Sri Lanka who were born in Switzerland. Switzerland offers an interesting context as its restrictive access to Swiss nationality and the correlated political rights in this country might push (second generation) migrants to keep or develop more transnational ties and practices with the ancestral homeland. Based on the principle of *jus sanguinis* access to nationality is not automatic after three generations in Switzerland and therefore descendants of migrants who did not naturalise are still recorded as foreigners. Being considered a foreigner in Switzerland might push some to seek other sources and sites of belonging.

The remainder of the chapter is in two main parts. First it reviews the literature on transnationalism among second generation. Secondly it draws on empirical research to shed light on the linkages between transnational ties and practices and the feelings and representations of adult children of refugees towards their ancestral homeland. We will show that these feelings affect all types of transnational activities and ties. Feelings of debts and loyalty, feelings of anger, feelings of otherness or feelings of being a stranger and idealisation of the ancestral homeland lead to various forms of transnational ties and practices. The comparative analysis of young people with parents who had been refugees from Turkey, Sri Lanka and Vietnam enables an understanding of the specificity of different refugee backgrounds and context on the activities of second generation.

Transnationalism among second generation from migration and refugee backgrounds

As highlighted by Bloch (2010), that whilst the bureaucratic distinctions of labour migrants and refugees do not reflect the mixed realities of displacement that are common to both categories, these constructed categories have, however, several consequences in terms of rights, which can in turn impact on transnational ties and practices given restrictions in regards to geographical mobility, family reunion, and access to the labour market and to welfare benefits. The extent and types of transnationalism will depend not only on this structural context both in the sending and settlement countries and correlated rights, but it will also be influenced at a micro- and meso-sociological level, for instance, by economic means, capabilities, the presence of the family and the form of the diaspora. All these will shape the desire and willingness to create or continue transnational ties and practices (Bloch, 2017a; Hammond, 2013; Koser, 2007; Rianõ-Alcalá and Goldring, 2014; Vickstrom and Beauchemin, 2016). The context of the initial migration, experiences of displacement and inter-generational influences will all impact on transnational activities among the second generation (Baldassar, Pyke and Ben-Moshe, 2017; Bloch, 2017b).

Most scholars agree on the multidimensionality of transnational practices among migrants (Faist, 2012; Portes, Guarnizao and Landolt, 1999; Dahinden, 2017). Transnational activities are classically categorised in three or four fields: economic, political, social-cultural (Portes, Guarnizao and Landolt, 1999) or economic, political, cultural and civil-societal (Itzigsohn et al., 1999). These classifications distinguish different levels, i.e., individual and community levels; various degrees of institutionalization of migrants' activities (from import-export activities to the involvement in an home country political cause); diverse intensity of engagement in transnational practices and along with Granovetters' (1973) classical analysis of social ties, multiple degrees of transnational ties, such as visits in the home country, distant communications, business, foreign investments and more.

The classifications produced to analyse transnational phenomenon are therefore numerous and varied, depending on who, where and how the transnationalism is considered, and depending on what is the focus, i.e., the activities, the social links, the practices, the identities or the feelings. Other categorisations of transnational activities and ties distinguish where the people focus their attention and efforts, which could be in the country of residence, in the homeland country or in a third country across international borders. Al-Ali, Black and Koser (2001) present a typology that disaggregates the broad categories of economic, political, social and cultural activities into those with a home-country focus and those with a host country focus. The historical classification into four transnational fields (economic, political, social and cultural) of practice remains, however, a major analytical framework (see among others King, Christou and Ahrens, 2011; Wessendorf, 2007). However in using three classifications, it is clear that there are important differences between generations which are linked to complex ideas of home, identity and belonging that are part of the inter-generational narrative as well as the specific experiences of the second generation.

Whilst second generation are automatically transnational, as they have 'multiple and constant interconnections across international borders' and their 'identities . . . configured in relationship to more than one nation-state' (Glick Schiller et al., 1995: 48) and benefit from both their own transnational willingness and that of their parents, they remit less than their parents, if at all (Lee, 2011, Bloch, 2017b). According to Lee (2011), this difference is not necessarily a question of quantity but of quality; second-generation migrants' transnational activities are frequently more indirect than among the first generation. For instance, rather than sending remittances directly, they might instead engage in NGO donations or fund raising or through cyber-transnationalism instead of actual visits which has created new norms of intra-diasporic relationships (Lee, 2011).

For second generation, home visits, whether voluntary or forced (Lee, 2011), are experienced in different ways; and some can separate more than link because they can emphasise the economic, social and cultural differences (Barber, 2017; Hammond, 2013). Affects and emotions play an important role in transnational motilities and return visits. McKay argues that 'emotion offers us a lens through which to theorise migrant subjectivities beyond the familiar narratives of victimization' (2007: 175). Analysing feelings, emotions and attachments in relation to long-distance social fields enables a better understanding of the process of identification, appropriation or rejection. These affects are sometimes clustered in the concept of 'emotional grammar' (Nussbaum, 2011: 149; Beatty, 2005), enabling a theorisation of transnational mobility in relation to new emotions and forms of intimacy (Mckay, 2007). Although the emotional aspect of the migration has a long history in refugee studies (Haines, Rutherford and Thomas, 1981), specific research on the intersections with transnationalism are much more recent (Brooks and Simpson, 2013; Conradson and Mckay, 2007; Jones and Jackson, 2014; Oeppen, 2013; Wise and Velayutham, 2017). In a recent account, Vathi and King (2017) discuss the various psycho-sociological implications of return for migrants and their families. It is timely to analyse further this particular aspect in regard to the specific situation of the second generation from refugee backgrounds, whose attachment to the home country may be more complex due to the exile dimension of their parents' migration (Alasuutari and Alasuutari, 2009; Binaisa, 2011; McMichael et al., 2017).

Methods and profile of the interviewees

The material which informs the empirical part of this chapter was gathered between June 2014 and October 2015 in the Geneva area of Switzerland as part of a cross-national collaborative project with colleagues who studied the same three groups, i.e., the Europe-born adult children of refugees from Sri Lanka, Turkey and Vietnam in Paris and London. The general aim of the study was to explore the lives of the children of refugees living in Europe who had diverse economic, social, cultural and religious backgrounds. A cross-national comparison of Switzerland (Geneva), France (Paris) and the United Kingdom (London) enabled us to examine the national, local, structural and contextual factors that may or may not impact on our respondents' experiences. A total of 135 qualitative interviews were conducted, 45 in each country (Bloch et al., 2015). We interviewed 76 women and 56 men, from 18 to 37 years old, born in Europe. This chapter is based on the interviews with the Switzerland-born children of refugees (30 female and 15 male).[2]

Depending of their parents' origin, the socio-economic background and context of arrival in Switzerland differed, and this can explain partly the difference between types of transnational practices and feelings toward the ancestral homelands. The Vietnamese refugees arrived in Switzerland as one of the first group of non-European refugees in a worldwide context of mobilisation for those who had left Vietnam by boat and were in camps. They benefitted from a relatively positive economic and political context in the late 1970s. The majority of the Vietnamese parents (12 out of 30) had a higher education (a post-secondary degree). In contrast, the Turkish (mostly Kurdish in our study) and the Tamil refugees arrived in Switzerland during the 1980s, when the economic context, the law and public opinion were less favourable to migrants and refugees (Mahnig, 2005). In addition, these refugees were less educated (in our sample, three Sri Lankan and four Turkish parents had a post-secondary degree) and had sometimes struggled to find jobs. Given this parental background, second-generation refugees with Turkish and Sri Lankan backgrounds suffered from more negative stereotyping and racialisation than interviewees from Vietnamese backgrounds. These stereotypes are in addition to the barriers in Switzerland for accessing Swiss nationality and the correlated political rights for all migrants and second generation.

Feelings and transnational ties with the ancestral homeland

Compared to the migration of guest workers in Switzerland – the main migration flow into the country – whose typical profile is of a male, migrating alone (Bolzman, Fibbi and Vial, 2003), many (especially those with Vietnamese background) among parents of our interviewees migrated collectively, with members of their family. This collective emphasis marks their social relations and trajectories in terms of family narratives, transnationalism, identity and belonging.

The collective Vietnamese-Swiss experience is marked by the persistence of anti-communism and opposition to the current regime in Vietnam. The collective Sri Lankan Swiss experience is marked by the civil war and discrimination of the Tamil minority, and the Kurdish-Turkish Swiss experience is also characterised by their experiences of discrimination. What these memories all have in common is the way in which they evoke the parent's country of origin in the minds of the second generation, sometimes creating ambivalent feelings ranging from indifference to nationalism (see also McMichael et al., 2017), and these affect transnational practices and ties. If the various feelings of attachment and belonging to the parents' country of origin influence the type of transnational practices and ties among the second generation, the classical socio-demographic factors such as age, gender and class also complete the explanation of the different type of transnationalism.

'Why me and not them?' – feelings of debt and loyalty to their parents' homeland

Although the connection with the country of heritage is necessarily less strong for the second generation than for their parents, who were born and raised there, the story of displacement creates a common past among the children of refugees, generating different feelings of debt and loyalty towards the country of origin of their parents and of those who stayed there. As highlighted by Reed-Danahay (2014) for Vietnamese Americans, the collective memories of the children of Vietnamese refugees reflect the politics of anti-communism associated with first-generation refugees. While the anti-communist ideology interferes with the idea of 'living together peacefully in an international community' (Werbner, 2008: 2) and 'reinforce[s an] antagonistic ideology of nationalism' among first-generation refugees (Reed-Danahay, 2014: 12), it creates a sense of unease for their children about their ancestral home. Although most of these children of refugees did not migrate themselves, many have the feeling of having deserted the country and left it in chaos. Whilst the majority had visited the country of origin, most of them developed a feeling of debt towards those who stayed.

The memories of exile affect the second generation's relationship not only with their country of heritage but also with the country of residence. Thus the common anti-communist ideology among the children of Vietnamese refugees also has consequences for their lives in Switzerland, as it appears as a backdrop to their economic ambition and actual economic success. The higher the social capital of those who fled Vietnam compared to other refugees, the welcoming reception they received in the host country (Brettell and Reed-Danahay, 2011) and the fact that some parents spoke French undoubtedly contributed to their success. The importance of the economic and professional position was a recurrent issue in our interviews, though it was sometimes described as a burden by those who did not fit the representation of the 'model minority' in which most of the community seemed caught (Espiritu, 2006; Lieu, 2011; Reed-Danahay, 2014). Similar feelings were expressed among the second generation of Kurdish origin who felt the duty to remember the history of Kurdish repression and be the messenger of the political cause in Switzerland. Even if most of them feel comfortable with their Swiss identity, they also feel obliged to mention their Kurdish origin to mediate the political cause in European countries.

> I am very proud to have Swiss nationality, to live here but I will always say that I'm Kurdish . . . since we do not have a state, it is important to mention it, otherwise nobody will mention it for us.
> (Lorîn, female, Kurdish background)

Like Lorîn, many others from Kurdish backgrounds felt an imperative to explain the origin and the situation of Kurdish people, the history of Kurdistan and the political dispute with the Turkish government. Very often, school appears to be a stage for young people to introduce and debate the political issue at the origin of their parent's exile. For instance, many of them have written academic work related to Kurdish questions.

These feelings of debt and loyalty to the ancestral homeland and the people who stayed behind there are crystallised in various forms of remittances. From a Maussian perspective (2012 [1925]), remittances can be understood as the fulfilment of (more or less important) obligations, as a counter-gift in recognition of the opportunity to have escaped suffering (Cliggett, 2003, 2005; Levitt, 1998). Through remittances, the children of refugees can show that they contribute to and care about their home communities, even though they themselves are not physically there. In our study carried out in Geneva, more than three-quarters of the families of the interviewees send or have sent remittances in the past, but their adult children – our interviewees – are less involved in this form of economic transnationalism which reflects the findings of other studies (see, for example, Crul, Schneider and Lelie, 2012; Lee, 2011). Life stage was certainly an aspect of remittance sending as more than half of those we interviewed were still students. Another reason appeared to be diversification of the form of economic participation linked to the country of origin of the parents. Indeed, with the second generation, the remittances take different forms: from classical remittances where people give money to their family (on a regular or on a more occasional basis), to other forms of economic involvement in transnational activities such as donations to charities or political organisations. This last type of remittance might more typically be sent by the children of refugees rather than by the second-generation offspring of guest workers and marks here a collective attitude in their relationship to their parents' homeland. This was the case, for instance, for Adan – a female of Kurdish background, who, with her friends, raised money for a charitable organisation to support Kurds in the city of Kobané during the conflicts with

Islamic State and, for Yâlhmani (a male of Tamil background), who mentions the tax his family paid to the Liberation Tigers of Tamil Eelam (LTTE) until 2009, after the organisation was condemned by EU as a terrorist movement in 2006.

> We are 40,000 Tamils in Switzerland [42,000 according to Moret et al., 2007]; almost everyone . . . paid the Tamil Tigers . . . you feel compelled, when you see what happened there, you came here and . . . you see in the newspapers that they [i.e., LTTE] managed to do this and that. So they were very well funded by [Tamil migrants] . . . Then they stopped . . . as it was seen as funding a terrorist movement.
>
> (Yâhlmani, male, Tamil Background)

Where the conflict in the ancestral home is on-going, transnationalism occurs through financial donations and sometimes active involvement in the political parties supporting their cause (for Kurdish people mainly the PKK) (see also Hess and Korf, 2014).

'If someone wanted to start a war to establish their democracy, I would be the first to sign!' – feelings of anger

The feelings of debt toward those left behind in a country struggling with a civil war or dictatorship is often linked with feelings of anger towards the government or the oppressing majority. Feelings of anger towards the ancestral homeland are related to experiences of oppression, violence, loss and more generally injustice. They identify the ancestral homeland as 'the location of [the] family's suffering' (Reed-Danahay, 2014: 10). All three groups, despite their different collective refugee heritage stories, expressed feelings of anger. What differed were the intensity and the transnational practices.

For those of Kurdish origin, the on-going persecution of their ethnic group in Turkey led them to be both more politically active than the other children of refugees whom we met, and to publicly defend their ethnicity, even though they no longer face any risk of persecution in the country of residence. It perpetuates the claims expressed by their parents, in both the countries of heritage and of residence, where antagonisms are also occasionally perceived.

> I can be emotional; my cousin has been murdered for his ideas and for sure, you cannot meet one Kurdish family without political related death among their relatives. Even if nobody tells you this during this interview, every family has his martyr (what they call a martyr anyway). Every family has been deeply touched by torture, it is difficult, there is a lot of emotions.
>
> (Zaraa, female, Kurdish background)

These feelings of anger towards the ancestral homeland are not only triggered by the physical torture endured there by the family but also by feeling of unjust economic loss and autonomy as mentioned by Tho, a male from a Vietnamese background.

> The communists . . . they always wanted to have control . . . They changed the currency value and implement a legislation [so] labor market earnings should be equally distributed to the people in the country . . . The problem was that my family had a shoe business . . . and it has became impossible to make it work with their new legislation because we did not have the money to buy shoes before reselling them, the government took all our cash flow.

But for some children of refugees, especially those with Kurdish and Tamil background, the feelings of debt and loyalty imply a strong and direct involvement in the political movement fighting for the rights of their oppressed people. This can occur in Switzerland, by taking part in local ethnic associations and public debate, in other European countries to protest, or in the ancestral homeland, continuing the battle that led their parents to flee. Many children of refugees participate in political transnational activities in various ways, degrees and places. Vayyam, a woman of Tamil heritage, was focussed on helping survivors of war crimes receive compensation. She saw herself within a humanitarian framework rather than as a political activist.

Rodi was actively involved with PKK, as he explained:

> When I joined the PKK, I travelled everywhere in Europe. That was what we did, we crossed borders whenever we want, it was illegal . . . With the party, I developed a whole network. When I got outside of Switzerland, I can go everywhere, I will always find a place to sleep. No need to pay a hotel! No! That's for tourists! For example, I was in Paris in 2013, when the two Kurdish women activists from PKK were murdered . . . I was out there, speaking in front of 7000 people, in front of a crowd of furious young people.
>
> (Rodi, male, Kurdish background)

Feelings of anger towards the ancestral homeland is not only related to politics and policies that caused their parents' exile. Pierre, a 30 years old male from a Vietnamese background, has never been to Vietnam, and in his interview he explained how he was not interested in Vietnamese culture or politics but he was fascinated by the military history of the war in Vietnam as part of his wider interest in military history, in Cold War novels and war video games. He has no interest in maintaining family traditions or cultural heritage. However, when asked if he would be interested in going to Vietnam, he answered that he was not particularly keen except if democracy was established, he then mentioned his thoughts on the current situation in Vietnam which tells a different story and one that is entwined with his own family history of loss and exile.

> If someone wanted to start a war to establish democracy, I would be the first to sign! I am serious! I mean it because when I see the human costs . . . One of my fathers' uncle died in a prisoner camp and a lot of people died trying to flee the country on boats.
>
> (Pierre, male, 28, Vietnamese background)

One must consider the differences in terms of attachment and engagement among the second generation to people, community and place and the anger toward the central government, the state and the institutions and agents of the state such as the police that has persecuted their parents; these differences result in mixed and complex emotions among the second generation.

Feeling a 'foreigner in the homeland of my parents'

Return visits could often evoke mixed and complex emotional responses, which included a separation between those who had remained and those who had left (McMichael et al., 2017; Vathi and King, 2017). The economic difference between 'here' and 'there' was felt acutely and according to Xuan Thu, when he returned to Vietnam it made him feel like 'a wallet with legs', which necessarily truncates the authenticity of the relationships there. This feeling of distance is as much self-perceived as it is reflected by 'others', even by those from the same family. In other words, they feel that they are perceived as foreigners. Sometimes this otherness is so strong that the children of refugees do not feel that they have any control over it or are able to hide it or decrease its importance. It takes place everywhere, embodied by the slightest gesture, word or behaviour. Even the way they speak sounds different: 'They can hear we have a French accent, so it makes them laugh to death each time' (Qûyen, female, Vietnamese background). Children of refugees also mention different mindsets: 'We think differently and have another way of acting . . . we learnt different things' (Cihan, female, Kurdish background).

The impossibility of feeling 'at home' in the homeland of their parents comes from these second-generation from refugee backgrounds having lived their entire life in Switzerland. But this cannot be the only explanation. Previous studies demonstrate cases of the children of migrants who idealised their parents' homeland – a minority even dream of a 'return' there (see, for instance, Christou, 2006 on Greeks from North America; Goulbourne et al., 2010 on Caribbeans from Britain; Wessendorf, 2007 on Italians from Switzerland). They speak of a 'return' even if technically it is not the case as the 'second generation' were by definition born elsewhere. However, once the idealisation turns into reality and the 'return' concrete, the experiences are often described in the literature in a more negative than positive way, as shown for instance by King and Christou (2014) about second-generation Greek-Germans and Greek-Americans 'returning' to live in Greece. None of the children of refugees we met seriously envisage going to live permanently in their parents' homeland. Unlike the second generation of European migrant workers whose country of origin is democratic and has known an economic adjustment over the past generation, children of refugees from Turkey, Sri Lanka or Vietnam have political (Tamil and Kurds are still persecuted in Sri Lanka and Turkey) or economic (Vietnam, Sri Lanka and east Turkey are still developing regions) reasons not to 'return' to their parents' country of origin.

Whilst the children of refugees, unlike their parents, do not necessary attribute their lack of connection to their ancestral homeland 'to its having been the location of [the] family's suffering' (Reed-Danahay, 2014: 10), they feel uncomfortable there, where they feel that they are automatically labelled a foreigner, a child of immigrants, despised, a 'wallet on legs', or a deserter of the homeland. In this context, they feel that they constantly have to prove their belonging and loyalty to the country of origin of their parents, as mentioned by Sibel, 'We have always to justify our identity [when in the homeland of their parents], we have always a label, we have to endorse a label' (female, Kurdish background). Their common memories of exile lead to antagonist feelings towards the ancestral homeland – anti-communism for the Vietnamese, anti-Turkish policy to counter their ethnic persecution and the denial of an autonomous state for the Kurds, and anti-Singhalese policy for Tamils not only concerning their ethnic persecution but also because of their economic deprivation in Sri Lanka.

All this influences their vision of the ancestral homeland and their ability to return as 'fully cosmopolitan subjects', i.e., open 'to different cultural experiences' (Hannerz, 1990: 239). As also argued by Reed-Danahay (2014) about the American Vietnamese, these antagonist views of the ancestral homeland create forms of anti-cosmopolitanism, as defined, *inter alia*, by Tremon (2009: 105): this antagonism limits their ability to formulate several simultaneous allegiances and to '"juggl[e]" different possible identifications, which allows the cosmopolitan to maximise (economic, political, social) benefits by exploiting power differentials'.

'The happiness itself was there' – idealisation of the country of origin

Opposite to the feelings of foreignness, the idealisation of the country of origin is a classical theme when it comes to the study of the relationship between immigrants and their home country. Among our sample, these feelings of idealisation may also be strong for some children of refugees. The idealisation of the country of origin is mostly made at the smallest scales: the village, grandma's house, the beach, etc., are idyllic but not the country. The favourite object of idealisation are the social relations, family relations (especially the place of old people in the society) and the nature, both thought of as more authentic in the country of origin compared to the one in Switzerland or other European countries which have been 'corrupted'. Among our interviewees the idealisation of the country of origin is stronger for the small number of those who started their lives there and arrived in Switzerland as young children. The example of Rodi, who arrived in Switzerland when he was seven, provides a good example.

> When we are in a village here [in Switzerland], the smell is not the same. So many chemical products have been spread in the nature . . . For example, I do not eat fruits here . . . But when I was spending holidays home, in Kurdistan, then, yes, I relived, I was vivified fully! For sure, they do not have a lot of material things, but the happiness itself was there because that particular smell of nature was there too! When you walk through the garden, you could smell, you could hear the birds singing, everything! . . . Through ages, this connection with nature has been written in our DNA.
>
> (Rodi, male, Kurdish Background)

For Piraï, the idealisation of the homeland of her parents is related to feeling of loss brought by the exile as in Switzerland they live in a small apartment and on social assistance whereas life in Sri Lanka looked better.

> In Sri Lanka, most people say that we live a nice life here in Europe, but I think it is the opposite! . . . Here, we live in small apartment, always inside but there it is totally different, they have big house with garden, they can live outside, enjoy the fresh air . . . Here, we must go outside of our home to do this, go to a park or else. They do not understand this . . . My parents live on social assistance and people in Sri Lanka still think we earn a lot of money, but really they have a better life than we do!.
>
> (Piraï, female, Sri Lankan background)

In this case the idealisation of the ancestral homeland is also linked to the circumstances in Switzerland so comparisons of the past with the present can result in seeing the ancestral country in a positive way.

Detachment

Feelings of detachment among children of refugees towards their country of origin are rare. Some children from Vietnamese background whose parents have a higher level of education and who never visited Vietnam have expressed partial feelings of detachment. Truc Linh, for example, has no desire to visit Vietnam.

> I have never been to Vietnam! But it is difficult because what we would like to see is the Vietnam of our parents, the one they described in their stories. The country has changed a lot, as everyone says. It is not anymore the Vietnam that my parents knew. Even them, now, they do not look Vietnamese. So, I do not really feel the necessity to go there.
>
> (Truc Linh, female, Vietnamese background)

Truc Linh's social network is in Switzerland and is not Vietnamese although she is, nevertheless, involved in diverse activities like charity and action to promote the memory of Vietnamese refugees in Switzerland and to contribute to the positive perception of this community in Switzerland. She has however become critical of the Vietnamese community.

> Outside of Geneva . . . Vietnamese people are less integrated, they behave more 'cliché', they have a stronger Vietnamese accent, they even look more Asian. My parents explain it by the habit to stay among Vietnamese people, eat only Vietnamese food, then they are not so tall.
> (Truc Linh, female, Vietnamese background)

Her point of view seems to be linked with the desire to stress her social situation, to distance herself from poorer economic and social conditions of 'regular' people outside of the metropolis from Vietnamese backgrounds. Her interest in Vietnamese affairs in Switzerland seems to be both a social duty linked to her privileged social status and part of a domination process.

Detachment seems correlated to a weaker involvement in community associations and a higher social and economic status in Switzerland as well as rare or no visits to the ancestral homeland and no family left there. These attitudes were more expressed by children of refugees with a Vietnamese background than those with a Kurdish and Tamil heritage who make frequent visits to their ancestral homeland and still have family there.

Conclusion

Transnational practices and ties, but also feelings of belonging and identity of the children of refugees, contrasts with both that of their parents and those of the second generation of migrant workers in Switzerland. While their parents have direct experience of flight and migration as well as the need to rebuild a whole life (work, housing, social relations) in Switzerland, the second generation grew up and were educated there. This means that they have developed stronger feelings of belonging in Switzerland but that does not mean that they are void of complex feelings about their parent's country of birth or are not engaged in transnational activities both within Switzerland pertaining to the ancestral home or more directly through economic, political, social and cultural activities. Whilst the data presented confirms the idea that second generation remit less in a direct way and have fewer transnational ties than their parents, it also shows that their transnationalism is more diverse. Whereas the first generations' transnational practices consist mainly in home visits, contacts with the family and remittances, the second generation make humanitarian and charitable donations, are politically involved and/ or maintain links with family in third countries, for example. In contrast to the second generation of migrant workers in Switzerland (Wessendorf, 2007), second generation from refugee backgrounds have less opportunity to travel to their parents' home country because of the distance and express no wish to 'return' permanently.

The fear about transnationalism historically was that it represents a barrier to integration in the residence country (Amelina and Faist, 2008; Dekker and Siegel, 2013; Haller and Landolt, 2005; Levitt and Waters, 2002; Louie, 2006). Whilst it is largely agreed that integration and stability help (the first-generation) migrants' transnational ties to develop overtime (Kasinitz et al., 2008; Portes, Haller and Guarnizo, 2002), it is expected that these ties and practices will disappear or are eroded from one generation to another (Alba and Nee, 2003). However, this is not the case, it is not so much eroded but different. Moreover, transnationalism and integration seem to be completely compatible among the second generation from refugee backgrounds in Switzerland. Nevertheless it seems that a higher level of education and incomes is correlated to less direct transnational practices and ties. The fact that our interviewees have succeeded at school and that they manage (or will manage) to have a better socio-economic situation than their parents may partly explain the shift in involvement from transnational direct involvement (such as travel, remittances to the family) to indirect involvement (such as donations to charity, humanitarian and political involvement in the residence country).

As already well described in previous literature, we also found that second generation have also mixed feelings towards the ancestral homeland. The gap they experienced between imagination and reality creates various forms of belongings to the ancestral homeland. As also argued by McMichael et al. (2017: 395), the discomfort related to these mixed feelings and experiences of not fitting in, is not necessarily negative as it can lead to more 'reflexivity' and supports 'new narratives of identity'. Finally we showed that these mixed feelings towards the ancestral homeland impact on the types of transnational activities and ties, reinforcing in turn the distance towards the ancestral homeland and underlining the inter-generational dimension of transnationalism; however, as argued, both sending and settlement countries should see an interest in supporting transnationalism as a tool for development and humanitarian aid as well as a driving force for integration.

Notes

1 We use the term 'second generation' although it is a marker of exclusion which underlines the fact that these young people are not seen as belonging to the country in which they were born and grew up or are even still perceived as foreigners and sometimes discriminated against on those grounds. However this category is useful to describe the social construction of a common experience.
2 The study on which this paper draws has been funded by the Swiss Network for International Studies. The study was part of a collaborative research project conducted in Geneva, London and Paris between June 2014 and December 2015 by Alice Bloch (University of Manchester), Milena Chimienti, Anne-Laure Counilh, Shirin Hirsch (University of Manchester), Giovanna Tattolo (CERI, Sciences Po Paris), Laurence Ossipow and Catherine Withol de Wenden (CERI, Sciences Po Paris). We thank all the participants in the study.

Bibliography

Al-Ali N, Black R, and Koser K (2001) Refugees and transnationalism: The experience of Bosnians and Eritreans in Europe. *Journal of Ethnic and Migration Studies* 27(4): 615–634.

Alasuutari P, Alasuutari M (2009) Narration and ritual formation of diasporic identity: The case of second generation Karelian evacuees. *Identities* 16(3): 321–341.

Alba R, Nee V (1997) Rethinking assimilation theory for a new era of immigration. *International Migration Review* 31(4): 826–874.

Alba R, Nee V (2003) *Remaking the American Mainstream: Assimilation and Contemporary Immigration*. Cambridge, MA: Havard University Press.

Amelina A, Faist T (2008) Turkish migrant associations in Germany: Between integration pressure and transnational linkages. *Revue Européenne des Migrations Internationales* 24(2): 91–120.

Baldassar L, Pyke J, and Ben-Moshe D (2017) The Vietnamese in Australia: Diaspora identity, intra-group tensions, transnational ties and 'victim' status. *Journal of Ethnic and Migration Studies* 43(6): 937–955.

Barber T (2017) Achieving ethnic authenticity through 'return' visits to Vietnam: Paradoxes of class and gender among the British-born Vietnamese. *Journal of Ethnic and Migration Studies* 43(6): 919–936.

Bauböck R, Faist T (eds) (2010) *Diaspora and Transnationalism: Concepts, Theories and Methods*. IMISCOE research, Amsterdam: Amsterdam University Press.

Beatty A (2005) Emotions in the field: What are we talking about? *Journal of the Royal Anthropological Institute* 11(1): 17–37.

Binaisa N (2011) Negotiating 'belonging' to the ancestral 'homeland': Ugandan refugee descendents 'return'. *Mobilities* 6(4): 519–534.

Bloch A (2010) The right to rights? Undocumented migrants from Zimbabwe living in South Africa. *Sociology* 44(2): 233–250.

Bloch A (2017a) Transnationalism and the state: Recurring themes and new directions. *Ethnic and Racial Studies* 40(9): 1508–1519.

Bloch A (2017b) Inter-generational transnationalism: The impact of refugee backgrounds on second generation. Keynote lecture, *World on the Move: Migration, Societies and Change*, Migration Lab conference, University of Manchester, Manchester. 30 October–2 November 2017.

Bloch A, Chimienti, C, Counilh, A-L, Hirsch, S, Tattolo, G, Ossipow L, et al (2015) *The Children of Refugees in Europe*. Final Report. Geneva: SNIS. Accessible au lien suivant. Available at: www.snis.ch/multimedia/files.

Bloch A, Neal S, and Solomos J (2013) *Race, Multiculture and Social Policy*. Houndmills, Basingstoke and Hampshire: Palgrave Macmillan.

Bolzman C, Fibbi R, and Vial M (2003) *Secondas, Secondos. Le Processus d'Intégration des Jeunes Adultes Issus de la Migration Espagnole et Italienne en Suisse*. Zurich: Seismo.

Brettell C, Reed-Danahay D (2011) *Civic Engagements: The Citizenship Practices of Indian and Vietnamese immigrants*. Stanford, CA: Stanford University Press.

Brooks A, Simpson R (2013) *Emotions in Transmigration: Transformation, Movement and Identity*. Basingstoke and New York: Palgrave Macmillan.

Christou A (2006) American dreams and European nightmares: Experiences and polemics of second-generation Greek-American returning migrants. *Journal of Ethnic and Migration Studies* 32(5): 831–845.

Cliggett L (2003) Gift remitting and alliance building in Zambian modernity: Old answers to modern problems. *American Anthropologist* 105(3): 543–552.

Cliggett L (2005) Remitting the gift: Zambian mobility and anthropological insights for migration studies. *Population, Space and Place* 11(1): 35–48.

Conradson D, Mckay D (2007) Translocal subjectivities: Mobility, connection, emotion. *Mobilities* 2(2): 167–174.

Crul M, Schneider J, and Lelie F (2012) *The European Second Generation Compared: Does the Integration Context Matter?* Amsterdam: Amsterdam University Press.

Crul M, Vermeulen H (2003) The future of the second generation: The integration of migrant youth in six European countries. *International Migration Review* 37(4): 965–985.

Dahinden D (2017) Transnationalism reloaded: The historical trajectory of a concept. *Ethnic and Racial Studies* 40(9): 1474–1485.

Dekker B, Siegel M (2013) *Transnationalism and Integration: Complements or Substitutes?* Maastricht, The Netherlands: Maastricht Graduate School of Governance.

Espiritu YL (2006) Toward a critical refugee study: The Vietnamese refugee subject in US scholarship. *Journal of Vietnamese Studies* 1(1–2): 410–433.

Faist T (2012) Toward a transnational methodology: Methodology to address methodological nationalism, essentialism, and positionality. *Revue Européenne de Migrations Internationales* 28(1): 51–70.

Glick Schiller N, Basch L, and Blanc-Szanton C (1995) From immigrant to transmigrant: Theorizing transnational migration. *Anthropological Quarterly* 68(1): 48–63.

Glick Schiller N, Salazar NB (2013) Regimes of mobility across the globe. *Journal of Ethnic and Migration Studies* 39(2): 183–200.

Goulbourne H, Reynolds T, Solomos J, and Zontini E (eds) (2010) *Transnational Families: Ethnicities, Identities and Social Capital*. Abingdon: Routledge.

Haikkola L (2011) Making connections: Second-generation children and the transnational field of relations. *Journal of Ethnic and Migration Studies* 37(8): 1201–1217.

Haines D, Rutherford D, Thomas P (1981) Family and community among Vietnamese refugees. *International Migration Review* 15(1/2): 310–319.

Haller W, Landolt P (2005) The transnational dimensions of identity formation: Adult children of immigrants in Miami. *Ethnic and Racial Studies* 28(6): 1182–1214.

Hammond L (2013) Somali transnational activism and integration in the UK: Mutually supporting strategies. *Journal of Ethnic and Migration Studies* 39(6): 1001–1017.

Hannerz U (1990) Cosmopolitans and locals in world culture. *Theory, Culture & Society* 7(2–3): 237–251.

Heckmann F, Schnapper D (eds) (2003) *The Integration of Immigrants in European Societies: National Differences and Trends of Convergence*. Stuttgart: Lucius & Lucius.

Hess M, Korf B (2014) Tamil diaspora and the political spaces of second-generation activism in Switzerland. *Global Networks* 14(4): 419–437.

Itzigsohn J, Cabral CD, Medina EH, and Vazquez O (1999) Mapping Dominican transnationalism: Narrow and broad transnational practices. *Ethnic and Racial Studies* 22(2): 316–339.

Jones H, Jackson E (eds) (2014) *Stories of Cosmopolitan Belonging: Emotion and Location*. Abingdon: Routledge.

Juhasz A, Mey E (2003) *Die zweite Generation : Etablierte oder Aussenseiter? Biographien von Jugendlichen ausländischer Herkunft*. Wiesbaden: Westdeutscher Verlag.

Kasinitz P, Mollenkopf JH, Waters MC, and Holdaway J (2008) *Inheriting the City: The Children of Immigrants Come of Age*. New York and Cambridge, MA: Russell Sage Foundation and Harvard University Press.

King R, Christou A (2014) Second-generation "return" to Greece: New dynamics of transnationalism and integration. *International Migration* 52(6): 85–99.

King R, Christou A, and Ahrens J (2011) Diverse mobilities: Second-generation Greek-Germans engage with the homeland as children and as adults. *Mobilities* 6(4): 483–501.

Koser K (2007) Refugees, transnationalism and the state. *Journal of Ethnic and Migration Studies* 33(2): 233–254.

Lee H (2011) Rethinking transnationalism through the second generation. *The Australian Journal of Anthropology* 22(3): 295–313.

Levitt P (1998) social remittances: Migration driven local-level forms of cultural diffusion. *International Migration Review* 32(4): 926–948.

Levitt P, Waters MC (eds) (2002) *The Changing Face of Home: The Transnational Lives of the Second Generation*. New York: Russell Sage Foundation.

Lieu NT (2011) *The American Dream in Vietnamese*. Minneapolis, MN: University of Minnesota Press.

Louie V (2006) Growing up ethnic in transnational worlds: Identities among second-generation Chinese and Dominicans. *Identities* 13(3): 363–394.

Mahnig H (ed) (2005) *Histoire de la Politique de Migration, d'Asile et d'Intégration en Suisse Sepuis 1948*. Zurich: Seismo.

Mauss M (1896/1897–1924/1925) Essai sur le don : Forme et raison de l'échange dans les sociétés archaïques. *L'Année Sociologique* 1(1923–1924): 30–186.

Mckay D (2007) 'Sending dollars shows feeling' – emotions and economies in Filipino migration. *Mobilities* 2(2): 175–194.

McMichael C, Nunn C, Gifford S, and Correa-Velez I (2017) Return visits and belonging to countries of origin among young people from refugee backgrounds. *Global Networks* 17(3): 382–399.

Moret J, Efionayi D, Stants F (2007) *Diaspora sri lankaise en Suisse*. Berne-Wabern: Office federal des migrations (ODM).

Nussbaum M (2011) *Upheavals of Thought: The Intelligence of Emotions*. Cambridge: Cambridge University Press.

Oeppen C (2013) A stranger at 'home': Interactions between transnational return visits and integration for Afghan-American professional. *Global Networks* 13(2): 261–278.

Portes A, Guarnizao L, and Landolt P (1999) The study of transnationalism: Pitfalls and promise of an emergent research field. *Ethnic and Racial Studies* 22(2): 217–237.

Portes A, Haller W, and Guarnizo LE (2002) Transnational entrepreneurs: An alternative form of immigrant economic adaptation. *American Sociological Review* 67(2): 278–298.

Portes A, Rumbaut RG (2001) *Legacies: The Story of the Immigrant Second Generation*. Berkeley: University of California Press.

Portes A, Zhou M (1993) The new second generation: Segmented assimilation and its variants. *The Annals of the American Academy of Political and Social Science* 530(1): 74–96.

Reed-Danahay D (2014) 'Like a foreigner in my own homeland': Writing the dilemmas of return in the Vietnamese American diaspora. *Identities* 22(5): 603–618.

Riaño-Alcalá P, Goldring L (2014) Unpacking refugee community transnational organizing: The challenges and diverse experiences of Colombians in Canada. *Refugee Survey Quarterly* 33(2): 84–111.

Sommerville K (2008) Transnational belonging among second generation youth: Identity in a globalized world. *Journal of Social Sciences* 10: 23–33.

Tamaki E (2011) Transnational home engagement among Latino and Asian Americans: Resources and motivation, transnational home engagement. *International Migration Review* 45(1): 148–173.

Tremon A-C (2009) Cosmopolitanization and localization: Ethnicity, class and citizenship among the Chinese of French Polynesia. *Anthropological Theory* 9(1): 103–126.

Vathi Z, King R (eds) (2017) *Return Migration and Psychological Wellbeing: Discourses, Policy-Making and Outcomes for Migrants and their Families*. London: Routldege.

Vickstrom ER, Beauchemin C (2016) Irregular status, territorial confinement, and blocked transnationalism: Legal constraints on circulation and remittances of Senegalese migrants in France, Italy, and Spain. *Comparative Migration Studies* 4(1).

Werbner P (ed) (2008) *Anthropology and the New Cosmopolitanism: Rooted, Feminist, and Vernacular Perspectives*. Oxford: Berg.

Wessendorf S (2007) 'Roots migrants': Transnationalism and 'return' among second-generation Italians in Switzerland. *Journal of Ethnic and Migration Studies* 33(7): 1083–1102.

Wise A, Velayutham S (2017) Transnational affect and emotion in migration research. *International Journal of Sociology* 47(2): 116–130.

Chapter 10

Reflecting on the past, thinking about the future

Forced migration in the 21st century

Giorgia Donà and Alice Bloch

Introduction

The chapters in this book have shown that there is an increased discrepancy between the realities of forced migrants and the language, legal frameworks and strategies that continue to be adopted to understand and respond to involuntary movements. While the chapters in the book do not offer explicit solutions, they do highlight the gaps and limitations of the current theoretical and policy frameworks and offer suggestions for change that might better engage with the realities of the 21st century. The chapters demonstrate the power of states, particularly those in the global north, but that power goes hand in hand with micro-level agency, solidarity and resilience, all of which can emerge and be cultivated in the most unlikely of circumstances.

Durable solutions: a tired paradigm

Chapters in the book highlight the discrepancy between the complex reality on the ground and the stasis of durable solutions: local integration, resettlement and repatriation. The empirical work in each chapter shows that forced migration is increasingly complex and that the dynamics of movements are fast changing. Yet, while refugee flows are increasingly complex, the solutions remain unchanged or similar to those adopted decades ago in a different era. This discrepancy is most evident in the continuing prominence of the rhetoric of permanent solutions: the same three solutions have been a central part of UNHCR's mandate since its inception in the post World War II period. It is clear that these durable solutions, local integration, resettlement and repatriation, certainly in the ways in which they are currently being executed, fall short of addressing the global refugee crises and demonstrate how state agendas act as barriers to solutions. For example, rather than local integration taking place, it is nation-state agendas of containment, border controls and security that keep refugees in camps and discourage or prevent local integration. The use of camps has a long history. In the post-war (1945) period, the Palestinian case is the most obvious example of a protracted refugee situation without local integration. Generations of Palestinians have been born, lived and died within refugee camps without the chance for integration into the society of residence and often without citizenship, rights or access to the labour market.

As the chapter by Hyndman and Giles has shown, camps are places that contain and keep people alive but do not offer the freedoms of economic, social, political and civil engagement in wider communities and societies. As well as protracted situations new camps are also emerging on what seems to be a regular basis. Most recently this includes camps in Turkey, Jordan, Bangladesh, the Greek island of Lesbos and France. Camps are clearly anything but a temporary solution. However, as Landau shows in Chapter 7, the rising awareness of and concerns about refugees in urban areas, some of whom are undocumented or certainly not in the asylum and refugee system, show a new type of informal local integration. It is in these new environments that we see refugees' agency and where choices are made to disappear in cities and to make a go of life outside of the constraints and containment of the bureaucratic systems, their labels and processes. However, because this type of refugee residence is often not made official, forced migrants continue to live in a condition of official invisibility and limbo, which again shows the discrepancy between top-down solutions and bottom-up resolutions.

Alongside local integration, another durable solution continuously exposed as inadequate is refugee resettlement. Part of the problem is that the numbers needing to be resettled far exceed the resettlement schemes. As we noted in the opening chapter of this book, less than 200,000 refugees were resettled in 2016 globally. States resist resettling refugees in anywhere near the numbers that would make a tangible difference to the numbers waiting to be resettled. Even where moments of apparent humanity are evident, for example, Germany's acceptance of refugees in the summer of 2015, the motives were not purely humanitarian, instead they also reflected changing demographics and the need for migrants to fill the shortages caused by ageing populations and declining birth rates (Castles, 2013). While Germany opened its doors in the summer of 2015. the responses to these new arrivals have been mixed and the warm welcome and formation of new friendships has been juxtaposed with racism, hostility and violence (Häberlen, 2016). The consequence in Germany has been a retreat away from openness to hotspots, deportation and the provision of financial aid to tackle smuggling. The poor federal election result for German Chancellor Angela Merkel, in the autumn of 2017, was attributed largely to her open policy towards Syrian refugees arriving in Europe.

The final durable solution is repatriation; more than 500,000 people were returned to the country from which they sought asylum in 2016 with the majority returned to Afghanistan. Return is not always voluntary but instead forced and in some cases includes non-refoulement, which is the return to countries where people fear persecution and on occasions the consequences can be imprisonment and/or death. Majidi and Schuster's chapter in this volume shows the forced nature of return and it demonstrates the impact of return. Return is clearly not a durable solution in many cases, as some returnees can and do simply leave again creating a constant strategy of mobility where the objective is to evade state authorities as new destinations are sought or old ones returned to (Schuster, 2011). In short, just because refugees are returned, it does not mean that they will stay especially where they fear persecution, where there are no economic opportunities and where they feel stigmatised due to perceptions of failure (Schuster and Majidi, 2015).

The limitations of durable solutions have become so clear that the UN Member States adopted the 'New York Declaration for Refugees and Migrants', in September 2016 and at the time of writing are consulting on the proposed Global Compact on Refugees. The Declaration sets out to develop a Comprehensive Refugee Response Framework, which contains a number of commitments as well as plans for building on the stated commitments. The commitments include protecting the human rights of all migrants. This commitment in itself is significant given that so few states – and no countries of the global north or west – have signed or ratified the already existing 1990 *International Convention on the Protection of the Rights of All Migrant Workers and Members of Their Families*. Other areas included in the Declaration are children's rights, responses to sexual- and gender-based violence, support for countries hosting large number of refugees, increasing resettlement opportunities and the support of a global campaign to condemn xenophobia. One key part of the strategy is a more equitable global approach to hosting and supporting the world's refugees. Of course, these are not novel ideas; the struggle will be to persuade governments to actually act on them in order to address the current global situation, which share similarities with previous eras but also differences due to political transformations, security and race and racialization.

Modern constructions: continuity and change

This book has captured existing continuities and discontinuities in histories and the experiences of forced migrants that unfold in global and local landscapes. The chapters highlight shifting refugees' geo-political significance, and its impact on processes of inclusion/exclusion and access to rights. Since World War II, refugees have been political subjects but the configuration of the political has changed. During the Cold War period, refugees had ideological and political value and were constructed as racialised, gendered and political subjects – that is 'white, male and anti-communist' (Chimni, 1998: 351). In Chapter 3 Banerjee and Samaddar map the continuities and discontinuities of the post-colonial forced migrant, which are being informed by a strong sense of history, awareness of the distinct nature of post-colonial politics and society and an appreciation of the migrant and the refugee appearing as the subject of history.

During the Cold War, the departure of refugees weakened the power of the (communist) ideologies in their countries of origin while strengthening those of the (western democratic) countries who welcomed them. As the Cold War came to an end, refugees started to arrive in the global north from developing countries in the global south. These new refugees did not fit the post–World War II Cold War construction and so, argued Chimni, the result was a paradigm shift to 'restrictive measures' and 'the non-entrée regime' (1998: 351).

In the historic transformations of the last few decades from the Cold War to the War on Terror and the New Wars that are emerging, refugees' geo-political significance has shifted. The War on Terror has generated a worrying perception that equates seeking refuge with being a potential terrorist threat. In December 2017, the Supreme Court ruled that Trump's executive order halting refugee admissions and temporarily barring people from six Muslim-majority countries and two others could be immediately imposed. The countries include Syria, Iran, Somalia and Yemen, where repression and violence continue, leaving refugees in flight and those who have family members in the United States unable to join them because of the perception that they are a threat. The problematic conflation of *refugee* with *terrorist* means that resettlement has changed from being the preferred durable solution to becoming the least preferred and sometimes impossible answer to the plight of millions of individuals fleeing conflicts. Globally, refugees are political in ways that reinforce global divisions between citizens and non-citizens, insiders and outsiders and those who are desirable and wanted and those who are unwanted and need to be prevented from entering the nation-state (Anderson, 2013).

The chapters in the book highlight the politics of inclusion and exclusion that are played out and monitored through physical and increasingly techno-bureaucratic borders. Donà and Godin expose the tensions between inclusion in networked globalised spaces and exclusion at the borders of nation-states. In a globalised world physical, administrative and discursive borders exist in tension with globalised and networked societies. Walls and border guards are physical embodiments of existing borders. Everyday bordering practices are constantly expanded to restrict access for some and contain them inside physical locations like camps and islands as well as social and bureaucratic spaces differentiating citizens and non-citizens. While modalities of inclusion and exclusion are not new, we see the increased relevance of borderscapes – interlocking physical, social, bureaucratic and discursive spaces- as core sites of inclusion and exclusion where forced migrants' opportunities to claim equal access to rights are increasingly limited. At the margins of the state, islands are natural spaces of isolation and exclusion. It is not accidental that they are borderscapes of contestation, peripheral places of power to the core site of government power, and where the unwanted can be relegated. However, the measures that governments use to contain, restrict and exclude are only partially successful. Regardless of the measures to increase the robustness of borders, they remain permeable but the costs are high both in terms of life and economically.

The emergence of new categories of refugees to be excluded and contained in a shifting geo-political context continues to be framed through an imperialist and post-colonial lens where race and racialization take centre stage but so too does gender where women are vulnerable or infantilised and men are threatening or emasculated (Jaji, 2009; Schuster, 2011; Griffiths, 2015). Responses to new forms of refugee movements are increasingly out of the touch with the complex contemporary realities. Of course the new type of refugee is not new, nor is the response of the global north who host such a tiny proportion of the global refugee population. However, even within the context of these small numbers who make their way to the most developed countries, refugees have become the embodiment of the 'other' to be excluded, labelled as undeserving, removed or relegated to borderscapes and where being male is constructed as dangerous.

Another way in which refugees are now constructed and reframed also links to their economic utility as workers and as such value is placed on their usefulness within the neo-liberal framework. However, this relationship is ambivalent because, on the one hand, refugees must be economically useful, but on the other hand they are excluded from economic engagement in camps and by government policies during asylum determination procedures forcing them into a lack of productivity and of dependency on the state, charity or the good will of others. One of the objectives of the New York Declaration is to 'strengthen the positive contributions made by migrants to economic and social development in their host countries' (United Nations, 2016). This is, of course, nothing new; historically much has been made of the successes of refugees and their attractiveness is based on their skills and value as workers but a model that links refugees with economic utility has, in effect, turned refugees into economic objects. No longer is a refugee a person who is persecuted and requires protection.

By working, refugees are, of course, contributing to local economies but more importantly employment can offer independence, self-esteem and opportunities to develop social networks. Employment can also challenge traditional gender roles and empower women who might otherwise have remained economically inactive (Nawyn, Reosti and Gjokaj, 2009). It is an impossible situation. Refugees are constructed as the neo-liberal subject, on the one hand, and vilified and repelled, on the other, for being dependent or requiring welfare assistance or humanitarian aid. The binary construction of the 'good' versus 'bad' forced migrant places individuals into value-laden stereotypes, informed by economic, political and/or security agendas, imposed from the top. These simplistic images do not match the complex reality on the ground. Of course, constructing refugees in certain ways – political, economic, deserving, undeserving, a threat, an asset, a burden, a responsibility, etc. – is not a recent phenomenon, it is the constructions that have varied across time and space. The chapters in the book have captured existing continuities and discontinuities in histories, experiences and constructions that unfold in the global and local landscapes. Above, we noted the juxtaposition between the refugee as the neo-liberal subject contributing economically and their forced dependency as a consequence of exclusion and containment. In the next section, we discuss another contemporary experience of forced migration, namely the increased precarity of status and experience, which is caused and reinforced by a reconfigured (hierarchical) welfare/crisis system.

Welfare, crisis and precarity

The links between immigration, welfare and politics have a long history, and these are played out in different ways in different contexts: from crisis management and humanitarian interventions to a more calculated curtailment of welfare provision in countries which traditionally had developed welfare states where new hierarchies of entitlement link closely to the thesis of insider/outsider or citizen and non-citizen (Sales, 2007; Anderson, 2013). The historic construction of refugees as victims, therefore dependent and warranting care, during the Cold War period, was as much led by compassion as by political expediency. After the Cold War, when the political climate changed, more asylum seekers arrived in Europe. As the financial costs grew, the construction of the *refugee* also changed with a new divisions merging between deserving and undeserving and genuine and bogus. Reductions in welfare linked to these constructions were central to policy (Bloch and Schuster, 2002; Sales, 2007).

However, many countries do not have developed welfare systems or indeed any formal welfare provision and in these contexts informal systems of community organisations, charities and places of worship have always been evident operating side by side with international humanitarian agencies and/or UNHCR (Bloch and Schuster, 2002; Jaji, 2009) offering food and sometimes shelter. The chapter by Voutira on informal hospitality and Landau's analysis of urban livelihoods offer examples of what Sitaropoulos (2002) described as a 'responsibility-shifting paradigm'. Added to this is another layer, the remittances sent by refugees to family and sometimes friends and communities. It is these remittances that do so much of the work in supporting displaced people in camps and cities mostly, though not exclusively, in the global south. The research on remittances shows a mix of the pressure, the obligations and the desire to help and support but most of all their significance as part of the support infrastructure (Lindley, 2010). Moreover it also demonstrates the role of the second generation from refugee backgrounds contributing to the family pool of remittances (Hammond, 2013). The chapter by Chimienti, Counilh and Ossipow shows that among the second generation, there is much diversity in terms of transnational engagement and little evidence of remittance sending. This diversity among second generation links to the circumstances of their parent's displacement and their engagement in transnational activities which are part of inter-generational transmission.

Statutory support for forced migrants is piecemeal and lacking in co-ordination where agendas can dictate provisions and outrage can influence interventions. The reconfiguration from welfare to crisis impacts on the lives of forced migrants because it determines their rights and can transform their experiences. While refugees have most of the rights associated with citizenship, others in the displacement spectrum do not. Fewer forced migrants are granted access to asylum and Convention refugee status than in the past (Gibney and Hansen, 2005). Arriving in Europe or Australia does not guarantee access to asylum procedures. In Australia, access depends on mode of arrival where those who arrive by boat are immediately denied the opportunity to seek asylum and strategies such as 'tow backs' and removal to off-shore island detention centres ensure removal, separation and containment (Mountz, 2011). In Europe bureaucratic systems are not fit for purpose. Even getting into the system can be impossibly difficult (Schuster, 2011): the inability of countries to process the large numbers of people arriving by boat on islands in Greece and Italy have exposed the lack of the infrastructure and resources dedicated to ensuring access to asylum procedures and appropriate reception conditions. Images of people walking from south to north and east to west in Europe reveal the problems with the Common European Asylum System. The system is not common or equal and the new border fences to block and contain evoke much more sinister images of Europe's past of the mass displacement, of genocides, and of divisions between east and west.

The chapters in the book have shown that the experiences of asylum seekers and refugees have shifted from a state of relatively safety to precarity including the threat and reality of forced return, explored by Majidi and Schuster in Chapter 6. Not being able to make an asylum claim or waiting for a determination on an asylum application, wandering across Europe without rights, contained and waiting in limbo are some of the ways in which precarity exists in the everyday lives of asylum seekers. Precarity comprises of many factors depending on the geographical context and can include economic, social and psychological dimensions, or the general precarity of place experienced by non-citizens (Banki, 2013). Precarity is no longer merely an economic idea, it now includes other vulnerabilities including, argues Butler, those associated with 'being socially constituted bodies, attached to others, at risk of losing those attachments, exposed to others, at risk of violence by virtue of that exposure' (2006: 20). For non-citizens, precarity can be experienced through the lack of security of residence and vulnerability to deportation, by exclusion from public services, civil rights and everyday discrimination (Bloch and McKay, 2016; Paret and Gleeson, 2016). However, as structural processes leave forced migrants in precarious situations, so too do moments of agency and solidarity emerge that lead to social change, even for those individuals who may be outsiders to conventional forms of citizenship. Those with the least power are not always powerless. For example, it is the ontological insecurity faced by undocumented migrants that opens up the channels that allow for change (Gonzales and Chavez, 2012).

Questions raised and looking forward

The chapters in this book have both raised and answered questions. The chapters have shown the ways in which narratives and constructions of and about forced migrants exist and persist and how these serve different interests often perpetuating the post-colonial world order. Striping refugees of their political, social and cultural subjectivities and the numerous potential contributions that they might bring with them is a goal in which governments in the global north are complicit: in fact they are leaders in the policies that stigmatise and humiliate. Core states with the economic power simply push back, separate and reject. There is an abject failure to take an historical approach that might shed light on the colonial period and its legacy and that might take a critical and reflexive look at contemporary military interventions and the propping up of regimes with money and weapons.

Despite living in a transnational, networked and information age, the knowledge that is used by high-level policy makers is almost exclusively produced in the global north. This is partly a function of funding and resources, but it is also about the voices that are heard and the voices that are actively sought. Clearly there is a massive disjuncture between where forced migration takes place, where forced migrants are and where decisions are made. Perhaps this explains the constant war of attrition and the race to the bottom when it comes to responsibility. Chapter after chapter in this book demonstrates the need to rethink existing durable solutions showing so clearly how the frameworks simply do not meet the contemporary demand and how these failures can have devastating consequences, for example, where people are 'repatriated' (see Majidi and Schuster, Chapter 6), where they lack protection in urban areas (see Landau, Chapter 7) and where displacement is protracted (see Hyndman and Giles, Chapter 5). All the chapters in the book suggest new ways of thinking. The chapter by Zetter encourages us to think conceptually about drivers, patterns and process of forced displacement while Banerjee and Samaddar position the post-colonial analysis of population movements at the centre of our understanding of forced migration and displacement. Voutira reminds us of the lessons that history repeating itself can teach us about protection and hospitality. The chapters by Hyndman and Giles, Landau, Donà and Godin, and Voutira all offer new paradigms for the care of forced migrants and refugees outside conventional spaces and forms of assistance and protection. It is our hope that the reader will consider the system through the lens of the everyday lived experiences that the empirical case studies clearly demonstrate, including among those from second generation who grow up in families where their parents have been refugees (see Chimienti, Counilh and Ossipow, Chapter 9)

The chapters point to a mismatch between what happens at international level, in different nation-states and on the ground and the tensions in the system between the different actors and their agendas. The different layers of bureaucracy and administration show a system that is creaking under the unmanageable weight of 21st-century realities of global inequality and a world order that the powerful states benefit from by maintaining inequality both outside and within their borders. For refugees, the micro-level interventions and demonstrations of generosity and hospitality (see Voutira, Chapter 4) show both the positive and the negative; positive because some individuals and even communities display acts of humanity and negative because of the abject failures of the system. Most of the informal strategies for welfare inclusion work in parallel to the bureaucratic chaos and inadequate responses of international and state-led assistance (Häberlen, 2016).

We are witnessing individual and group agency and refugee-led initiatives and solidarity (see Landau, Chapter 7 and Voutira, Chapter 4) and the use of mobile technologies for inclusion and belonging but also for shared information and the maintenance and development of networks (see Donà and Godin, Chapter 8). Refugee agency and initiative go hand in hand with the more formal structures and local informal hospitality and volunteering that are now evident across Europe as a mechanism for managing the state welfare deficits that can leave refugees destitute. The chapters look both backwards and forwards. An area of particular importance, but usually overlooked, in terms of forward thinking are the experiences of second generation from refugee backgrounds and those who are displaced as young children who grow up in a displacement context. There are millions of people globally who have grown up or are currently growing up in families that have been displaced and these numbers are increasing. Chapter 9 by Chimienti, Counilh and Ossipow focuses on transnational links to the ancestral home of parents among the European born second generation from refugee backgrounds. These connections and disconnections will have longer-term impacts in relation to remittances, development and possible return and therefore form part of the larger picture that needs to be considered within the wider analyses of forced migration. However it is not just connections to sending countries, the experiences of second generation from refugee backgrounds as well as those who are displaced as children should be more central to understandings of protracted refugee situations and issues of resettlement, integration, race, racism, identity and belonging (Bloch et al., 2015). Forced migration does not just happen to the migrant generation it can also be omnipresent in the lives of their children. Generation, which is often omitted from analysis, should be a central facet of forced migration policy, theory and practice.

Looking forward, we also need to reflect on methods and methodology that still have a tendency to fall into the pitfalls of methodological nationalism (see Wimmer and Glick Schiller, 2003). To counteract these tendencies we included research at the border, across borders and at the geographical and symbolic edges of national territories. Moreover, the lens of methodological nationalism is challenged by the emerging borderscape methodological approaches (Brambilla, 2015). While some of the field sites examined in the book may be located in national contexts, they also push their boundaries from the core of nation-states to their peripheries, which can be within the same territory or external to them. This borderscape edge can be geographical, it can be social, it can be administrative and it can be a cultural creation (Rajaram and Grundy-Warr, 2007). Our contention is that scholars need to rethink how research is done at borders, in peripheries and spaces of transit rather than those centres of power that are spatially fixed or that implicitly assume the existence of the fictitious homogenous nation-states.

In addition we concur with the view of Colson (2007) that working with the concept of linkages rather than more local and time bound approaches is more useful methodologically. This is because it enables a more reflexive line of enquiry by incorporating the centrality of historical processes whose impacts are far from local or time-limited and implicate both those who move and those who become hosts whether willingly or unwillingly. As forced migrants move across places and inhabit transnational spaces, there is a need to rethink our methodologies. We need to disaggregate contexts from processes (Donà, 2010) and shift from levels, groups and contexts to nodes of connection. Some of the chapters in this book move towards an analysis of the connecting spaces and practices and therefore take an approach based more on linkages and nodes than on traditional approaches. Future research should continue to explore the shift towards an inter-linkages framework for the analysis and intervention in forced migration studies that does not separate fields of knowledge but builds on conceptual, political and responsive 'linkages'.

No one book can deal with the range of issues or geographical locations that characterise contemporary forced migration, and we are mindful of the theoretical, policy, geographical and disciplinary gaps as well as some of the key themes that have been referred to chapters that could in themselves have become stand-alone chapters. Here we are thinking about undocumented migration, incarceration through detention, climate change and displacement, the intersections of race and racism with forced migration and the ever-growing body of research and scholarship that focuses on sexual violence and sexuality in conflict and post-conflict reconciliation including the International Criminal Court. Finally, as researchers, practitioners and activists, we are also mindful of the on-going need to unpack the intersectional forms of race, gender and class that are so deeply embedded in existing frameworks of asylum, protection, reception and humanitarianism. Unless we recognise these embedded colonial forms of racism that are embodied in policies and practices, we will be completely unable as a global community to even begin to offer protection to those who are still viewed as racialised and gendered bodies, capitalist workers or objects of neo-liberalism.

Bibliography

Anderson B (2013) *Us and Them: The Dangerous Politics of Immigration Control*. Oxford: Oxford University Press.
Banki S (2013) Precarity of place: A complement to the growing precariat literature. *Global Discourse* 3(3–4): 450–463.
Bloch A, Chimienti M, Counilh A-L, Hirsch S, Tattolo G, Ossipow L et al (2015) *The Children of Refugees in Europe: Aspirations, Social and Economic Lives, Identity and Transnational Linkages*. Final Report – Working Paper. Geneva: SNIS.
Bloch A, McKay S (2016) *Living on the Margins: Undocumented Migrants in a Global City*. Bristol: Policy Press.
Bloch A, Schuster L (2002) Asylum and welfare: Contemporary debates. *Critical Social Policy* 22(3): 393–414.
Brambilla C (2015) Exploring the critical potential of the borderscapes concept. *Geopolitics* 20(1): 14–34.
Butler J (2006) *Precarious Life: The Powers of Mourning and Violence*. London: Verso.

Castles S (2013) The forces driving global migration. *Journal of Intercultural Studies* 34(2): 122–140.
Chimni BS (1998) The geopolitics of refugee studies: A view from the south. *Journal of Refugee Studies* 11(4): 350–374.
Colson E (2007) Linkages methodology: No man is an island. *Journal of Refugee Studies* 20(2): 320–333.
Donà G (2010) Rethinking wellbeing: From contexts to processes. *International Journal of Migration, Health and Social Care* 6(2): 3–14.
Gibney M, Hansen R (2005) Asylum policy in the West: Past trends, future possibilities. In: Borjas GJ, Crisp J (eds) *Poverty, International Migration and Asylum*. Basingstoke: Palgrave Macmillan, 70–96.
Gonzales RG, Chavez LR (2012) "Awakening to a nightmare": Abjectivity and illegality in the lives of undocumented 1.5-generation Latino immigrants in the United States. *Current Anthropology* 53: 255–281.
Griffiths M (2015) 'Here man is nothing!' gender and policy in an asylum context. *Men and Masculinities* 18(4): 468–488.
Häberlen J (2016) Making friends: Volunteers and refugees in Germany. *German Politics and Society* 34(3): 55–76.
Hammond L (2013) Somali transnational activism and integration in the UK: Mutually supporting strategies. *Journal of Ethnic and Migration Studies* 39(6): 1001–1017.
Jaji, R (2009) Masculinity on unstable ground: Young refugee men in Kenya. *Journal of Refugee Studies* 22(2): 177–194.
Lindley A (2010) *The Early Morning Phone Call*. New York and Oxford: Berghahn Books.
Mountz A (2011) The enforcement archipelago: Detention, haunting, and asylum on islands. *Political Geography* 30: 118–128.
Nawyn SJ, Reosti A, and Gjokaj L (2009) Gender in motion: How gender precipitates international migration. *Advances in Gender Research* 13: 175–202.
Paret M, Gleeson S (2016) Precarity and agency through a migration lens. *Citizenship Studies* 20(3–4): 277–294.
Rajaram PK, Grundy-Warr C (eds) (2007) *Borderscapes: Hidden Geographies and Politics at Territory's Edge*. Minneapolis, MN: University of Minnesota Press.
Sales R (2007) *Understanding Immigration and Refugee Policy: Contradictions and Continuities*. Bristol: Policy Press.
Schuster L (2011) Turning refugees into 'illegal migrants': Afghan asylum seekers in Europe. *Ethnic and Racial Studies* 34(9): 1392–1407.
Schuster L, Majidi N (2015) Deportation stigma and re-migration. *Journal of Ethnic and Migration Studies* 41(4): 635–652.
Sitaropoulos N (2002) Refugee welfare in Greece: Towards a remodelling of the responsibility-shifting paradigm? *Critical Social Policy* 22(3): 436–455.
United Nations (2016) *UN Summit for Refugees and Migrants*. New York: United Nations. http://refugeesmigrants.un.org/declaration
Wimmer A, Glick Schiller N (2003) Methodological nationalism, the social sciences, and the study of migration: An essay in historical epistemology. *International Migration Review* 37(3): 576–610.

Index

activism and digital securitisation 131–132
Afghanistan: refugees from, in Pakistan 93–94; return of refugees to 97
African cities, displacement in: allure of 120; as durable solution 114–120; methods and site profiles 108–109; urban lives 109–112; vulnerability and protection 112–114
agency: individual 11–12; move to urban locations and 36, 164; permanent temporariness and 115; psychosocial well-being and 99; of refugees 25–26, 28, 38, 120–121, 171; tension between perceived victimhood and 80
Al-Shabaab 82, 94
ancestral homeland: anger toward 152–154; debt and loyalty to 150–151; detachment from 156–157; feelings of foreignness in 154–155; idealisation of 155–156; visits to 148, 154–155
anger, feelings of, toward ancestral homeland 152–154
armed conflict, as driver 30–31
asylum, definition of 5
asylum at sea 63
asylum seekers: deportation as deterrent to 94; in global north 80–81; nation-state sovereignty and 5; numbers of 1; protection granted to 96; recorded testimonies of 131–132
asylum system, access to 168–169
Australia: access to asylum system in 168–169; Pacific Solution and 8

belonging, mobile technologies for 127–129
borders, borderscapes and bordering practices: in Calais 133–140; digital 131; overview 5–8, 166; partition 51–54; research and 171; techno-border-scapes 133–140; technologically secured 132
Braudel, Fernand 60, 68–69
business of deportation 99–100

Calais, migrants in transit at border in 133–140
camps: in Calais 133–140; decline of 36; informal 127; in Kenya 81–83, 84n4, 94; on Lesbos 66; long-term 77; numbers in 106; for Palestinians 163–164; in Turkey 70n2; UNHCR and 79
care and hospitality, principles of 57
carriers sanctions 7
categories and rights 3–4
children: in displacement contexts 171; rights of 10
'citizen detectives' 6
classification of transnational activities 147–148
climate change, as driver 31–32
Cold War 76, 79, 165–166, 168
conjuncture 68–69
containment: in Greece 64; policies of 6–7; see also camps
Convention on the Rights of the Child 10
Convention Refugee 77
country of origin see ancestral homeland
credit, access to 113
criminalisation of migrants 56–58

crisis: forced migration as 44; intractable 36; precarity and 168–169; use of term 21, 29
critical forced migration studies, post-colonial analysis of 45–48

debt, feelings of, toward ancestral homeland 150–152
dependency pyramids 111
deportability 91, 98–99
deportation: business of 99–100; constraints on 95–98; deterrent effect of 94; as form of forced migration 90–91; history of 92–95; impact of 98–99; as inhumane and illiberal 100; need for monitoring after 97–98; research on 91–92; terminology for 88–90
deportation gap 88, 95
detachment, feelings of, toward ancestral homeland 156–157
development, as driver 32–33
diasporas, mobile technologies for belonging in 127–129
difference, and security/insecurity in forced migration 45–48
digital humanitarianism 132, 136–138
digital surveillance 130–133
displacements: children, impact on 171; conceptualisation of 28–33; internally displaced people 2, 34, 53–54, 84n6; by natural disasters 21, 33; numbers of 1, 37; to or within cities of global south 107–108; prolonged, and durable solutions 8–10; research on 23–28, 121; into urban areas 106–107; see also African cities, displacement in
drivers of forced migration 20–21, 22, 28–33
Dublin Convention 5, 7
durable solutions: deportation as 100; displacement to or within Southern cities 107–108, 114–120; limitations of 163–165; need to rethink 170; to protracted refugee situations 9–10, 36

economic welfare of urban refugees 114
economies, mobile-focused 138
'emotional grammar' 148
environmental degradation, as driver 31–32
Eurodac database 7, 131

European Convention on Human Rights and Fundamental Freedoms 96
European Union: access to asylum system in 169; bi-lateral agreement with Turkey 6–7; deal signed with Turkey 96–97; deportations to Afghanistan from 97; refugee 'crisis' in 129, 132
e-volunteers 65
exclusion: global geopolitics of 80–81; inclusion and, tension between 15–16, 166–167; 'second generation' as marker of 158n1
expulsion 89; see also deportation
externalization: of asylum 80; of borders and border controls 7

feminization of asylum 81
food security 113
forced deportation 4; see also deportation
forced migration: contemporary landscape of 3–5; defined 19; global context of 11; overview 1–2; patterns and processes of 34–37; post-colonial aspect of 44–45; themes of 2–3; types of 37–38; use of term 23–28
forced migration studies: overview 3, 44; power and subjectivities in 54; see also critical forced migration studies
forced return 89, 92; see also deportation
Frontex 7, 66, 131
fundraising, digital 137–138

gendered aspects of forced migration 4
gender inequalities in mobile technologies 139
generational divide in mobile technologies 139
Geneva Convention on the Status of Refugees (1951) 4–5, 19, 77
geopolitics and protracted refugee situations 74–76
Germany, acceptance of refugees by 164
global cities 106
global north: asylum seekers in 80–81; policies of 169–170
global South: displacement to or within cities of 107–108; theorizing from 121
'grannies' 64, 65

176 Index

Greece: border between Turkey and 62–63; hot spots of Aegean islands of 63–65; policy response of 69
'Greek refugee past' 67–68

hard deportation 95
history/historical times, types of 68–69
humanitarianism: de facto protection and 117–118; digital 132, 136–138; direct service provision and 118–119; forced repatriation and 96; as ideology 57; local institutional literacy and 116–117; in municipalities 115–116; political authority and 119–120; reforms to systems for 120; UNHCR on 83
human rights: bordering practices and 8; forced migration and 10–11

idealisation of ancestral homeland 155–156
IDP (internally displaced people) 2, 34, 53–54, 84n6
India: Chin people in 50–51; colonial trade and resources in 48–49; migrants from Bangladesh and Myanmar in 52–53; notion of dialogue in 56; 'racial difference' in 46–48; sentiments regarding 'foreigners' in 49–50
inequality, global 170
information and communication technologies (ICTs) 126; *see also* mobile technologies
infrastructure support for smartphones 138–139
integration, local: as durable solution 9, 163–164; transnationalism and 158
internally displaced people (IDP) 2, 34, 53–54, 84n6
international obligations and asylum at sea 63
internet and migrant transnationalism 128, 129
intersectional divide, digital 139–140
'irregular migrants' 35–36

jus sanguinis access to nationality 146

Kenya, Dadaab refugee camps of 81–83, 84n4, 94

labels: evidence from praxis on 20–22; research and 23–28
Lesbos, refugee crisis in 62, 65–66
lifelines, mobile phones as 134–135
local institutional literacy 116–117
longue durée 68–69
loyalty, feelings of, toward ancestral homeland 150–151

mass involuntary repatriation 93, 96
Mediterranean: arrivals and fatalities in 64; as conceptual category 60–62; mobility and immobility of 69
microhistory 68
mixed movements of people 35
mobile technologies: for belonging 127–129; at border in Calais 133–140; defined 126; for digital surveillance, activism and humanitarianism 130–133; in migrants' lives and journeys 126–127; for survival 129–130; use of 171

national inequalities in mobile technologies 139–140
natural disasters, displacement by 21, 33
networked societies 126
New York Declaration for Refugees and Migrants (2016) 165, 167
New York Protocol Relating to the Status of Refugees (1967) 4, 5, 19
non-refoulement, principle of 4, 89, 164

onward trajectories 37

Pakistan, Afghan refugees in 93–94
Palestinian refugee camps 163–164
palliative aid 84n4
paradox of willing hosts and uninterested guests 66, 69
partition and making of borders 51–54
patterns and processes of forced migration 34–37
'permanent temporariness' 77, 115
physical security 113–114
post-colonial analysis of forced migration 45–48
precarity: in camps in Calais 133; in global cities 15, 107–108, 110–111, 112, 120; information precarity 136; movement and 121, 134; welfare system and 11, 168–169
prima facie refugees 77

protracted refugee situations (PRS): consequences of 77; global geopolitics of exclusion and 80–81; as global phenomenon 74–76; intractable crises and 36–37; on Lesbos 66; overview 8–9; Palestinians and 163–164; research on 78–80; study of 78; use of term 76
psychosocial well-being and deportation 98–99

racism in policies and practices 172
reconfiguration of borders 5–8
Refugee Act of South Africa 118
refugees: agency of 25–26, 28, 38, 120–121, 171; defined 4; developing regions as hosts of 2; economic usefulness of 167; geo-political significance of 165–167; in Lesbos 62, 65–66; numbers of 1; as 'others' to be excluded 166–167; *prima facie* 77; from Syria 62; use of term 23–28; *see also* protracted refugee situations; urban refugees
refugee status determination 77
refugee studies 3, 44–45
remittances 96, 151–152, 168
repatriation 92, 164–165; *see also* deportation
research: at borders 171; on deportation 91–92; on displacement 23–28, 121; on linkages 171–172; on protracted refugee situations 78–80; risks of 101n3; on transnationalism 145
resettlement 9, 164
resources and security 48–51
Rohingya people 9, 55
routes of migration 35

safe return 93
second generation from refugee backgrounds: diversity of 168; experiences of 171; feelings and ties with homeland 149–157; methods and interviewee profiles 149; transnationalism and 145–148, 157–158
securitisation: digital, 131–132; minorities, women and 53; mobile technologies and 135–136; as process 81
security/insecurity in forced migration: difference and 45–48; resources and 48–51

slavery: in India 47; of Rohingya women 55
social invisibility of urban refugees 111, 115
social networks and urban refugee success 114
soft deportation 95
Somalia: refugees from, in Kenya 81–83, 84n4, 94; security conditions in 82–83
Sri Lanka, refugees from, in Switzerland 149, 156
statelessness and trafficking 55
state sovereignty and asylum cases 5
stereotypes of refugees 167
stigmatising of refugees 169
surveillance, digital 130–133
survival, mobile technologies for 129–130, 134–135
'survival migration' 27
Switzerland: access to nationality in 146; second generation refugees in 149
Syria: civil war in 62; refugees from, in Turkey 97

tea labourers in India 48–49
technological devices to manage migration 126
terrorist, conflation of refugee with 166
time-space discontinuities of displacement 34
trafficked people 54–56
transit countries 37
transit spaces of exception 8
transnationalism: feelings and ties with homeland 149–157; research on 145; second generation from refugee backgrounds and 145–148, 157–158; *see also* ancestral homeland
transnational spaces and mobile technologies 127–129
trauma, inter-generational 67–68
Turkey: bi-lateral agreement with European Union 6–7; border between Greece and 62–63; camps in 70n2; deal signed with EU 96–97; refugees from, in Switzerland 149, 151, 152, 153, 156; Syrian refugees in 62, 97

UNHCR (United Nations High Commissioner for Refugees): 'boat people' and 63; durable solutions of 163–165; imposed return and 93;

Nansen Award of 62–63; Policy on Alternatives to Camps 79; protracted refugee situations and 9; refugee status determination 77; repatriation and 92–93; resettlement and 92; urban areas and 106; *see also* protracted refugee situations

urban refugees: agency and 164; challenges facing 109–114, 120; churning and 120–121; defined 107; economic welfare of 114; increase in 36; local institutional literacy and 116–117

Vietnam, refugees from, in Switzerland 149, 150–151, 153–154, 156–157
voluntary migration 35–36
voluntary repatriation 9, 36, 94–95

War on Terror 76, 166
welfare system and precarity 168–169
women: securitising migration and 53; trafficking of 54–56; as urban refugees 112, 113
workforce, deportability of 91
World Humanitarian Summit 22

#0141 - 310818 - C190 - 234/156/10 [12] - CB - 9781138653221